the home guide to
CRAFT

the home guide to
CRAFT

Katherine Sorrell

Photography by Howard Sooley

bay books

Contents

a note on measurements

Both imperial and metric measurements are
given for each project, where appropriate.
Sometimes, in order to avoid awkward fractions,
some measurements have been slightly
adjusted. This will not affect the finished
project, but it is important to work within one
measurement system only in each project and
not jump from metric to imperial or vice versa.

contents

Introduction

Whether you want to perfect a single technique or dabble in a variety of projects, you'll discover that half the fun of craft is simply discovering just how creative you really are.

Above: Ceramic painting might not be quite as simple as it looks but with a steady hand and a bit of practice, you'll be delighted at how professional your work can look.

Right page: Efficient storage of materials becomes ever more important as you develop and diversify your craft skills.

It wasn't so long ago that people made things because they had to. Without 'craft' they wouldn't have had clothes to wear, implements to eat with, vessels to drink from, toiletries to wash with or bedlinen to sleep in. These days, of course, most of us can just go out to the shops and buy more or less everything we need — we're 'cash rich, time poor' and there's no great necessity to spend hour after hour laboriously knitting, sewing, dyeing or weaving. So why is craft still so popular? Perhaps it's the very fact that we aren't obliged to do it that makes it attractive; perhaps it's the inherent satisfaction of being able to say 'I made that'; it could be because it's enjoyable for adults and children alike; or maybe it's just a basic human urge to create, to counteract the predominance of soulless, machine-produced items that normally surround us.

Certainly, craft has enjoyed a resurgence in recent years. For so long it was the object of scorn and derision, associated with lumpy, rustic, quirky pieces. But just as developing technology has resulted in the emergence of new craft forms, so traditional crafts have been revived and reinvented, and the result is that today's craftspeople frequently combine the best of old and new in a way that perfectly suits our eclectic, comfortable, modern homes. Craft may be highly functional or it may come close to fine art, but if it is well designed and well made it adds quality to our everyday lives. Craft has always been personal and meaningful, affordable and pleasurable; what is changed is that now it is also fashionable and inspirational.

This book is an exploration of the exciting possibilities of modern craft, demonstrating how one can take an ancient or traditional technique and adapt it to 21st-century living or, conversely, take a high-tech method and adapt it so the results are accessible. What makes this book unique is its breadth of coverage — we have selected 30 different types of

Below: Felt is the oldest textile on earth and felt making is surely one of the most satisfying and simple of all textile crafts. A combination of fleece, hot water and agitation produces a unique bonded fabric.

Right page: Once you've made your first batch of hand-made paper you'll want to explore all the wonderful variations you can achieve by adding texture and color to the basic mix of paper pulp.

craft, from the well-known (knitting, soap making, basketry) to the almost-forgotten (crochet, cyanotype, wirework) and the cutting-edge (resin casting, acrylic molding, complex textiles) and produced a pair of projects for each, resulting in 60 projects that range from table linen and jewelry to handbags and bowls, all of them beautiful and all eminently easy to live with.

Each project has been devised by a maker who is an expert in his or her field. And while you can see (and buy) their work in some of the world's leading galleries and stores, now you can also make your own version of their designs. It is possible to carry out each project on a kitchen table (or sometimes in a garage or back yard) with the minimum of equipment and only a certain amount of dexterity. Some, naturally, require greater skill than others, but the clear, step-by-step photographs and

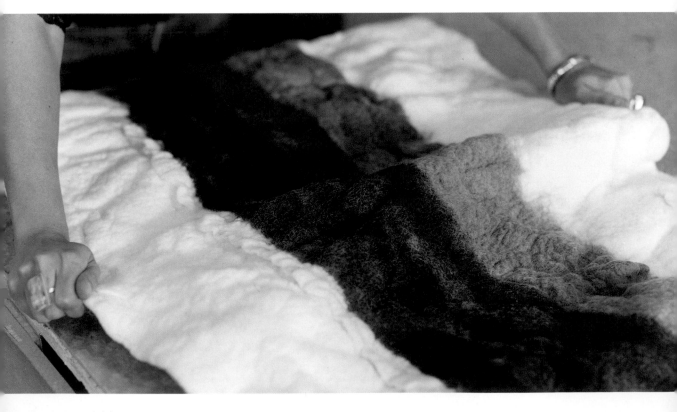

written instructions, as well as templates and, where necessary, more detailed instructions at the back of the book, should enable anyone to carry them out without much difficulty. A comprehensive list of materials and equipment at the start of each project will also tell you exactly what you will need to buy or prepare.

The other unique feature of this book is a concise history of each craft, which outlines how it arose and developed around the world. While it is not essential to know that the first beads probably date back to around 38,000BC, or that it was Roman legend that gave soap its name, it is, however, fascinating and illuminating, and will, hopefully, add an extra dimension of interest to your work. A blend of practical and intellectual is the ideal catalyst for craft, and this book provides a little of the latter alongside a great deal of the former, in a format that is both attractive and easy to follow. Explore one craft in depth (there's nothing to stop you developing your own ideas once you've mastered the techniques shown here) or take your time and learn numerous different ones — but, whatever you do, have fun with the process of making things and, above all, enjoy your gorgeously individual finished results.

Painting, Printing & Dyeing

Stenciling

It is the very simplicity of stenciling that makes it such an effective and enjoyable craft — perfect for decorating surfaces large or small. But although the process is straightforward, the results can be wonderfully intricate and unique, as demonstrated by Japanese masters over the centuries.

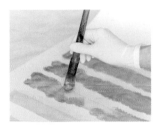

The practice of stenciling, or the art of painting repeated patterns through cut-out holes in a flat surface, has probably been around since prehistoric times, either to tell stories or just for decorative purposes. Cave-dwelling man produced stencil-like images of animals, and the ancient Egyptians used them extensively both inside and outside their elaborate tombs. The people of Fiji applied vegetable dyes onto bark cloth through primitive stencils cut from banana leaves, and in the Roman Empire stencils were first used commercially, to make the banners that advertized the popular games.

It was in 8th-century Japan, however, that stenciling was first given truly artistic form. The process was developed to such a superb level that amazingly fine details and intricate patterns became possible. In a technique known as *katazune*, expert craftsmen strengthened their cut paper — which could be so complex it resembled a web of holes with tiny, fragile links — with fine silk threads or hair. They used sheets of waterproofed paper made from mulberry fiber, in two layers at once — the threads or hair glued between them for extra support. The paper could be used several times, but when it became too damp, another stencil, exactly the same, was cut from a master, and registered using tiny pin holes. The color was applied with a large, soft brush, or sometimes a rice-based resist paste was stenciled on and the cloth later immersed in a dye bath. Some fabrics were relatively simple; others were stenciled with many different patterns one after the other, and then embellished with hand-painting and embroidery for unsurpassed effect. This type of stenciling was the sole method of printing used in Japan until the 19th century. Elsewhere, meanwhile, more basic stencils could be found. The craft was brought to medieval Europe by returning Crusaders, and used for religious pictures and manuscripts, and also in grander manor houses for wall decorations, using rich colors and simple, repeated patterns — perhaps shields, crowns or *fleurs de lys*.

Similarly, stencils became a popular substitute for expensive wallpaper in America during the late 19th and early 20th centuries. The method was also used for chairs, trays, boxes, bedspreads and other textiles, and there was a corresponding fashion for stenciled pictures, on a velvet background, of baskets of fruit and flowers.

In the 21st century, stenciling is still an admired craft. It may no longer be commonly practiced professionally, but it is a means of producing patterns at home easily and inexpensively, using ready-made stencils or your own designs. On fabric, paper, walls, floors, furniture and accessories, the permutations of design and color are practically limitless, whether simple or sophisticated, traditional or modern.

Devoré drape

You will need

- Felt-tip marker pen
- Sheet of acetate
- Masking tape
- Cutting mat and craft knife
- Ruler
- Piece of dark blue or black cross-dyed silk/viscose velvet, long enough to cover your window and to allow 4in/10cm at the top and bottom for hemming, and at least one-and-a-half times the width of the window. It should be pre-washed in a mild detergent to remove any finish
- Iron
- Pins
- Large printing surface (see page 18)
- Protective mask
- Light spray adhesive
- Overalls, apron or an old shirt
- Plastic gloves and safety goggles
- Stippling or stencil brush, or a small piece of sponge
- Ready-mixed devoré paste (about 1 pint/ 500ml should cover one square yard/ one square metre of fabric)
- Mild detergent
- Sewing machine
- Thread to match the fabric

This glorious full-length drape has a sumptuous feel, and the stenciled devoré effect is a clever way to diffuse light and disguise a window or a view.

The devoré technique is ideal for making a drape because, as seen so strikingly here, it can be used to create sheer and opaque areas through which the light is filtered in a series of fascinating and beautiful patterns. An excellent way to apply the devoré paste is through a stencil, as in this project, resulting in crisp edges and regular motifs. Choose any base color you wish for the velvet, though darker shades will inevitably have the most impact.

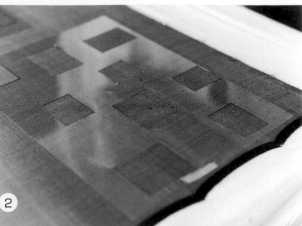

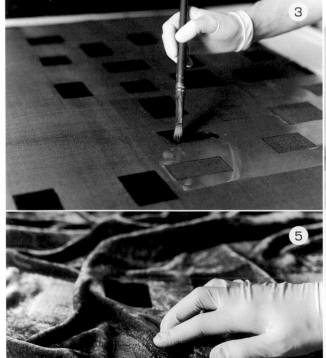

printing surface
Use plywood or fiberboard covered with a blanket and a sheet of plastic, both stapled firmly to the underside of the wood and wrinkle-free.

alternative fabrics
You can buy other fabrics for devoré, such as silk, viscose, satin and poly-cotton.

how to make:
Devoré drape

1 Photocopy to enlarge the stencil design on page 411 and then trace it onto the acetate. Tape to the cutting mat and cut out the squares and rectangles neatly with a craft knife. This is your stencil.

2 Press the velvet and, using pins or tape, attach it to your printing surface, pile-side down. Wearing a protective mask, lightly spray the stencil with adhesive and place on the fabric.

3 Wearing overalls, gloves and goggles, use the brush or sponge to apply the devoré paste through the stencil, brushing from the edges into the center to avoid the paste leaking underneath. Apply the paste evenly all over, as thicker areas will devoré more and may cause holes in the fabric. Pull away the stencil carefully and reposition randomly, avoiding areas of wet paste, until you have covered the whole fabric.

4 When you have finished, wash your brush or sponge immediately and allow the entire piece of fabric to dry thoroughly. Then, wearing a protective mask and gloves, press the back of the fabric carefully with a hot iron for 30–60 seconds. Stop ironing when the fabric changes color.

5 In a well-ventilated area, and still wearing a protective mask and gloves, gently rub the right side of the fabric so that the pile comes away and you can see the design. A stiff residue of paste will be left behind. Hand wash the fabric in warm water with a small amount of mild detergent. Rinse thoroughly in cold running water and allow to dry. Press the fabric and hem it neatly around all edges, then hang it at your window.

Floor cushion

You will need

(To make a cushion measuring 26 x 26in/ 65 x 65cm)

- Sheet of wallpaper lining paper
- Ruler
- Pencil
- Scissors
- Masking tape
- Cutting mat and craft knife
- Piece of white suede (or leather), 27 x 78in/67 x 195cm
- Large printing surface (see page 18)
- Tailor's chalk
- Light spray adhesive
- Overalls, apron or an old shirt
- Plastic gloves
- Protective mask
- Safety goggles
- Stippling or stencil brush, or a small piece of sponge
- Approx 1 pint/500ml ready-mixed silver textile pigment dye
- Piece of calico or other light fabric
- Iron
- Sewing machine, with a leather needle
- Thread to match the suede
- Pillow form, 26 x 26in/65 x 65cm

The luxury of suede is brought to life in this fabulous floor cushion. It's ideal for lounging on and is wonderfully fashionable in a casual, relaxed way.

As modern interior design is influenced more and more by Eastern styles, we are increasingly eating, drinking and sleeping at a lower level. This superb floor cushion is not particularly either Eastern or Western in its design, but bridges the gap between the two in an unselfconscious, quietly luxurious way. The long, 'envelope'-style flap is another feature that gives the cushion a contemporary appearance, while the bold stripe design in silver adds just enough of a decorative element without going over the top.

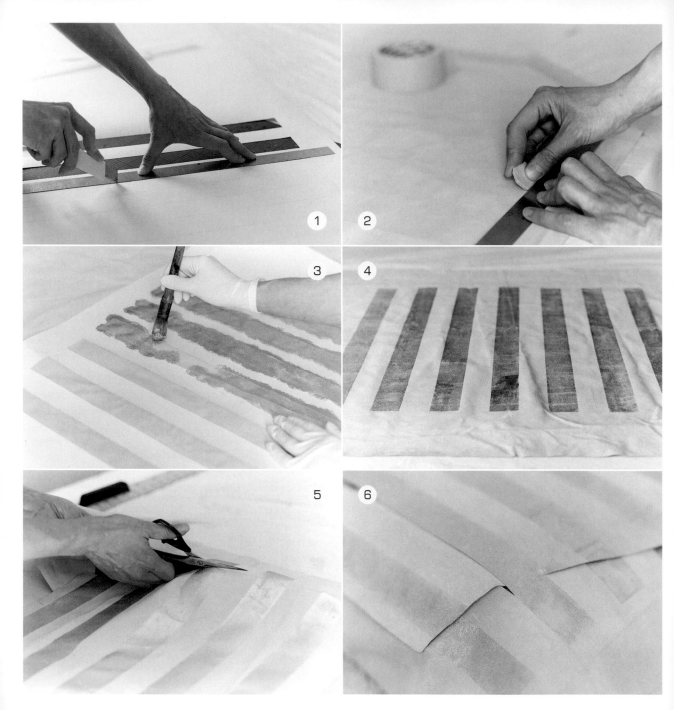

how to make:
Floor cushion

1 Cut a piece of lining paper 78in/195cm long. Rule up 21 rectangles within this larger rectangle, according to the template on page 112. Tape the paper securely to the cutting mat and cut out each of the rectangles neatly, using a craft knife. This is your stencil.

2 Using masking tape, attach the suede to your printing surface right-side up. With the tailor's chalk, rule a straight line down each side of the fabric, 4½in/11cm in from the edges.

3 Place the cut stencil on the suede, lining up its cut edges with the two lines, and attach lightly with spray adhesive. Wearing the overalls, gloves, mask and goggles, use the brush or sponge to apply the dye evenly through the stencil, brushing from the edges into the center to avoid the dye leaking underneath the stencil.

4 When you have finished, carefully pull away the stencil, wash your brush or sponge immediately and throw the stencil away. Allow the suede to dry thoroughly, then lay the calico over the back of it. Press the suede carefully with a hot iron, through the calico, for about 3–5 minutes to fix the dye.

5 Fold over one third of the suede, wrong sides together. Stitch neatly up each side, leaving a ½in/1cm seam allowance. Cut away a narrow edge from the remaining third, on a slight diagonal, so that it forms a flap.

6 Cut two slits in the main body of the cushion, along the edges of one printed stripe, wide enough to insert the flap. Fill with the pillow form and carefully tuck in the flap.

> ### variations
> You can vary this project by printing the stripes in different colors, or cutting them to different widths.

Screen printing

Most of the patterned fabrics we buy today have been industrially printed — a relatively new process that is fast, precise and hugely versatile. But screen printing by hand still has many advantages, enabling artists and craftspeople to produce images that are graphic, eye-catching and individual.

Patterning dyes onto fabric was a process carried out in ancient Greece, Rome and Byzantium, but the first real printing technique was almost certainly developed by the Chinese, who were printing paper with carved woodblocks two millennia ago. This, the oldest method of direct printing, has also been practiced in India for centuries, in the form of vividly colored and intricately patterned cottons, and was in use in medieval Europe as a minor textile craft. From woodblock printing came, in the late 18th century, a method of printing from engraved copperplates, particularly for the one-color, scenic prints known as *toiles de Jouy*. From this developed the first mechanized printing process, cylinder (or roller) printing, which was patented in 1783 and revolutionized the Western textile industry, speeding up production to thousands of yards per day.

Screen printing is the youngest of all the direct printing methods, though it has a long and distinguished ancestry in the form of stenciling, to which it is closely related. But while stenciling can be wonderfully intricate and highly effective, it has the disadvantage of always requiring the 'ties' that link the cut-out patterns together. Screen printing was a refinement that no longer needed ties, thanks to the fact that the print is made by the dye being pushed through a fine mesh held taut in a frame, with areas blocked out by paper stencils, varnish or photochemicals. It was in 1850 at Lyons that the first recorded stencil prints were made that were supported all over by silk gauze — though it is entirely possible that this process had been discovered in Japan long before. In 1907 an Englishman took out a patent for a 'tieless stencil' and during the First World War, posters and banners were produced by screen printing. But it was not until the 1920s that European and American screen printing became a viable industry, and the term 'serigraphy' was coined, from the Latin *seri*, meaning 'silk', and Greek *graphos*, meaning 'to draw or write'.

For several decades, screen printing remained a hand process, then in the 1950s the fully automated flat bed screen printer came into operation, followed soon after by the rotary printer, both of which have made possible the printing of huge runs of fabric and paper in sophisticated, detailed and precise patterns of many colors. But the artistry of the hand screen print remains undiminished, and evidence of its qualities can be seen not only in the work of artists, including Andy Warhol, famous for his Marilyn Monroe and Campbell's Soup prints, but also in the ground-breaking designer fabrics produced by the European textile houses in the 1930s, '40s and early '50s. Colorful and creative, these fabrics epitomize all that is best about screen printing and show why it is still highly regarded today by artists, designers, craftspeople and couture houses.

Wall hanging

You will need

- Sheets of unprinted newsprint (or wallpaper lining paper), measuring 20 x 28in/50 x 70cm, or the size of your screen
- Cutting mat
- Craft knife
- Ruler
- Masking tape
- Screen measuring about 20 x 28in/ 50 x 70cm (see page 406)
- Roll of 1200 or 1400 grade lining paper
- Large printing surface (see page 18)
- Overalls, apron or an old shirt
- Plastic gloves
- Safety goggles
- About 1 pint/500ml ready-mixed pearlized textile pigment dyes in each of two or three pastel colors
- Specialist screen-printing squeegee (see page 406)
- Brick (optional)
- Wallpaper paste, tacks or adhesive-backed Velcro

Discreet but still effective, a paper wall hanging such as this makes an unusual and individual way to add character to a room, and is quick and easy to make.

In this project, a choice of strong, hard, geometric shapes has been tempered by the use of pale, pearlescent colors, creating a wall hanging that would be delightful to install almost anywhere in the house (though it may not last too long in a bathroom or a steamy kitchen). Because the technique is so straightforward, once you feel confident with it you can develop your own shapes and patterns, and choose your own colors, in order to tailor the design to the personality and style of your home.

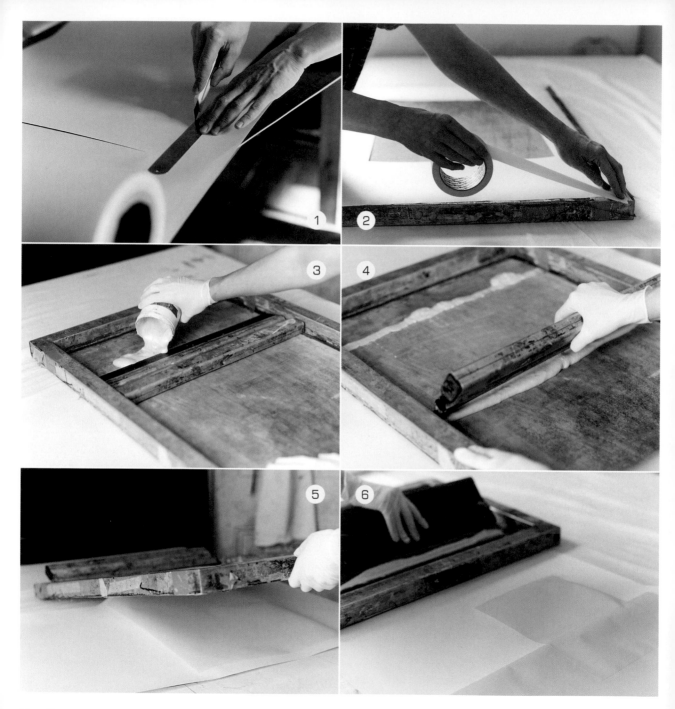

how to make:
Wall hanging

1 Put a sheet of newsprint on the cutting mat and use the craft knife to cut out a rectangle within it — the rectangle should be no longer than 20in/50cm and no wider than 15in/38.5cm. This will be the first stencil pattern (see page 413 for template).

2 Tape the stencil to the back of the screen, positioned so that a reservoir area of 4–6in/ 10–15cm is created at one end of the screen. Hold the screen up to the light to check that all non-printing areas are covered by the stencil.

3 Tape the lining paper (either way up) to your printing surface and place the screen on it anywhere you like, allowing at least 8in/20cm at the top for hanging. Wearing overalls, gloves and goggles, pour about 10fl oz/300ml of your first color dye into one end of the screen.

4 Then, holding the frame with one hand and the squeegee with the other, pull the paste firmly and smoothly across the screen two or three times. Vary the angle of the squeegee and the pressure to apply more or less paste (the lower down the squeegee, the more ink you will squeeze through). You could place a brick on one end of the screen to hold it in place and use both hands.

5 Carefully lift the screen away from the paper and place elsewhere to start printing a pattern. You will need to print quickly to prevent the paste from drying on the screen.

6 After printing as many rectangles in this color and size as you wish, scrape any excess paste back into the pot, throw away the paper stencil and clean the screen and squeegee under cold running water. Make another paper stencil in a smaller size and choose another color, then repeat steps 2–5 to build up a varied pattern. If you decide to overlap any printing areas, ensure that the dye on the area you have already printed is dry. When you have decorated your desired area, neatly trim the lining paper top and bottom and allow to dry. Paste onto the wall as normal wallpaper, or use tacks or a strip of adhesive-backed Velcro.

Spiral scarf

You will need

- (To make a scarf measuring 9 x 77in/ 24 x 198cm)
- Pencil and pen
- Screen measuring 20 x 28in/ 50 x 70cm (see page 406)
- Paintbrush
- 5fl oz/150ml light-sensitive screen coating
- Cerise silk organza measuring 20 x 79in/ 50cm x 2m (washed in a mild detergent to remove any finish)
- Iron
- Masking tape
- Large printing surface (see page 18)
- Tailor's chalk
- Overalls, apron or an old shirt
- Plastic gloves and safety goggles
- 10fl oz/300ml ready-mixed acid textile dye (dark pink)
- Specialist screen-printing squeegee (see page 406)
- Piece of calico or other light fabric
- Aluminum foil
- Wok or pressure cooker
- Mild laundry detergent
- Pins
- Sewing machine
- Thread to match the fabric

This pretty pink scarf in vivid magenta features a lovely spiral symbol. As it has been screen printed onto semi-transparent fabric, the result is a dazzling, multi-layered moiré look.

Long scarves in a striking sheer fabric are always useful and versatile, and the advantage of screen printing is that it enables you to cover vast lengths of fabric with the same design in no time at all. This project uses light-sensitive screen coating painted around a template, and employs a spiral motif that is highly stylish. But it would be just as easy to create a different pattern that could be printed to an equally fabulous effect.

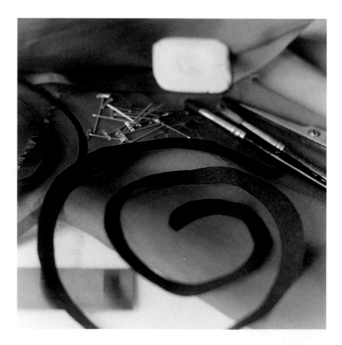

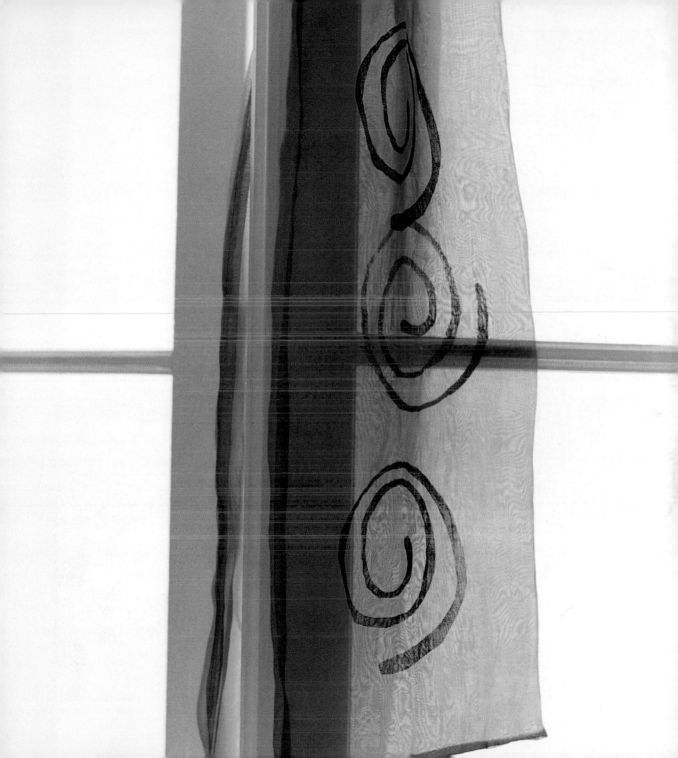

how to make
Spiral scarf

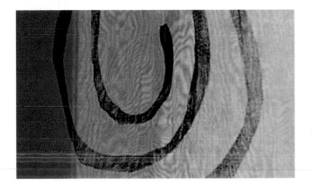

1 Trace the template on page 414 onto the center of your screen mesh. Paint around this with light-sensitive screen coating, leaving the design area unpainted. Allow to dry, then develop and fix it by leaving out in bright sunlight for 30–60 minutes until all the coating has changed color. Ensure all of the non-design area mesh is covered in the emulsion, including a large enough reservoir space on the screen for the printing ink.

2 Press the fabric carefully and tape it, right-side up, to your printing surface.

3 Place the screen sideways at the top of the fabric and place masking tape to indicate the positions of the corners of the screen (stick the tape onto the printing base). Label these number 1. On both edges of the fabric, draw a short line with the tailor's chalk to indicate the top and bottom of the design area within the screen. Then move the screen along, judging by eye where the next printed design area should be. Indicate the corners of the screen again with masking tape and label as number 2. Repeat along the entire fabric, numbering 3, 4, 5 and so on.

4 Place the screen back into position number 1. Wearing overalls, gloves and goggles, pour about 8fl oz/250ml of the dye into one end of the screen (the reservoir area). Then, holding the frame with one hand and the squeegee with the other, pull the paste firmly, smoothly and evenly across the screen at least twice. Vary the angle of the squeegee and the pressure to apply more or less paste (the lower down the squeegee, the more ink you will squeeze through). If you find this hard, place a brick on one end of the screen to hold it in place, and use both hands to push and pull.

Spiral scarf

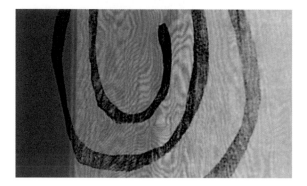

5 Carefully lift the screen away from the fabric and place within the registration marks numbered 3. Squeegee the ink across again. Continue printing alternate areas until you have covered the whole length of the fabric with the pattern. You will need to print quite quickly to prevent the paste from drying on the screen. When you have finished, scrape any excess paste back into the pot, wash the screen and squeegee under cold running water and leave the fabric and screen to dry. Then repeat step 4 to print the remaining alternate areas, starting with the tapes labeled 2, and so on. Clean the screen and squeegee again. (You can use the screen again if you wish to re-print this pattern.) Leave the fabric to dry.

6 Detach the fabric and roll in the calico to make a sausage shape. Wrap the sausage in aluminum foil, sealing the edges. Place on a raised tray in the wok or pressure cooker with a small amount of water and steam for 30 minutes in order to fix the dye. Rinse in cold running water, then in hand-hot water with a small amount of mild detergent. Then rinse in cold running water again. Leave to dry completely.

7 Press the fabric with a warm iron, then fold over lengthwise, right sides together, and pin. Leaving a seam allowance of ⅜in/1cm, stitch around the long side and one of the short sides. Turn out, fold in the edges of the remaining side, press and stitch neatly across. Press once more to finish.

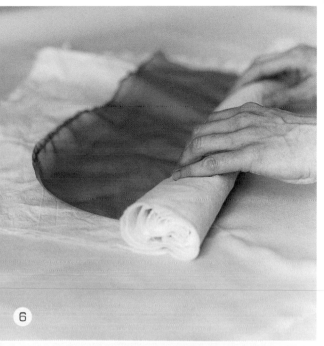

5

6

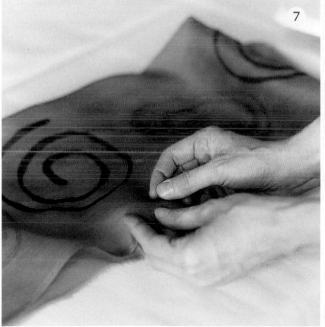

7

re-using the screen

To reclaim the screen for re-use, you will need to buy some reclamation paste. Wearing rubber gloves, overalls and goggles, spread it over the side of the screen you do not squeeze through and leave for the manufacturer's recommended amount of time. Then, simply use a high-pressure washer to blast the old coating away from the mesh. As long as you are able to see through the mesh, you can re-use the screen.

Cyanotype

In cyanotype, a forerunner to photography, the appeal of vivid blue color combines with the satisfaction of creating charming and unconventional images. The process has changed little since its invention in 1842, but today's practitioners are finding that it can be used in very modern ways.

A medium that has truly changed our perception of the world, photography was invented only 175 years ago. Its basic principles were discovered by four different men. In 1816 French physicist Joseph Nicéphore Niepce produced the first negative and, 11 years later, the first known photograph. Niepce worked with the painter Louis Jacques Mandé Daguerre who, in 1839, revealed his method of making a direct positive image on a silver plate, known as the *daguerreotype*. In England, scientist William Henry Fox Talbot was experimenting along similar lines, and had found a means of making endless positives from a paper negative, as well as of permanently 'fixing' images. His compatriot, the astronomer Sir John Herschel, was also an early experimenter with photography on glass.

All four men were vital to the establishment of photography as we know it, and in 1844 the first book illustrated with conventional photographs was published — Talbot's *The Pencil of Nature*. But in this time of intense experimentation, various other photomechanical processes were discovered and explored, including one by Herschel himself — cyanotype. The process is similar to the experiments of Thomas Wedgwood and Sir Humphry Davy who, early in the 19th century, placed objects on paper soaked in silver nitrate and exposed them to sunlight, creating effective — though impermanent — black and white images. Herschel's method, however, employed light-sensitive iron salts, also known as Prussian Blue (hence cyanotype, from 'cyan', the Greek word for blue), rather than silver nitrate. It is believed that Herschel had been looking for a means of accurately copying his notes, drawings and calculations, and the resulting images were, literally, 'blueprints' of their subject matter.

Herschel made his discovery public in 1842, and in 1843 — one year before Talbot's book of photography — a book containing cyanotype images was published by Anna Atkins, a family friend of Herschel's, who had made nearly 400 prints of dried coastal algae. Quick, inexpensive and simple, cyanotype soon became a popular means of printing images on paper — for family portraits, artistic endeavors and in commerce (particularly for photographic proofs and for copying architectural and engineering drawings). As other photographic methods improved, however, cyanotype fell out of favor, though it was still widely used for architects' plans, thanks to the large-scale production of blueprint paper from the 1880s onwards.

Today, photographers, artists and craftspeople are once again experimenting with labor-intensive photographic processes, and have rediscovered the appeal and charm of cyanotype, producing images that can be displayed as artworks or transformed into beautiful home accessories or even clothing.

Fern lampshade

You will need

- Overalls, apron or an old shirt
- Rubber gloves
- 18g ferric ammonium citrate
- 8g potassium ferric cyanide
- Small metal or glass bowl
- Measuring cup (metal or glass)
- Metal spoon
- Wide decorating paintbrush
- White cylindrical paper lampshade and sheet of heavyweight paper large enough to cover it
- Newspapers
- Board slightly larger than the paper
- Two or three dried fern sprigs
- Sheet of clear acrylic the same size as the board
- At least 4 clips
- Ruler
- Pencil
- Craft knife or scissors
- Spray adhesive
- All-purpose clear adhesive
- Ribbon to trim edges of shade

    (Any kitchen equipment should not be used for food afterward)

The crisp contrast between the attractive blue of the cyanotype dye and the bright clean white of the fern outline is what gives this lampshade a unique and inspirational character.

The cyanotype process is now used for art and craft purposes rather than professional photography, but it has lost none of its charm and appeal. The technique itself seems almost magical, and you will find that you achieve different results every time, depending on the length of exposure, amount of sunlight and base color of paper you work with. This project employs classic inky blue, trimmed with a contrasting ribbon, which brings out the detailing of the fern's silhouette with the utmost clarity.

how to make:
Fern lampshade

1 In a darkened room and wearing overalls and rubber gloves, mix the ferric ammonium citrate and potassium ferric cyanide in the bowl. Add 10½fl oz/ 300ml of cold water and stir well until the chemicals have completely dissolved. This mixture is now light sensitive — do not expose it to light. It should be a pale yellowish-green color.

2 Paint the solution evenly over the paper, protecting the surface underneath with plenty of newspaper, and allow to dry in the dark.

3 Still in a darkened room, put the dry, coated paper on the board, place the ferns evenly on the paper, and cover with the acrylic sheet. Clip the acrylic firmly to the board so that the fern is flat against the paper.

4 Take the board outside and expose to direct light. The longer you leave it, the darker the paper will become. About 20 minutes in average daylight will give a good image. In direct sunlight it may only take around ten minutes. Overcast days will require a longer exposure time. The paper will gradually turn a dirty gray color. Bring the board back inside and remove the paper from the frame (discarding the ferns).

Fern lampshade

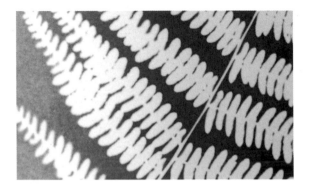

5 Develop the image by rinsing the paper well in cold water (wearing rubber gloves). Take care not to rip the paper — it will become quite fragile. Leave the paper, image side down, in cold water for five minutes, then carefully rinse off any remaining chemical until the water runs clear. The background will slowly turn blue, leaving a white image where the ferns were placed. Leave flat to dry (not in strong sunlight). Once dry, the image will be permanently printed.

6 Measure the lampshade and mark its dimensions on the printed paper, adding an overlap of ¼in/5mm on one vertical side. Cut out this shape.

7 Spray the back of the paper lightly with spray adhesive and carefully wrap the printed paper round the existing shade, gluing the vertical seam overlap.

8 To finish, glue ribbon around the top and bottom of the shade to give a neat edge.

variations

You can make cyanotype prints in different colors. For purple, use a red paper and for green, use yellow.

Other leaves that are suitable for this technique include rosemary, ivy, eucalyptus and wild grasses.

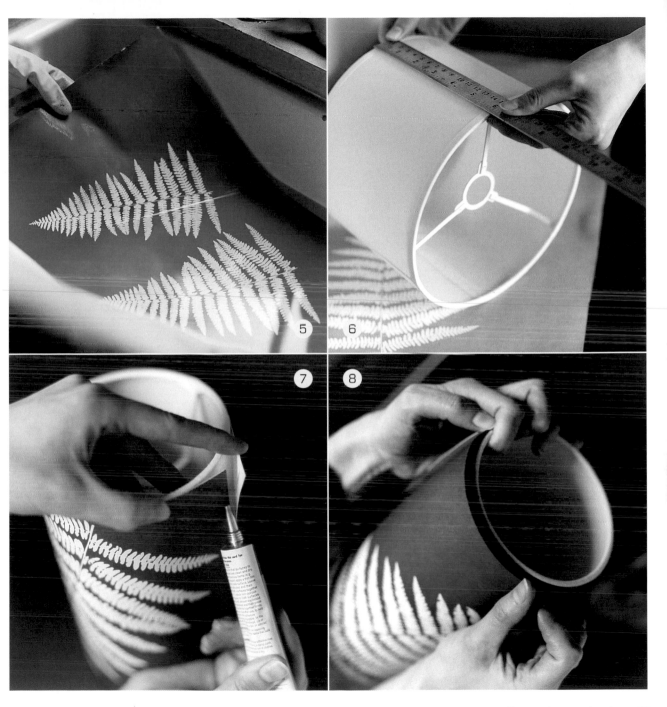

Feather floor cube

You will need

(To make a cube measuring
18 x 18 x 18in/ 45 x 45 x 45cm)

- Four pieces of white or cream silk, each measuring 19 x 19in/48 x 48cm
- Overalls, apron or an old shirt
- Rubber gloves
- 55g ferric ammonium citrate
- 25g potassium ferric cyanide
- Large metal or glass bowl or pan
- Measuring cup (metal or glass)
- Metal spoon
- Newspapers
- Board measuring 20 x 20in/50 x 50cm
- Six or seven pigeon feathers or similar
- Sheet of clear acrylic measuring 20 x 20in/50 x 50cm
- 4 clips
- Iron
- Pins
- Sewing machine
- Blue thread
- Scissors
- 40in/1m heavyweight furnishing linen, in deep blue (at least 24in/60cm wide)
- Foam rubber cube, 18 x 18 x 18in/ 45 x 45 x 45cm

(Any kitchen equipment should not be used for food afterward)

Wonderfully practical yet beautifully decorative, this attractive floor cube blends science and nature to fabulous effect, and would make a striking addition to a living room or bedroom.

The cyanotype process may be more than 150 years old, but used like this it could not possibly look more modern. Although you could employ the same technique to make a cushion cover or perhaps a slipcover for a dining chair, the choice of a sculptural floor cube is ideal for a contemporary esthetic. The cube's straight lines are offset by its rich metallic blue hue and the softness of the feathers; as an alternative, you could choose a more random pattern, or use feathers of varying shapes and sizes.

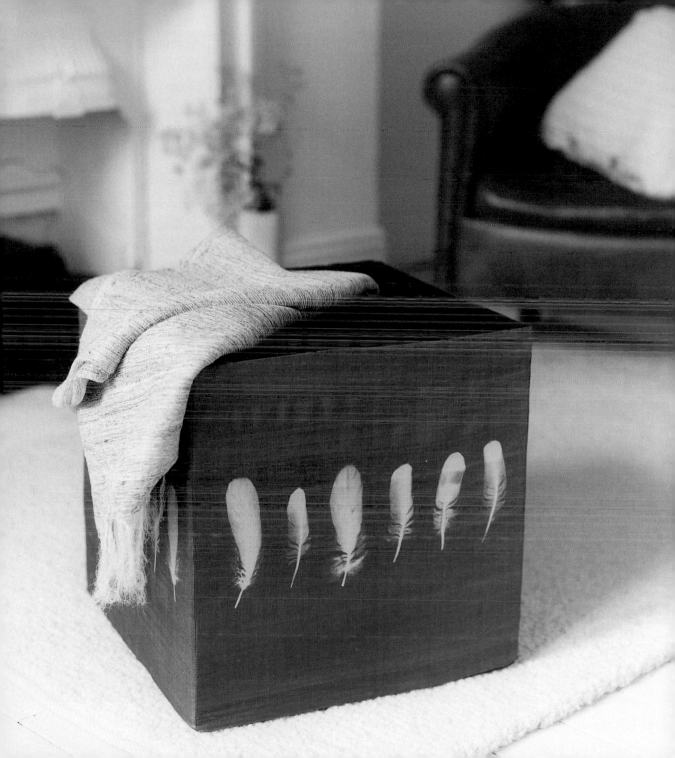

how to make:
Feather floor cube

1 Rinse the silk in warm water (to remove any residue or detergent). Squeeze out and leave damp.

2 In a darkened room and wearing overalls and rubber gloves, put the ferric ammonium citrate and potassium ferric cyanide together in the bowl or pan, add 28fl oz/800ml of cold water and stir well until chemicals have completely dissolved. This mixture is now light sensitive — do not expose to light. It should be a pale yellowish-green color.

3 Wearing gloves and still in the darkened room, dip the silk into the solution so that it is completely covered in the chemical, to ensure an even coating. At this stage you can either work on all four pieces of silk at once, or one at a time. Put newspaper on the floor to catch any drips, and hang the fabric up to dry, ensuring that it is taut and horizontal. When the fabric is dry — it will be a dark greenish-blue color — put one piece on the board and place the feathers evenly on the fabric, then cover with the sheet of acrylic.

4 Clip the board securely to the acrylic, so that the feathers are completely flat against the fabric. Take the board outside and expose to direct sunlight. The longer you leave it, the darker the silk will become. Allow between 20 minutes and an hour, depending on whether it is bright sunlight or an overcast day.

Feather floor cube

5 Bring the board inside and remove the acrylic sheet and the feathers. Wearing rubber gloves, rinse the fabric under cold running water until the water runs clear. You may find it necessary to leave the silk in a bucket of cold water for some time to allow the residue chemical to leach out. When the feather images are white, the fabric is completely fixed. Leave to dry — once the fabric is dry it will be permanently printed. Repeat from step 3 with the other three pieces of silk.

6 Press the four pieces of printed silk and pin in a row. Stitch down the side seams, right sides together, allowing ½in/1.5cm seam allowance, then join down the final seam to make a circle. Cut two rectangles of linen 12 x 19in/30 x 48cm for the base of the cube and hem one long side on each piece. Press. Cut another piece 19in/48cm square for the top of the cube.

7 Pin the square of linen to the top edges of the circle of printed silk, with the right sides together, and stitch into place on a sewing machine to make a cube shape without a base.

8 To finish off, pin the hemmed linen rectangles to the bottom edge of the silk, right sides together and with the hemmed edges overlapping the center, to make a base with a neat flap opening. Stitch the pieces together, then pull the finished cover carefully over the top of the foam cube. Smooth down the fabric so that it sits in place neatly.

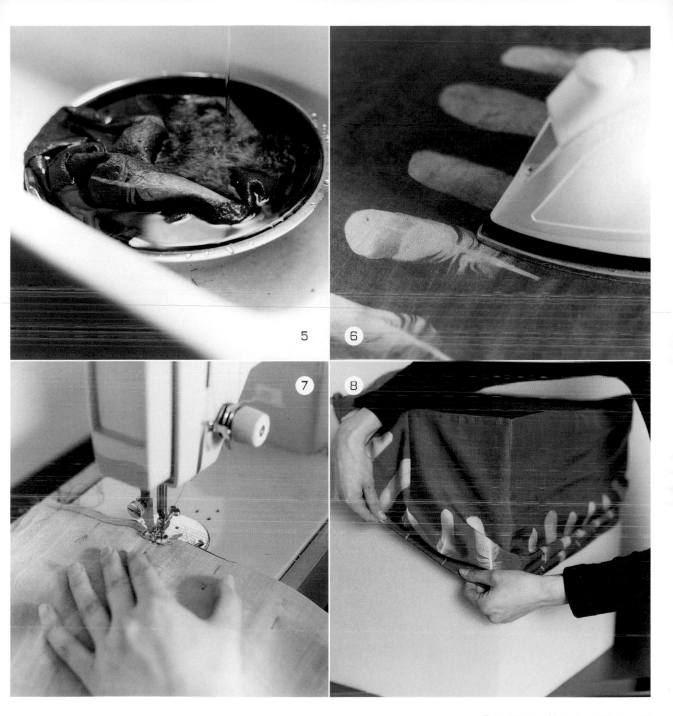

5

6

7

8

Silk painting

For thousands of years, the secrets of sericulture, or silk cultivation, were closely guarded by the Chinese, who prized the luxurious fabric above all others. Strong, fine and glossy, silk is wonderfully wearable — and is the ideal fabric for sophisticated and creative decoration.

We have only legends to describe how the Chinese first learned to cultivate the silkworm, but it was probably at least 5,000 years ago. At first, the precious fabric, spun from the silkworm's cocoon, could be worn only by members of the royal family and their dignitaries, but gradually other classes were also permitted to wear silk, and it was used for home decoration and in commerce, too. In time, it became essential to the Chinese economy. Inevitably, it was also used as a form of money, too, and by the second century BC it was being exported along the trade route (known as the Silk Road) that linked East to West.

But the Chinese could not hold onto their monopoly forever. Despite capital punishment for anyone caught smuggling silkworms out of the country, it is thought that sericulture reached Korea around 200BC, India around 300AD and Byzantium around 550AD. By the Middle Ages it had reached Europe, and in Spain, France and England, silk was sought after by royalty and the aristocracy.

While man has decorated all types of fabric ever since he began spinning and weaving, it is silk that is most highly regarded for this purpose. Its texture, luster and ability to absorb dye make it eminently suitable for painting and coloring. Ancient records indicate that textile dyes were used in China around 2,500BC, if not before. All over the world, however, different techniques were developed for coloring silk, from the block prints of India to the shibori (a sophisticated form of tie-dyeing, see page 64) techniques of Japan and the batik of Java. In fact, wherever silk was traded or cultivated, it was decorated in myriad ways. In Japan, in particular, silk decoration was developed to a particularly marvelous art form, and it was here, during the Middle Ages, shibori was sometimes combined with resist techniques, embroidery and free painting to create beautiful kimonos of immense complexity in pattern, though of extreme simplicity in cut.

Until the 19th century, of course, all dyes were made from either vegetable, animal or mineral sources — madder red, saffron yellow and woad blue, for example. By 1900, however, a whole range of chemical-based colors had been developed, many of them more lightfast and easily washable than natural colorings. Since then, synthetic dyes have been widely used for silk decoration, creating intense, easy-to-use, permanent colors, whether for direct printing, resist work, free painting or immersion in a dye bath. Some craftspeople, these days, are experimenting with natural dyes once again, while more types of synthetic dye are available than ever before. This makes the possibilities almost limitless for contemporary silk painters, who employ a wide range of traditional techniques but also add a modern interpretation, to make the most of this very ancient and beautiful fabric.

Wall hanging

You will need

(To make a hanging measuring 33 x 43in/ 85 x 110cm)

- Overalls, apron or an old shirt
- Rubber gloves, goggles and dust mask
- Length of satin silk pavona, 36 x 45in/ (91 x 114cm)
- 6 tablespoons soda ash
- Large plastic bucket (about 5 gallons/20 liters)
- Iron and pins
- Large printing surface (see page 18)
- Layout paper (9 tabloid-size/A3 sheets stuck together to the size of hanging)
- Soft pencil and embroidery pen
- 10 tablespoons urea
- Measuring spoons and measuring cup
- 2 large (1 quart/1 liter) plastic pots, one with a lid
- Mixing spoons or spatulas
- 1 teaspoon water softener (powder form)
- 4 tablespoons sodium alginate F
- Hand or electric whisk
- 1½–1¾fl oz/40–50ml each of procion dyes (see right)
- 17 empty glass jars or plastic lidded pots
- Paintbrushes of various sizes, flat and round
- About 4¾fl oz/140ml water based resist
- Hairdryer (optional)
- Newspapers (without color pictures)
- Large saucepan with wire rack (steamer)
- Mild laundry detergent

To add a decorative element to a room or simply brighten up a plain wall, a fabric hanging makes a wonderful change to a conventional painting, drawing or photograph.

If you love the look of silk painting, you will be unable to resist making this wall hanging, with its simple, repeated shapes and muted colors. And not only is the finished project lovely to look at, but also the technique of actually making it — mixing the dyes, masking out areas and painting with soft brushes — is thoroughly enjoyable. This project uses dyes in the following colors: lilac, ice blue, brown rose, antique gold, bubblegum, pearl gray, navy, chocolate brown, midnight blue, warm black and bronze.

how to make:
Wall hanging

1 Firstly, read the safety advice on page 57. Wearing overalls, gloves, goggles and a dust mask, soak the fabric in the soda ash dissolved in 3 gallons/12 liters of water for 30 minutes, and leave to dry (unrinsed). Press, then pin to the print table, fairly taut.

2 Copy the design on page 415 onto the layout paper and pin it to the stretched fabric, allowing for a ¾in/2cm hem at the bottom and sides, and 1½in/4cm at the top. To transfer the design to the fabric, make holes through the paper with a pin along all the drawn lines at about ⅜in/1cm intervals, then draw with an embroidery pen over the pierced lines The design will be visible on the silk, defined by a series of dots.

3 Wearing the protective clothing, prepare the thickening paste by first dissolving the urea in 13fl oz/375ml of hot water. In the other pot, add the water softener to 1 pint/500ml of cold water, then beat in the sodium alginate with a whisk. Add the urea solution to the alginate solution, beat together and leave to stand overnight, with lid on.

4 Still wearing the protective clothing, prepare the dye stock solutions by adding 1 teaspoon of dye powder to 4fl oz/125ml hot water and mixing until completely dissolved. Store each dye stock solution in a separate lidded container, labeling the contents clearly. To mix the shades used in this project, add measured amounts of dye stock solution to measured amounts of thickening paste as follows: Lavender: 4fl oz/125ml paste, 1 teaspoon lilac dye stock, 1 teaspoon ice blue. Rose: 4fl oz/125ml paste, 2 teaspoons brown rose, 1 teaspoon antique gold, 2 teaspoons bubblegum. Beige: 4fl oz/125ml paste, 8 teaspoons pearl gray. Gray: 4fl oz/125ml paste, ½ teaspoon navy, 2 teaspoons brown. Light Brown: 4fl oz/125ml paste, 2 teaspoons antique gold, 2 teaspoons bronze, 5 teaspoons chocolate brown. Purple: 4fl oz/125ml paste, 4 teaspoons lilac, 2 teaspoons midnight blue, 1 teaspoon ice blue, 3 teaspoons warm black.

Wall hanging

5 Paint the design, beginning with the ovals, spots and squares. Use smallish rounded brushes for outlining shapes and larger brushes for filling in. (For even results, fill in while the outline is still wet.) Let dry or use a hairdryer.

6 Paint resist over the ovals, spots and squares, so you can paint the large areas of color without painting around all the shapes. Working like this also adds interest to resisted areas, as the background color soaks through the resist in some places. Leave to dry (or use a hairdryer), then paint background areas and the border. Let dry again.

7 Roll the silk in newspaper, place in a saucepan with a wire rack, put a little water in the bottom and steam for 10 minutes with the lid on to fix the dye. Do this in a well-ventilated area. Remove the fabric from the newspaper and rinse in cold running water, then in hand-hot water with a little mild detergent. Then rinse in cold running water and let dry. Press when the fabric is still slightly damp. Hem the side and bottom edges by turning over once, pressing, and then pressing again with fusible hemming tape sandwiched between the fabric. For the top edge, press a 1½in/4cm hem, then press with the hemming tape so that there is a pocket of ¾in/2cm at the top edge in which to insert the dowel.

to finish, you will need
- 4½yds/4m fusible hemming tape
- Measuring tape
- 48in/1.2m x ¼in/5mm dowel

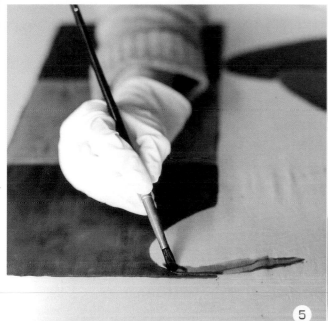

⑤ ⑥

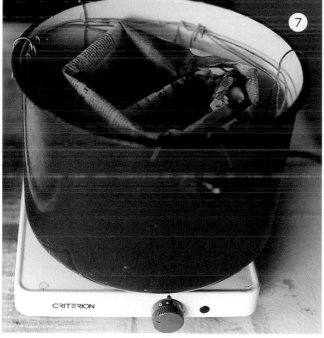

⑦

safety advice

Work in a well-ventilated area separate from living or eating areas and do not eat, smoke or drink in your work area. Do not use kitchen utensils for dyes and chemicals. Wear protective clothing and wash your hands well after working with dyes and chemicals.

Abstract scarf

You will need

(To make a scarf measuring 17½ x 68½in/ 44 x 174cm)

- Protective clothing (see page 52)
- Piece of crepe satin silk, 18 x 69in/ 45 x 175cm
- 6 tablespoons soda ash
- Large plastic bucket (5 gallons/20 liters)
- Iron
- Pins
- Large printing surface (see page 18)
- Embroidery pen and/or colored paper and scissors
- Measuring spoons and measuring cup
- 2 large (1 quart/1 liter) plastic pots, one with a lid
- Mixing spoons or spatulas
- 10 tablespoons urea
- 1 teaspoon water softener (powder form)
- 4 tablespoons sodium alginate F
- Hand or electric whisk
- 10 empty glass jars or plastic lidded pots
- About 1½–1¾fl oz/40–50ml each of procion dyes (see right)
- Paintbrushes of various sizes, flat and round
- About 4¾fl oz/140ml water-based resist
- Hairdryer (optional)
- Newspapers (without color pictures)
- Large saucepan with wire rack (steamer)
- Laundry detergent and fabric softener
- Needle and thread to match main color

A painted silk scarf is a beautiful object to own. This one can be dressed up or down as you wish, and is delightfully easy to wear.

If you've been put off trying silk painting because of its emphasis on 'artistic' imagery and vivid colors, this project takes a more contemporary, understated approach. Simple geometric shapes are repeated in a small range of soft colors — a design with as much validity as traditional silk painting, but a much more modern style. Vary the colors if you wish to coordinate with your wardrobe, but bear in mind that subtle shades are best. This project uses the following colors: antique gold, bronze, chocolate brown, navy, ice blue, midnight blue and warm black.

how to make:
Abstract scarf

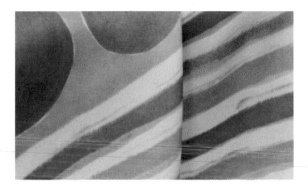

For safety guidelines, see page 57.

1 Wearing overalls, rubber gloves, goggles and a dust mask, soak the fabric in the soda ash dissolved in 3 gallons/12 liters of water for 30 minutes and leave to dry (unrinsed). Press, then pin to the printing table, so that it is fairly taut.

2 Plot out your design on the fabric, using an embroidery pen and/or cutting out shapes in colored paper. If you wish, you can copy the design on page 416.

3 Wearing the protective clothing, prepare the thickening paste by first dissolving the urea in 13fl oz/375ml of hot water. In the other pot, add the water softener to 1 pint/500ml of cold water, then beat in the sodium alginate with the whisk. Add the urea solution to the alginate solution, beat and leave overnight with the lid on.

4 Still wearing all your protective clothing, prepare the dye stock solutions by adding 1 teaspoon of dye powder to 4fl oz/125ml hot water and mixing until completely dissolved. Store each solution in a separate lidded container, labeling the colors clearly. To mix individual shades, add measured amounts of dye stock solution to measured amounts of thickening paste as follows: Light brown: 4fl oz/ 125ml thickening paste, 2 teaspoons antique gold dye stock, 2 teaspoons bronze dye stock, 5 teaspoons chocolate brown dye stock. Light blue/gray: 4fl oz/125ml thickening paste, 2 teaspoons warm black, 3 teaspoons ice blue. Dark blue: 4fl oz/125ml thickening paste, 1 teaspoon warm black, 2 teaspoons navy, 4 teaspoons midnight blue, 1 teaspoon chocolate brown, ½ teaspoon antique gold.

Abstract scarf

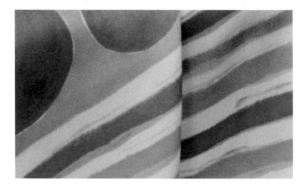

5 Paint the areas to remain white (the rings and stripes) with resist. Paint the colored spots and stripes with thickened dyes. Use smallish, rounded brushes for outlining shapes, and larger brushes for filling in. (Fill in before the outline dries or the brushstrokes will show.) For neat stripes, use a flat brush; for looser stripes, a rounded brush. Let dry or use a hairdryer.

6 To paint the background color of the areas patterned with spots, paint resist over each spot then, using a large flat brush, paint over the area to be colored. On patterned areas reserved white with the resist, paint the background color over the resisted areas.

7 Roll the scarf in sheets of newspaper, place in a large saucepan with a wire rack, put a small amount of water in the bottom and steam for 10 minutes with the lid on to fix the dye. Do this in a well-ventilated area away from areas used for food preparation. Remove the fabric from the newspaper and rinse, first in cold running water, then in hand-hot water with a small amount of mild detergent. Then rinse in cold running water again. Soak in fabric softener and rinse again. Leave to dry.

8 Press when the fabric is still slightly damp, and hem the edges by rolling over twice, pinning, then stitching by hand with small hemming stitches.

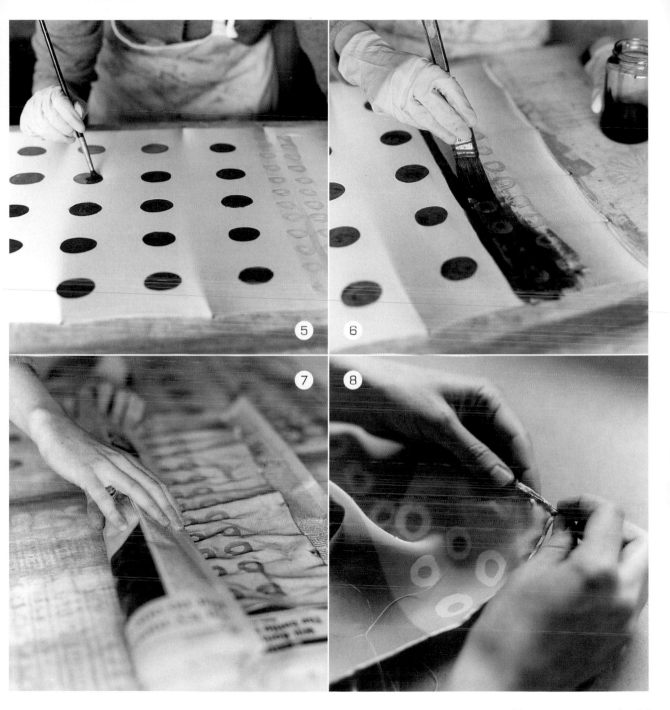

Shibori

The practice of tying and dyeing fabric has been around for many years — sometimes from the need to re-use old cloth; sometimes for the beauty of the effect. Shibori-dyed fabric is especially appealing — its traditional patterns are centuries-old, but its attraction is fresh, modern and exciting.

Shibori is the Japanese word for resist-dyed textiles that have first been shaped, perhaps by folding, braiding, crumpling or twisting, and then secured, by stitching, knotting or binding. What makes them so special is their pretty soft-edged patterns, which appear completely different from the sharply dyed edges that result from using resists of wax, paste or stencils. And like all dyeing processes, there is an element of chance in the method — depending on how the fabric is shaped, the strength of the dye and the length of time in the dye bath — which gives a wonderfully lively, characterful appearance.

The oldest known shibori cloth was discovered in Peru, and dates back to the first or second century BC. At different times, shibori has been made in Ecuador, Guatemala, Bolivia, Paraguay, Argentina and Mexico, involving fine, hand-woven woolen and cotton cloth. In India, shibori was practiced mainly in western areas, using muslin or silk, often with hundreds of tiny spots forming patterns on a dyed background, and used for saris, veils and turbans. There it was (and still is) known as *bandhana* work; in Indonesia, another important tie-dye area, it is called *plangi* (bound cloth) and *tritik* (stitched cloth), depending on the specific technique involved. Silk was generally the base fabric, perhaps bound and sewn with leaf fibers and intricately dyed in colorful, contrasting colors. The nomadic tribes of North Africa dyed simple spot and circular patterns onto woolen loincloths, and it is thought that the Bedouin and Berber people passed on their knowledge to other areas of the country. The processes were developed over the years, and today shibori is still flourishing in West Africa. For the Yoruba people of West Nigeria it is called *adire*, and is dyed with indigo to create magnificently patterned cloth.

While shibori has been practiced all over the world for centuries, it is in Japan that it has been most fully explored. It is believed that shibori reached Japan from China around the end of the sixth century, after which it developed rapidly and became particularly fashionable among the aristocracy. During the Middle Ages it was more widely available, reaching an unprecedented level of popularity, used for samurai garments, government officials' uniforms and ordinary people's clothing. A wide variety of complex techniques was developed, which required an extraordinary amount of skill, so shibori dyers were respected and admired members of society.

Today, shibori is still a living craft in Japan, widely practiced commercially and now entering new areas. Until recently it was used mainly for kimonos, but it is now being applied to fashion accessories such as scarves and wraps, and to other interior items including bed covers and lampshades, demonstrating the virtuosity of its makers and the magical effects of this intriguing craft.

Monochrome scarf

You will need

(To make a scarf measuring 20 x 20in/ 50 x 50cm)

- 21in/52cm square piece of white silk georgette or fine silk
- Weighing scales
- Laundry detergent (liquid)
- 20in/50cm length of smooth, rigid, plastic pipe or tube, about 6in/15cm in diameter
- Steel wool pads
- Furniture polish
- Ball of string
- Strong thread
- Scissors
- Overalls, apron or an old shirt
- Rubber gloves
- Protective mask
- Packet of black dye (cold dye is ideal)
- Two plastic buckets (one stainless steel, if heat is required for the dye)
- Fabric conditioner
- Iron
- Needle (or sewing machine)
- Thread to match the dye color

Wonderfully floaty and feminine, this scarf possesses both delicacy and a bold, striking design — the result of a technique that is ancient in form, but thoroughly modern in esthetic.

Some tie-dyed fabrics can appear a little clumsy and unsubtle, but if you employ the shibori technique with a certain dexterity, as demonstrated here, you can achieve a look that is superbly impressive and unmistakably sophisticated. The visual intrigue of this appealing project lies in its bold juxtaposition of graphic black and white stripes, delicately narrow and pleasingly irregular. This is a vibrant design that would be worn equally well with either a casual outfit or a smart business suit.

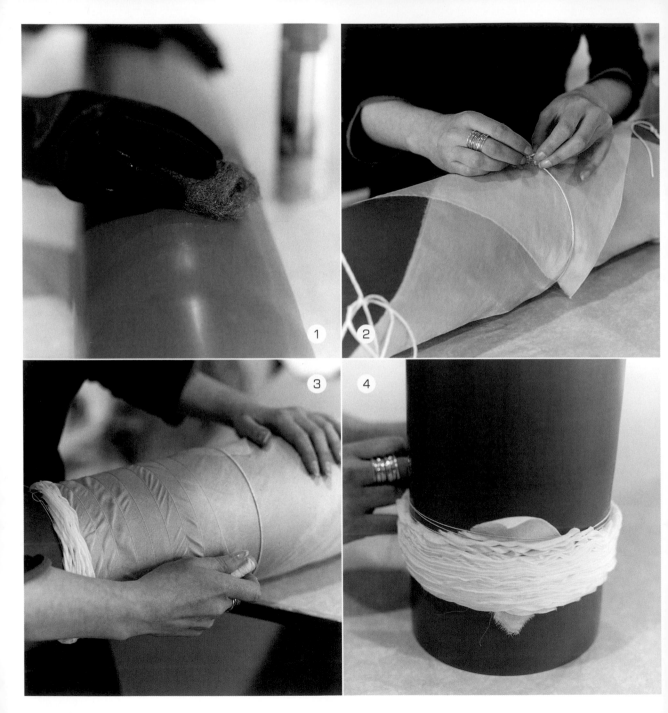

how to make:
Monochrome scarf

1 Weigh the silk in order to determine how much dye to use. Hand wash it in hand-hot water with a little detergent to remove any finish, and spin to remove excess water. Also ensure that the pipe is really smooth by polishing with steel wool and furniture polish.

2 Roll the damp fabric around the pipe at 45 degrees to form a diamond shape. To hold the silk in place while it is wrapped, tie the ends and the center with string. Take the strong thread and knot around the base of the pipe.

3 Holding the pipe in one hand, firmly wrap the thread around the silk, leaving about ¾in/2cm between each line of thread (the further apart the thread, the more fabric will be exposed to the dye). After about 4in/10cm, push the fabric down (toward the end of the pipe) to form concertina folds. Remove the string when the thread reaches it.

4 Continue wrapping the thread until all of the fabric is condensed into folds. Cut off the thread and knot securely. Soak the wrapped fabric in tepid water for an hour.

wrapping the thread
When you wrap the length of thread around the pipe, make sure that you keep the tension fairly taut. If you wrap it round too loosely, the dye will get under the thread and you will not achieve the desired striped effect.

Monochrome scarf

5 Wearing overalls, rubber gloves and a mask, mix up the dye in the bucket, following the manufacturer's instructions and observing safety recommendations. Make sure there is enough water to cover the fabric on the pipe. Place the pipe in the dye bath. Leave in for the recommended length of time to give a strong color, moving the pipe around a little occasionally to prevent the dye from settling.

6 Remove the pipe from the dye and rinse away excess dye under the cold tap. Carefully unwind the fabric from the pipe, discarding the thread.

7 Thoroughly rinse the dyed fabric with cold water until the water runs clear. Hand wash and condition the fabric in a bucket full of hand-hot water, and then leave to dry.

8 Press the fabric. To hem the edge by hand, fold over the raw edges about ⅜in/1cm. Start with the needle at the raw edge and make a couple of stitches to secure the thread. Slip the needle into the fold and run it along inside for ½–¾in/1–2cm. Take it out and pick up a tiny piece of the fabric just below the exit beside the raw edge. Repeat by putting the needle into the fold again, just beside where it came out. Continue all the way round to give a good rolled hem. Alternatively, you could machine stitch the hem.

Velvet throw

You will need

(To make a throw measuring about 77 x 41in/195 x 105cm)

- 2¼yds/2m white velvet, at least 43in/110cm wide
- Weighing scales
- Sewing machine
- Laundry detergent (liquid)
- Basting thread
- Needle
- Scissors
- Ball of string
- Weights
- Quilting thread
- Overalls, apron or an old shirt
- Rubber gloves
- Protective mask
- Packet of dark gray dye (ideally cold dye)
- Small glass jar
- Plastic bucket (stainless steel, if heat is required for the dye)
- Fabric conditioner
- 2¼yds/2m satin at least 44in/115cm wide
- Pins
- Silk thread to match the velvet
- Iron

The subtlety of the shibori technique has to be seen to be believed, and this throw is an utterly glamorous example of just how beautiful and impressive it can be.

The delicious deep slate gray of this soft velvet combines perfectly with its irregular shibori-dyed pattern to create an irresistible piece that is almost decadent in its luxury. Other colors could have an equally eye-catching effect, depending on the décor you would like them to match — a deep red, perhaps, or emerald green, midnight blue, dove gray, pale lilac or burnt orange. Alternatively, for a very unusual effect, try the same technique using several shades of a color and cut the fabric into smaller pieces to create a beautiful patchwork quilt effect.

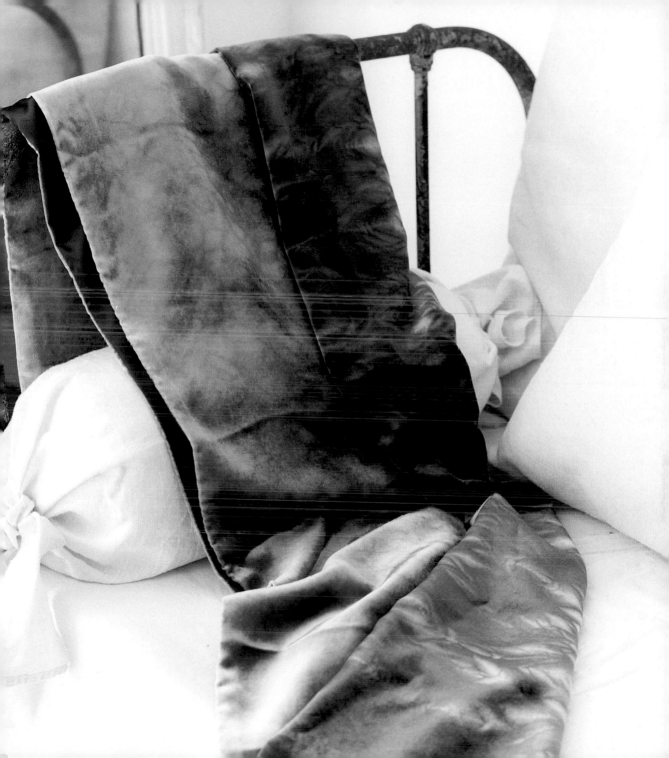

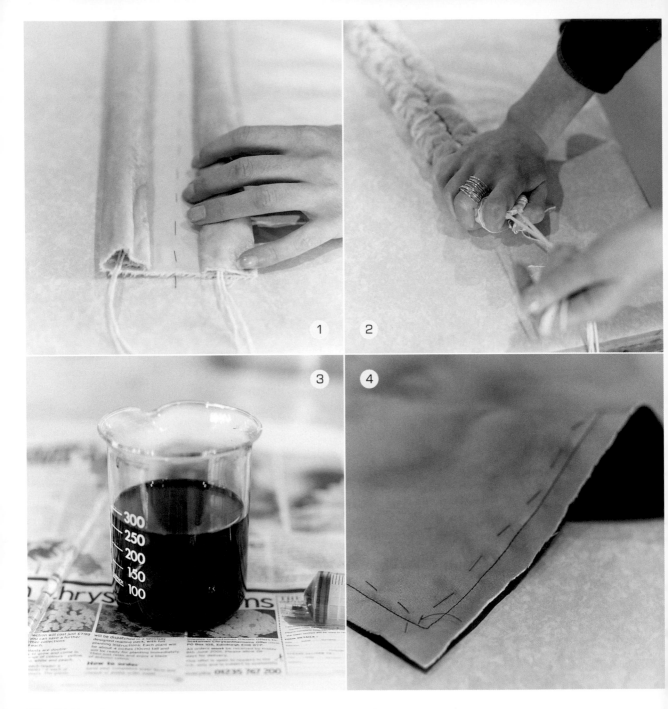

how to make:
Velvet throw

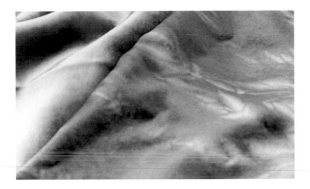

1 Weigh the velvet in order to determine how much dye to use. With the sewing machine, overlock the edges of the velvet so that it does not fray, then machine wash (on a low temperature, using a gentle cycle) to remove any finish. Spread the damp velvet right-side down on a large table. With basting thread, mark the center lengthwise. Cut a double length of string and lay it along one of the long edges. Starting at the edge, roll the fabric around the string. Continue rolling until you reach the basting thread in the center, then use weights to hold the rolled velvet in place. Repeat from the other side.

2 Tie short lengths of quilting thread loosely around the double sausage-shaped fabric, leaving gaps of about 2–4in/5–10cm between them, all the way along. At one end, take the ends of the 'core' string and tie them together firmly. At the other end, hold both of the core strings in one hand and with the other hand push the fabric so it wrinkles up. When the fabric has been concertina'd, tie the core strings securely. Submerge in lukewarm water for at least an hour.

3 Wearing overalls, gloves and a mask, mix up the dye in a glass jar, following the manufacturer's instructions and carefully observing any safety recommendations, then pour into the bucket. Place the fabric in the dye bath. Leave until the dye has produced a strong color, stirring regularly. Once dyed, rinse thoroughly under cold running water. Untie, wash (as in step 1) using fabric conditioner, spin and let dry.

4 Cut off the overlocked edges of the velvet, then place it on top of the satin, right sides together, and pin around all the edges. Baste over the pins about ¾in/2cm from the raw edge. Remove the pins.

Velvet throw

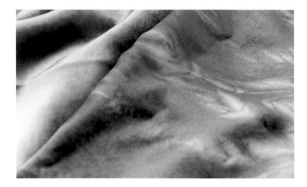

7 Lay the throw out completely flat. In its center, pin through both layers. Then pin again, working from the centre at 10–12in/25–30cm intervals both horizontally and vertically, to produce a grid shape of pins holding the layers firmly together.

8 Thread a needle with a double length of silk thread. At one of the pinned points, make two small stitches on top of each other through both layers (starting at the reverse of the throw), leaving a tail of thread when you start and finish. Tie the two tail ends together, being careful not to distort the fabric by pulling too tightly. Trim the ends to about ⅝in/ 1.5cm (if you cut them too close to the fabric they may come undone). Do not worry about leaving loose threads on the reverse of the quilting — this is a traditional feature of quilting and will give your work authenticity. Work over the entire throw, removing the pins as you go.

5 Cut the satin to the size of the velvet (the velvet may have shrunk). Machine stitch ⅝in/1.5cm from the raw edge, leaving a gap of about 6in/15cm in the middle of one long side. Remove the basting and trim excess fabric from the corners.

6 Turn right side out. Press the edges flat, taking care not to crush the pile, and neatly hand stitch the opening edges together.

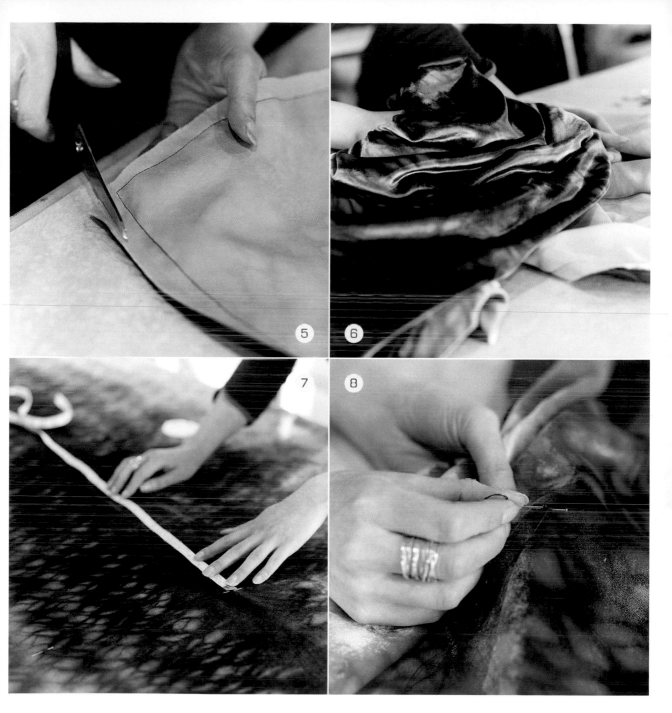

Knitting &
Stitching

Knitting

While the basic knitting stitches are extremely simple, this is a craft that can be used to create fabrics in which color, pattern and form combine in the most complex and harmonious ways. Useful, everyday items can be plain and unassuming or highly sophisticated, creative works of art.

The word 'knit' comes from the Old English *cnotta*, 'knot', but it is not a traditional English technique. In fact, it is thought that knitting originated in the Middle East (possibly among the Arabian nomads), and from there spread across North Africa and to Spain. By the 10th century it was certainly a well-developed craft, as demonstrated by the complex knitted socks that have been discovered in Egyptian tombs.

Various portraits of a 'knitting Madonna' show that knitting had reached Europe by the 14th century, and by the 15th and 16th centuries it was a well-established commercial business. It as organized into men-only guilds of professionals, who made caps, stockings and other knitted articles for the domestic market and for export. While the aristocracy enjoyed fine silk knitwear, the less well off knitted their own, more humble garments, giving rise to distinctive community knitting styles such as fishermen's ganseys (close-fitting sweaters with distinctive monochrome patterning) and, later, Fair Isle and Aran knits. Then, in 1589, English clergyman William Lee invented a knitting machine that could work 100 times faster than any hand-knitter (interestingly, the modern machine differs little from Lee's centuries-old design in its basic technology). At first Lee's invention could only deal with thick, woolen yarn, but eventually it was refined to cope with silk and to produce intricate patterns. This led to a cottage knitting industry in Britain, in which families rented out a hand-frame machine, children wound the yarn, men operated the machine and the women sewed up the garments. This thrived until the Industrial Revolution.

In the 18th and 19th centuries, meanwhile, thanks to increased prosperity and leisure time, in combination with rigid views on how women should conduct themselves, hand knitting gradually changed from being a poor person's necessity to a rich woman's pastime. Refinements were made — needles were given capped ends, for example — and printed patterns became extremely popular, often for small accessories such as pen-wipers or pincushion covers. In the 20th century, even after the emancipation of women, hand knitting continued to be a popular hobby, inexpensive and useful. Women knitted all sorts of items — from baby clothes and sweaters to underwear and entire coats. But it was not until the 1960s and '70s that there was an explosion of knitting as a real craft form, when art students discovered its potential and began to experiment, combining unusual stitches, mixing yarns of different types and textures and taking inspiration from fine art for pattern and color. Since that time, knitting has been seen as fashionable, ingenious and experimental. Its basic stitches may be linked to the past, but fresh ideas and interpretations have given it an adventurous, exciting future.

Chunky cushion

You will need

(To make a cushion measuring about 20 x 20in/50 x 50cm)

- Saw
- 2 broom handles (about 1in/2.3cm diameter)
- Ruler or measuring tape
- Sandpaper (optional)
- Glue (optional)
- 2 discs/knobs (optional)
- Small amount of olive oil (optional)
- 6½lb/3kg thick, unspun cream merino wool yarn (tops — 64 quality)
- Steam iron
- Scissors
- Pillow form 20 x 20in/50 x 50cm
- 2 buttons
- Large-eyed needle
- Twine

(See page 402 for instructions on how to knit)

Experience the comfort of a giant, plump cushion, knitted in softest merino wool. Its neutral color ensures that this project will complement any style of décor.

Hand knitting may not currently be in its heyday, but the satisfaction that one can gain from this classic domestic craft is just as great as it ever was. Though the skill is traditional, the results can be anything but; this cushion, for example, is overscaled in both its dimensions and its wonderfully chunky rib — which is achieved by using broom handles instead of conventional needles. The finishing touch is a pair of mother-of-pearl buttons, whose iridescence provides a contrast to the texture of the wool.

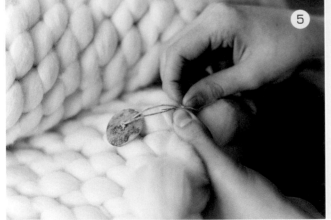

joining lengths of wool

When you are joining two balls of wool, just leave a long end of wool (about 6in/15cm) from your knitting and join on the new ball alongside — knit the two lengths of wool together until the first one runs out.

how to make:
Chunky cushion

1 Saw the broom handles to about 28in/70cm long each so you can use them as knitting needles. If necessary, sand the rounded ends with sandpaper. It will make knitting easier if you glue discs or a door knob to the ends to stop the knitting dropping off. It will also be easier to knit if you lightly oil the 'needles' with olive oil.

2 Practice knitting with the needles and thick yarn until you are used to the feeling. As you wrap the yarn around the needles, twist it slightly. This sample can be easily unraveled and the yarn used again.

3 To make the cushion, cast on enough stitches for a 22in/55cm width. Then knit, using stockinette/ stocking stitch (one row knit, one row purl), for 43in/110cm, slipping the first stitch of each row except the first row (transfer the stitch from the left to the right needle without working it). Bind off/ cast off loosely on a purl row.

4 Press flat with a steam iron and fold the knitting in half crosswise. Cut a 60in/1.5m length of yarn and neatly join the two sides together, using your fingers to push the yarn in and out of the knitted stitches, as if you were using a needle and thread.

5 Insert the pillow form. Attach the buttons to a length of twine and stitch to one open side. Fasten, using a stitch as a buttonhole. Press completed cushion with a steam iron.

Casual bag

You will need

(To make a bag measuring about
9¼ x 12in/24 x 30cm)

- One hank (12¼oz/350g) natural
  merino wool roving (prespun wool),
  wound into two balls
- One hank (12¼oz/350g) raspberry
  ripple, space-dyed merino wool roving,
  wound into two balls
- US Size 19/15mm knitting needles
- Laundry detergent and conditioner
- Measuring tape or ruler
- Iron
- Sewing machine
- Thread to match the wool
- Piece of linen measuring 10 x 24in/
  26 x 58cm
- Needle
- Pins
- Button

(See page 402 for instructions
on how to knit)

This cute little knitted bag — with a delightful
raspberry-ripple effect — slips neatly over the
shoulder for a look that is both fun and casual.

No one could argue that this sweet handbag is too formal
— in fact, its chunky ribbed texture and slightly uneven
shape make it just right for a walk in the park or a relaxed
weekend in the country. Once you've mastered the
project's basic principles, you could easily adapt its height,
width and, of course, color, to match any outfit in your
wardrobe. The bag fastens with a simple button pushed
through the stitches; a nice alternative might be a small
toggle or maybe a leather knot.

how to make:
Casual bag

1 Using two strands of roving, knit a sample swatch 4in/10cm square and count the number of rows and stitches. Felt the square (see step 4) and, when dry, measure its size in order to establish both the gauge/tension and how the felting affects the wool. From this, work out the number of stitches and rows you will need to knit for this project. (As a general guide, you will need to knit the bag a little bigger to allow for the felting, but all wool behaves slightly differently so it is necessary to check. If the bag does not come out to the exact measurements given here, don't worry — just remember to adjust the size of the lining accordingly.)

2 Using two strands of natural roving, cast on enough stitches to make a finished (after felting) width of 10in/26cm. Knit, using stockinette/stocking stitch (one row knit, one row purl), to make a finished length of 4in/10cm. Break off one strand of natural, leaving a tail of wool about 6in/15cm long, and tie in a pink strand. Continue for a further finished length of 4in/10cm. Break off the second strand of natural wool and tie in the second strand of pink. Continue, using two pink strands, for a further finished length of 8in/20cm.

3 When the total length is equal to a finished length of 16in/40cm, break off one pink strand and tie in a natural strand. Continuing in stockinette/stocking stitch, knit for a finished length of 4in/10cm. Break off the second pink strand and tie in the second strand of natural. Continue, using two natural strands, for another finished length of 4in/10cm, until the total length is equivalent to a finished length of 24in/60cm. Bind off/cast off on either row.

4 Gently felt the knitted rectangle by washing in hot, soapy water and kneading it for a few minutes, until you feel the quality of the fabric change. Rinse with cold water. Repeat if necessary. Add fabric conditioner and rinse again. Spin in a washing machine and dry flat, pulling the knitting into shape while still wet. The bag should shrink to 10 x 24in/ 26 x 60cm. (For more information on felting, see pages 171–172.)

Casual bag

5 Fold the knitted rectangle in half, right sides together, and press. Allowing ⅜in/1cm for the seams, machine stitch the two long sides together.

6 Take the linen and stitch a 1¼in/3cm hem at each of its short ends. Fold in half, with right sides together and stitch the two long sides together, allowing ⅜in/1cm for the seams. Turn out.

7 Place the knitted bag (inside out) inside the linen bag — it will protrude by about 1½in/4cm. Hand sew the lining to the knitting at the top and turn out. The top edge will curl over.

8 Using two strands of natural roving, knit a strap 2 x 32in/5 x 80cm, casting on an uneven number of stitches. Slip the first stitch of each row (transfer the stitch from the left to the right needle without working it) to create rolled edges on the underside of the strap. Felt as in step 4. Sew the strap to the top of the bag and the button to the inside of the knitting, above the lining. Use a stitch as a buttonhole.

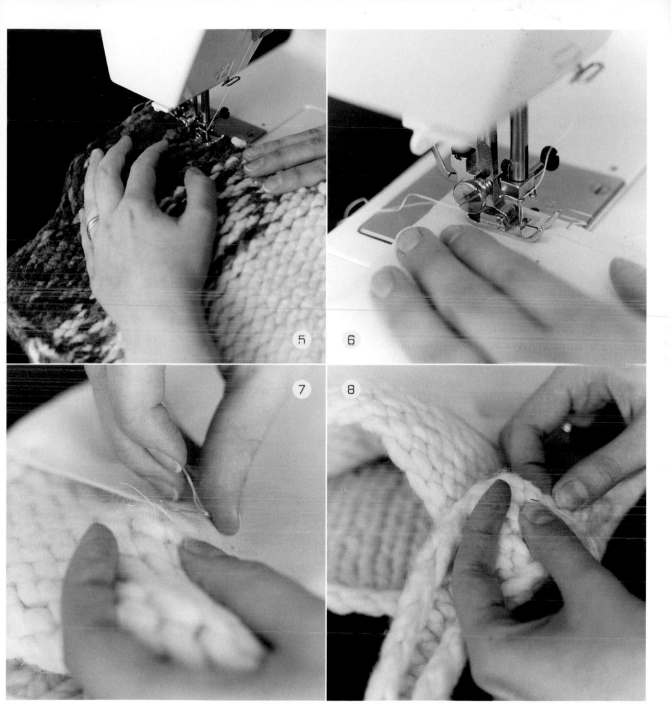

Crochet

Developed in the 18th century as a means of imitating costly lace, crochet has been used as an embellishment to clothing and all sorts of accessories. Its heyday was in Victorian times, but today's makers are experimenting with methods and materials that bring this classic craft right up to date.

It seems logical to assume that crochet has as long a history as knitting, but in fact no one knows exactly how or when crochet came into being. Theories are wide-ranging — some indicate that it came from Arabia and then spread via trade routes to the Mediterranean; some that it was a primitive ceremonial craft used in South America; some that it originated in early China; and others that it developed in the 16th-century Catholic church in Europe. What is known is that there is no evidence of crochet in Europe before 1800, but that it was probably an offspring from an ancient form of embroidery, called 'tambour work', known in China, Turkey, India, Persia and North Africa. In this technique, a background fabric is stretched onto a frame and worked with a hooked needle and thread. In late 18th-century Europe, the stitches came to be worked without a backing, and it was named 'crochet in the air', the word 'crochet' coming from the old French word *croc*, meaning 'hook'.

For many decades, crochet was made using fine cotton, linen or silk thread in an attempt to replicate expensive lace. It was taught to girls in European convents (who later took the craft to Britain and America) and for a while, being lavish and time-consuming, it was considered suitable only for the wealthy to practice. An exception, however, was in Ireland, where proceeds from the sale of crochet saved some people from starvation during the terrible potato famine of 1845–7.

Gradually crochet became a more widespread craft, and by the 1850s it had reached England, Wales and the Scottish lowlands, where it was known as 'poor man's lace'. Designs and pattern books proliferated. During Victorian times, its popularity increased, influenced partly by the fashion for covering up almost every item of furniture, and partly by the commonly held belief that Queen Victoria herself was a keen crocheter. When it was not employed to make covers for sugar bowls, milk pitchers and chair backs, it was used for babies' bonnets, edgings for handkerchiefs, pillowcases and tablecloths, collars and purses. But after the First World War, although some patterns for wool crochet started to appear, lack of free time and changes in fashion meant that the craft came to be practiced by fewer and fewer people.

Crochet enjoyed a brief resurgence in the 1960s and '70s, when it was taken up by some makers as an experimental form of textile art, and featured in mainstream fashion, but then almost disappeared again. Crocheters today use the traditional range of stitches but in increasingly exciting ways, perhaps employing intriguing patterning, contrasts of color and texture, or unusual materials, such as string, raffia or twine, to give a conventional craft form a desirable contemporary twist.

Sisal vase

You will need

(To make a vase measuring about 4in/
10cm diameter and 15in/38cm high,
depending on the type of string used
and your gauge/tension)

- Two balls of sisal string
- US Size G6/4mm crochet hook
- Scissors
- Empty jar or tin can
- Spray starch (optional)

(See page 404 for instructions on
how to crochet)

This crocheted vase makes a lovely accessory in a
natural, subtle interior. Its design is deceptively simple,
but has been given a clever twist with the use of
interestingly textured string.

Modern crochet — in vogue again after decades in fashion
wilderness — takes simple shapes in combination with
contemporary colors and materials. This vase is made
from inexpensive garden string and it uses only three
different stitches. Its impact comes from its pared-down
profile and rough, ribbed texture. For a brighter look, you
could use a combination of colors in bold stripes and,
of course, you can easily adjust the pattern to make the
vase as wide or narrow, tall or short as you wish.

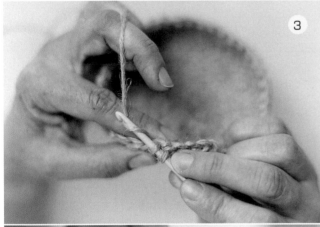

experimenting with yarns

As well as sisal, you could make a vase like this in other yarns and textures, such as nylon, leather strips, raffia or even fabric cut into thin strips and knotted together. Search your local hardware as well as traditional sewing stores for inspiration. Remember to try different-size hooks with these unusual yarns, in order to achieve the desired firmness.

how to make:
Sisal vase

1 Take the sisal string and, using the US Size G6/4mm hook, make 4ch to start. Join into a ring with a sl st into the first ch.

2 Make five rounds, as follows: Round 1: 1ch, work 2sc into each stitch to make 8 stitches. Join with a slip stitch into the first stitch. Round 2: 1ch, work 2sc into each stitch to make 16 stitches. Join with a slip stitch into the first stitch. Round 3: 1ch, * 1sc into next stitch, 2sc into next stitch. Repeat from * to make 24 stitches. Join with a sl st into the first stitch. Round 4: 1ch, * 1sc into each of next 2 stitches, 2sc into next stitch. Repeat from * to make 32 stitches. Join with a sl st into the first stitch. Round 5: 1ch, * 2sc into next stitch, 1sc into each of next 3 stitches. Repeat from * to make 40 stitches. Join with a sl st into the first stitch. This completes the base of the vase.

3 In order to build up the sides of the vase, work 1ch, then 1sc into each stitch. Join with a sl st into the first stitch. This is one round.

4 Continue working in rounds of single crochet until the vase reaches your desired height. Fasten off by cutting the string about 4in/10cm from the hook, and drawing this 'tail' through the slip stitch. Trim neatly.

5 Finish off by carefully inserting the jar or tin can into the completed sisal sleeve, in order to make the vase waterproof. For extra stability and durability, you may wish to apply spray starch to the vase.

---

abbreviations

ch = chain   sl st = slip stitch

sc = single crochet   dc = double crochet

* = repeat stitches as indicated

Mohair throw

You will need

(To make a throw measuring about
51 x 61in/130 x 155cm. Each motif
should measure approximately 7 x 7in/
18 x 18cm. Measure the first one
you make and, if it differs a great deal,
you may wish to swap to a larger or
smaller hook)

- 16 x 2oz/50g balls chunky lilac pink
  mohair yarn (or 17 balls if you wish to
  use this color for your trim)
- Two crochet hooks, US Size H8/5mm
  and US Size 7/4.5mm
- 1 ball contrasting- or complementary-
  colored mohair to trim (optional)

(See page 404 for instructions
on how to crochet and page 99
for abbreviations)

Irresistibly soft and delicate, this bed cover has a look
that combines the best of classic and contemporary.
While it may appear complex, the pattern can actually
be built up quite simply and speedily.

A gorgeously soft, velvety yarn, in a fashionable color and
a pretty, feminine pattern, is what makes this project so
appealing. Use two or three toning shades if you want to
create a more varied look; they could be combined in
stripes or blocks, or even radiate out from the center.
Finally, the beauty of the project is, of course, that you can
make as many or as few squares as you wish, to create any
size of cover — for a cushion or a baby's cot to a sofa or
even a king-size bed.

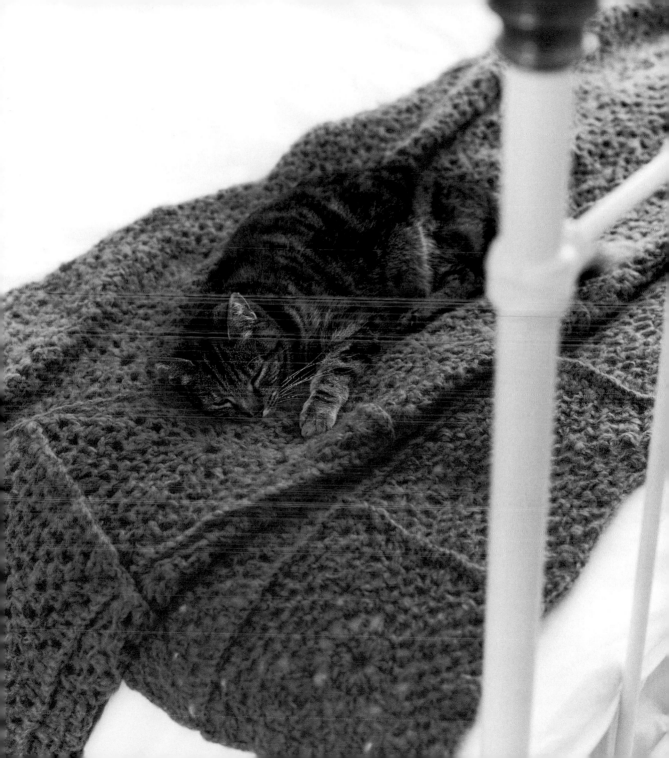

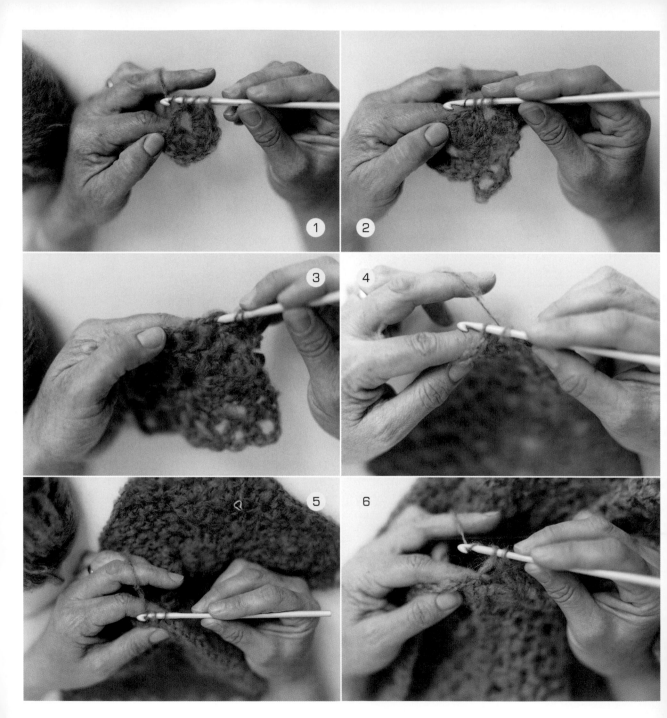

how to make:
Mohair throw

1 With the mohair yarn and the US Size H8/5mm hook, make 8ch to start. Join into a ring with a sl st into the first ch, then work in rounds. Round 1: work 3ch. Work 15dc into the ring. Join with a sl st to 3rd of the 1st ch.

2 Round 2: 5 ch, * 1dc into next dc, 2ch. Repeat from * 14 times then join with a sl st to 3rd of the 5ch.

3 Round 3: sl st into first space, 3ch, then 1dc, 3ch, 2dc into same space. * (2ch, 1sc into next space) 3 times. 2ch, then 2dc, 3ch, 2dc into next space. Repeat from * twice more. (2ch, 1sc into next space) 3 times. 2ch, and join with a sl st to 3rd of first 3ch. Round 4: sl st into next 3ch space, 3ch, then 1dc, 3ch, 2dc into same space. * (2ch, 1sc into 2ch space) 4 times. 2ch, then 2dc, 3ch, 2dc into 3ch space. Repeat from * twice more. (2ch, 1sc into 2ch space) 4 times. 2ch, join with a sl st to 3rd of first 3ch.

4 Round 5: as round 4, but working the repeats in parentheses 5 times each. Round 6: as round 4, but working repeats in parentheses 6 times. Round 7: sl st into 3ch space, 3ch, then 2dc, 2ch, 3dc into same space. * (1ch, 2dc into 2ch space) 7 times. 1ch, then 3dc, 2ch, 3dc into 3ch space. Repeat from * twice more. (1ch, 2dc into 2ch space) 5 times. 1ch, join with a sl st to 3rd of first 3ch. Fasten off by cutting the yarn 4in (10cm) from the hook, and drawing this 'tail' through the sl st. Trim.

5 Make enough motifs for the size of throw (this project needed 42, six motifs wide and seven long). Sew in any loose ends, then join the squares. To crochet, place two motifs together (right-sides out) and with a US Size H8/5mm hook work sc through the edges of both. This gives a ridged detail. For a flatter look, stitch together.

6 With the US Size 7/4.5mm hook, work one row sc around the edge of the finished throw. You may wish to do this in a contrasting or complementary color.

Hand embroidery

The word 'embroidery' comes from the Old French *broder*, 'to decorate', and that is what it does — in one or two colors or a dazzling range of hues; with simple stitches or in an array of techniques. Embroidery embellishes, enlivens and enriches fabric using needle, thread and a vivid imagination.

While the exact origins of decorative embroidery are rather hazy, it was certainly practiced all around the world by the Middle Ages. And in Europe, embroiderers formed guilds, whose workshops supplied the fine vestments and hangings for the church, often under the direction of a professional painter. Belgian embroiderers, for example, were known as 'painters with the needle', and Botticelli and Dürer were among those who supplied cartoons for the craft.

The most admired form of embroidery at this time was an English style known as *opus Anglicanum*. Its designs were fluid and detailed, worked in delicate stitches on a background of gold and colored silks, often embellished with pearls and precious stones. Though some was made for aristocratic households and military purposes, it was mostly produced for ecclesiastical garments.

Religion, war, trade and social changes all played their part in the history of embroidery. In Spain, the conquering Moors set up embroidery workshops and made 'blackwork' predominant, using geometrical motifs on linen cloth. In Hungary, which was controlled by the Turks but connected with Italy, Italian threads were used with Turkish designs to create floral patterns. And when northern India was conquered by the Moghuls, the second emperor brought Persian craftsmen to collaborate with the Indians. The result was a mingling of the two styles, employing Persian motifs but naturalistic details.

After European traders reached India in the early 17th century, Indian fabrics became hugely influential in Europe. A craze developed for what was known as 'chinoiserie', where fabrics were embroidered with exotic birds, flowers and foliage, and Asian designs also inspired Jacobean crewel work, in which heavy linen was embroidered in beautifully toning woolen stitches. Today, Indian hand embroidery is still considered among the best in the world — intricate, delicate and painstakingly detailed.

In the West, 19th-century industrialization nearly put paid to embroidery as an art form. Crude synthetic dyes gave garish colors, while pre-printed canvases offered no room for creativity, and it was not until the rise of the Arts and Crafts movement, when William Morris promoted the hand-crafted over the machine-made, that embroidery came into its own again. In the second half of the 20th century the circle was completed as embroidery once again became associated with fine art and trainee embroiderers were encouraged to use stitchery as a means of artistic self-expression. Since then, hand embroidery has regained more and more respect, whether practiced as an art form or simply an enjoyable means of relaxation, and whether pushing back the boundaries in terms of new concepts and experimentation, or reinforcing its rich history by using the traditional techniques of the past.

Flower napkins

You will need

(To make six napkins, each 16in/
41cm square)

- Six pieces of natural linen, each measuring 16in/41cm square
- Sewing machine
- Cotton thread to match the linen
- Scissors
- Pencil
- Tracing paper
- Dressmaker's carbon paper
- Masking tape
- 8in/20cm diameter embroidery hoop
- Size 3 embroidery needle
- 1 skein each of cotton embroidery floss in red, pink, pale pink, lilac, pale blue, dark green, pale yellow and bright green
- Iron

This napkin is so pretty, it's almost a shame to use it! The charming motif of a fantastical flower combines whimsy and daintiness to enliven an otherwise classic table setting for today's more casual style of dining.

Traditional embroiderers may find that this project strays too far from the usual realm of tiny stitches and standard motifs. But it shows how a combination of time-honored hand embroidery stitches can be interpreted in a way that is thoroughly modern, yet still highly appealing. The colors shown here are soft and pretty, though it would also be interesting to use vivid shades for a bold, bright look. The attractive fringed edging is a thoughtful touch that complements the napkin's lively informality.

how to make:
Flower napkins

1 Take the linen squares and use the sewing machine to stitch a line all the way round, ⅝in/ 1.5cm in from the edges of the cloth, following the warp and weft as much as possible. Fray the edges of the fabric almost up to the stitching.

2 Trace the design on page 417 onto a piece of tracing paper. Lay this over a piece of dressmaker's carbon paper and tape both of them onto the fabric, so that the design is in one corner. Draw over the design. As an alternative, you could draw out your own pattern. Experiment on a piece of paper first.

3 Remove the paper and sandwich the fabric into the embroidery hoop. Start to embroider the design, using three strands of floss for all colors. Begin with the flower head, and stem stitch along the outer and middle lines to define its shape. On the inside of this line, fly stitch to create definition, adding a French knot at the end of each fly stitch.

4 Between the two middle lines at the center of the flower, stitch a line of blanket stitches. The stamens are three lines of stem stitch, each finished with a French knot (use six strands of floss for these knots).

Flower napkins

5 Create the stalk by sewing two parallel lines of stem stitch, then two leaves and a central vein, also in stem stitch. Oversew a line of blanket stitch along the leading edge of both leaves to create definition.

6 Sew a line of fly stitches along the inside of the bottom edge of the leaves. In the center of each fly stitch make one short stitch and finish each stitch with a French knot.

7 To finish off, embroider a double cross stitch and a French knot in all four corners of the napkin, plus a single French knot in between.

8 Press carefully with a warm iron on the wrong side of the napkin, to ensure that you do not damage the finished embroidery.

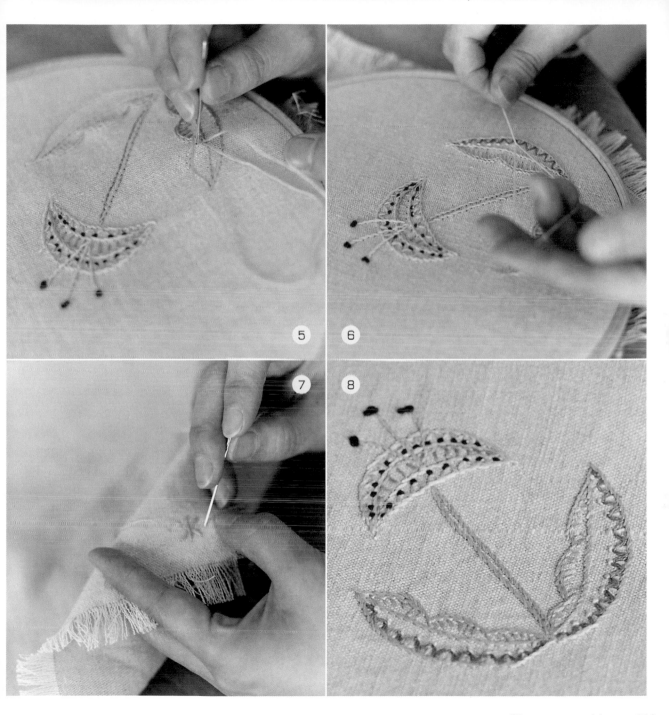

Hot water bottle cover

You will need

- Hot water bottle
- Large sheet of plain paper
- Pencil
- Pins
- Scissors
- Polar fleece measuring 20 x 36in/
  50 x 90cm
- Tailor's chalk pencil
- Piece of cotton measuring 20 x 36in/
  50 x 90cm
- Sewing machine
- Cotton thread to match the fleece
- Iron
- Needle
- Basting thread
- 8in/20cm diameter embroidery hoop
- Size 24 tapestry needle
- One skein each of tapestry wool in lilac,
  dark pink, pale yellow, pale blue, green
  and pale green

On a cold winter's night there's nothing nicer than to cuddle up in bed with a cozy hot water bottle. Warmth, softness and comfort are the bywords for this lovely — and surprisingly easy — project.

Although it would be possible to make this hot water bottle pouch in other fabrics and colors, the warmth of this deep red fleece really is irresistible. In fact, everything about it is friendly and welcoming, which means that although your stitches should be relatively neat, they don't by any means have to be perfect — a little irregularity is crucial to the appeal. And by all means adapt the design and colors of the stylized motif, as experimenting is all part of the fun.

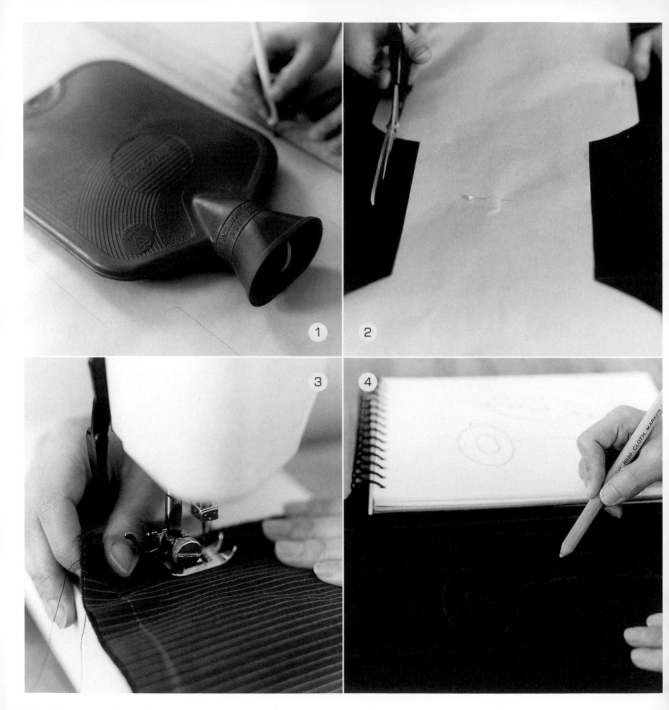

how to make:
Hot water bottle cover

stitches used

Chain stitch, stem stitch, basket stitch, cross stitch, satin stitch, French knot.
(See pages 408–9 for Embroidery stitch guide.)

1 Place the hot water bottle on a large sheet of paper. Draw around it, but make the bottom 2in/ 5cm shorter. Flip the bottle over at the neck and draw around it again, but this time extending its length by one third (see page 418). Allowing an extra ¾in/2cm all round, cut out.

2 Pin the paper pattern to the fleece and draw a line around it with the tailor's chalk pencil. Cut out, allowing an extra ¾in/2cm all round. Repeat with the cotton (this will act as a lining and help the fleece keep shape).

3 Sew a ⅜in/1cm hem on the top and bottom edges of both the fleece and the cotton. Press.

4 Baste the fleece to the cotton, wrong sides together (you will embroider through both layers). Using the tailor's chalk pencil, copy the design on page 419 onto the fleece in the position shown.

Hot water bottle cover

7 Sew flower stamens using a series of French knots all over the basket stitch area. Scatter a few cross stitches with a center French knot around the rest of the cover to finish.

8 Fold the fabric, right sides together, at the neck, and then fold over the flap at the bottom too, as shown by the line on the diagram on page 418. Machine stitch both side seams, following the chalk line you drew in step 2 (this gives a ¾in/2cm seam allowance), and clip any curves. Turn out and press.

5 Sandwich the fabric into the embroidery hoop. Begin to embroider the design. Start with a single line of chain stitch to create the stem and the stalk of the leaf. Next, sew a line of stem stitch to make the leaf itself. Chain stitch three separate lines to define the veins of the leaf. Make a French knot at the end of each vein.

6 At the top of the flower stem, basket stitch the center of the flower head. Create the surrounding petals by sewing satin stitches.

protecting the fabric
To prevent the embroidery hoop from marking the fleece, always remove the fabric at the end of each sewing session.

cutting thread
When sewing, cut each length of wool floss to about 10in/25cm — any longer and it will be difficult to work with and show signs of wear.

Machine embroidery

Although machine embroidery differs from hand stitching, it offers as much potential for decorative effect. For almost 150 years embroiderers have been exploring its creative uses, producing work that can be entirely disciplined or random and free, yet is expressive, vital and full of variety.

The advances of the Industrial Revolution changed Western society beyond all recognition. Among them was the sewing machine, which transformed the lives of women and made clothing far more affordable. The first sewing machine was invented as long ago as 1790, by an Englishman named Thomas Saint, and in the next 25 years patents for similar devices were granted to an Austrian, a German, a Frenchman and a Scot. The latter, John Duncan, had devised a machine to make embroidery, using a number of needles. By the 1830s, Barthelemy Thimonnier was running a factory, machine-sewing uniforms for the French army, but it was twice destroyed by the Parisian tailors, who feared for their livelihoods.

Then, in America, another battle began, between Massachusetts farmer Elias Howe and New York actor/inventor Isaac Merrit Singer. Howe had patented his sewing machine in 1846; Singer his improved version in 1850. Howe sued for patent infringement and won, but Singer went on to dominate the sewing machine market in the US, Britain and further afield — despite competition from more than 200 other companies — developing affordable machines featuring a table to support the fabric, a presser foot to hold the fabric down and a roughened feed wheel. His machines were also capable of both continuous and curved stitching.

While the merits of a sewing machine for ordinary stitching were obvious, early manufacturers were keen to emphasize their products' capacity for more decorative work as well. Sewing machines were a welcome new way to make the fancy trimmings that were used profusely in home furnishings and clothing, and it was not long before they were being employed to create 'art' embroidery, too. It was painstaking and difficult, carried out using a treadle machine that could perform only straight stitches (the first zigzag machine was not introduced until just after World War II), yet it often resulted in exquisite work that demonstrated the creative potential of this new innovation.

When electricity in the home became widespread in the 1920s and '30s, portable domestic sewing machines were introduced, and gradually their use for crafts purposes became more highly valued. Once viewed as no more than a cheaper, quicker and lower-quality version of hand embroidery, machine stitching is now widely practiced by craftspeople and amateur embroiderers. It is enjoyed for its different qualities — speed, freshness and immediacy, with a vast repertoire of stitches. Nowadays, machine embroidery could hardly be more fashionable, found in haute couture and in everyday design. It is also used along with other techniques to create a mixed-media craft form that combines the ancient art of embroidery, the skills of the 19th-century inventors and the avant-garde ideas of the new millennium.

Lavender pouch

You will need

(To make a pouch measuring 7 x 8in/
18 x 20cm)

- Length of mauve silk dupion measuring
  9 x 15in/22 x 38cm
- Two colors of synthetic thread, one
  matching the silk and one in pink
- Sewing machine (preferably with the
  facility to do freehand embroidery)
- Iron
- Ruler
- 'Invisible' embroidery pen or pale-colored
  tailor's chalk
- 4in/10cm embroidery hoop (optional)
- Scissors
- ¾–1oz/20–25g dried lavender
  (about a cupful)
- Pins

The very simplest machine embroidery can be highly
appealing and enormously effective, as this beautiful
lavender pouch, with its minimal motif and elegant
colors, so beautifully demonstrates.

This lavender pouch is really easy to sew and would make
a lovely treat for yourself or a wonderful gift, as well as
being an ideal introduction to the craft of machine
embroidery. Once you have become accustomed to working
with freehand embroidery using a hoop, you could adapt
the basic principles outlined here and develop more
elaborate, perhaps larger, designs using a variety of colors
— maybe a lavender neck rest, a small cushion, or a
heart-shape sachet to hang in a closet.

how to make:
Lavender pouch

1 Zigzag the edges of your fabric. Fold in half and press. On one side of the folded fabric, mark a rectangle for the lavender — about 1½in/4cm in from the folded edge and 2in/5cm in from the zigzag edges. Use the embroidery pen to draw ten horizontal lines at regular intervals in the center of this.

2 For this stage, it is possible to use an ordinary sewing machine, but the finished result may be neater if you use an embroidery machine and hoop. Embroider the design, creating a satin stitch by zigzagging very close together about ¼in/5mm long. The hoop will have to be moved across in order to complete the design. For an irregular effect, you can change the width of the stitch with each line you sew. Press on the wrong side on a well-padded surface to make the embroidery stand out.

3 Fold the fabric in half, this time with the good embroidery side in, and stitch the side seams with a ⅜in/1cm seam allowance, leaving one end open.

4 Turn out and, with the right side of the embroidery facing you, stitch along three sides of the rectangle marked in step 1, leaving the same side open as in step 3.

5 Pour the lavender into the small rectangle and pin it closed. Stitch neatly along the remaining line.

6 Turn in ⅜in/1cm on the remaining open side and press to make a neat edge. Stitch together, keeping the stitching as close to the edge as you can

filling the pouch
Be careful not to overfill the pouch with lavender or it will be difficult to stitch closed.

variations
If you want to experiment with the stitching, you could create your own design using continuous zigzag lines in toning shades of more than one color.

Laundry bag

You will need

(To make a bag measuring 20 x 28in/ 52 x 72cm)

- 2¼yds/2m oyster-white linen, at least 43in/110cm wide
- Ruler
- Scissors
- Iron
- Sewing machine, preferably with the facility to do freehand embroidery (a freehand embroidery foot is helpful, too, though not essential)
- Satin-finish synthetic thread to match the fabric
- Safety pin
- 'Invisible' embroidery pen or pale-colored tailor's chalk
- 8in/20cm diameter machine embroidery hoop
- Pins

The elegant beauty of this classic design just never seems to date. Ivory lettering on an unbleached linen background is chic and simple for both contemporary townhouse or country cottage.

Anyone who has ever been even vaguely interested in the art of calligraphy will appreciate the subtle beauty of pared-down, flowing lettering. This project borrows a little from that craft and translates it into another — machine embroidery — and substitutes fabric for paper, thread for ink. The result is truly lovely, taking an old-fashioned drawstring bag design in plain, soft linen, and combining it with loose, modern stitchcraft to transform a very functional object into something that is an absolute joy to use.

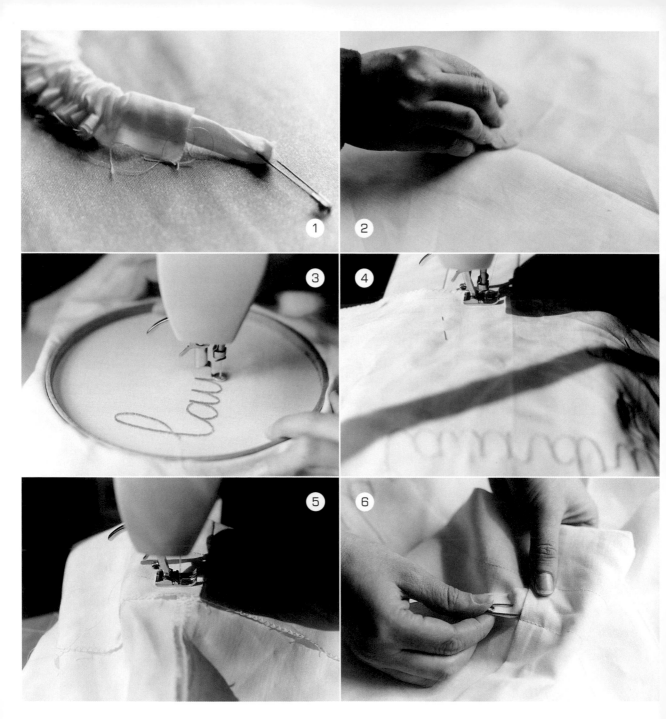

how to make:
Laundry bag

1 To make the drawstring, cut a rectangle of linen 2½ x 79in/6cm x 2m. Fold it right sides together lengthwise and press. Stitch along, leaving ⅜in/1cm seam allowance, then turn out, using a safety pin. Press again. Tuck the ends into the tube and stitch across neatly to secure them.

2 Cut out two rectangles of linen each 21 x 33in/ 52 x 85cm and zigzag along the raw edges. Using the ruler and embroidery pen or tailor's chalk, mark a horizontal line on the right side of one of the rectangles, about 6in/15cm up from the bottom edge. This indicates the positioning of the center of your lettering. Test how long the word will be by practicing on a piece of spare fabric, then mark three dots on the line for the first letter, the middle and the end. (If you wish, you can write out the whole word, though if you embroider freely you will create a looser, 'handwriting' style.)

3 Sandwich the fabric, with the marked embroidery area visible, into the embroidery hoop so that it is as taut as possible. Carefully embroider your letters, creating a satin stitch by zigzagging about ¼in/5mm long and very close together. Remove the fabric from the hoop. Press on the back of the embroidery on a well-padded surface to make the letters stand out.

4 Pin the two large pieces of fabric together with the right (embroidered) side in. Stitch three sides (with ⅜in/1cm seam allowance), leaving the top open.

5 Keeping the bag inside out, turn the top edge out 5in/12cm. Press, then mark two horizontal lines around the bag, 2in/5cm and 3¼in/8cm from the top edge — this is for the drawstring. Stitch along both lines. When you stitch over the side seams, go back and forth a few times to fasten the stitches beneath securely. Turn the bag right side out and, on the right-hand side seam, unpick the 1¼in/3cm of stitching between the two casing rows that you have just stitched.

6 Attach a safety pin to your drawstring, and pull it through the gap between the two stitched lines. Gather and tie in a bow.

Quilting

Quilting developed out of the need for warmth, but became a decorative medium too, used by rich and poor for clothing and home furnishings. There are many types of quilt, from sparse and simple to richly complex, but they all have an uninhibited vitality and keen enjoyment of form and color.

The word 'quilt' often implies a patchwork bed cover made in a pattern of hexagons or diamonds. The true definition of a quilt, however, is rather different — layers of padded fabric stitched together, which, although they could be pieced and patterned, or even appliquéd, are just as likely to be made from plain cloth. The stitching may form lines, crosses, shells, pineapples, feathers or ropes, or it may follow a printed or patchwork pattern. In 'batted' quilting, the filling is continuous, while 'trapunto' quilting is only partially filled; 'tied' quilts use knots rather than lines of stitching.

It is thought that quilting developed thousands of years ago in northern peasant communities. It was an ancient craft in China, where quilted clothing and armor were common, and it is likely that the Crusaders brought new patterns back with them from their travels. By the 16th century, quilts were used by the European nobility as bed covers and canopies, made from expensive fabric and metal threads, and by the early 1700s quilted garments were fashionable, too. The less well-off, meanwhile, would have used scraps of fabric, piecing and layering them to make clothes and bedding. With the rise of imported Indian chintzes and manufactured textiles, fabric became more widely affordable and quilting, therefore, even more prevalent.

The earliest American settlers are thought to have brought quilting techniques with them from Britain and Holland. Not only were quilts used as bed covers, but also mattresses, rugs, tents and window and door hangings — even crop protectors. Quilting 'bees' became a social activity, and professional quilters arose, who traveled from town to town selling their skills. Economical, practical and also decorative, quilting exploded in Britain and North America, particularly in the 19th century. Wales and North East England were centers of quilting in Britain, renowned for their wholecloth, 'medallion' or 'strippy' styles, while American quilters were associated with exuberant block quilts. The most highly regarded American quilts today, though, are those of the Amish people, whose simple but often unconventional designs were always made to the highest quality, with strong, dark colors and ornate patterns.

By the 1940s quilting had almost died out in Britain, and been relegated to a hobby in America. But the 1970s saw a huge revival of interest, sparked by a New York exhibition that demonstrated that these domestic objects, particularly Amish and other abstract quilts, had much in common with modern art. Since then, the craft has developed into a contemporary medium, given new freedom by machine sewing, modern batting and unusual fabrics, and often combined with painting, printing or dyeing. Simple or complex, patterned or plain, quilting is respected once again, now no longer practiced out of economic necessity but for enjoyment and enrichment.

Bed cover

You will need

(To make a bed cover measuring 39 x 78in/1 x 2m)

- Tailor's chalk
- Ruler
- 2⅓yds/2.1m cornflower blue silk satin (at least 39in/1m wide) for the top of the quilt
- Pins
- 2⅓yds/2.1m silk satin to match the top silk satin (or cotton; must be at least 39in/1m wide) for the bottom of the quilt
- Sewing machine with a fine 70s needle
- Thread to match the top color fabric
- Scissors
- Iron
- 2¾yds/2.5m of 12oz batting (36in/90cm wide)
- Sewing needle
- Long, fine quilting needle

Cozy and comfortable, this bed cover takes a classic design and updates it with modern fabric. Chic, clean and sophisticated, it is a perfect blend of old and new. It could happily grace a bedroom of any style.

Although quilted satin bed covers are the height of contemporary fashion, this version employs tied quilting, one of the craft's oldest forms. Quick and highly effective, it simply involves knotting the layers together with a small stitch at regular intervals. For variety, you may wish to make the reverse side from a patterned fabric. Or use thinner batting and machine stitch a decorative pattern — criss-cross lines, in a square or diamond pattern, would be a pleasantly subtle, modern interpretation of the theme.

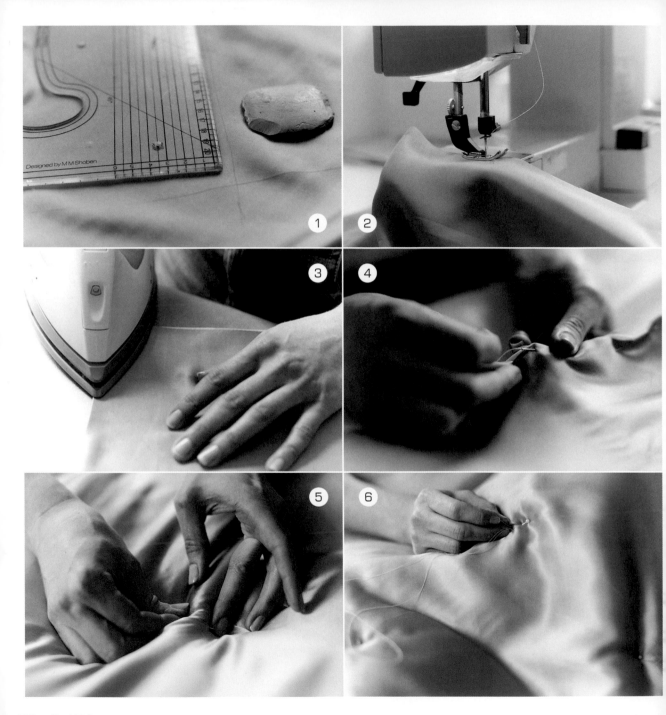

how to make:
Bed cover

5 Pin at the chalk dots, checking that both the front and back of the fabric are smooth. With a long quilting needle threaded double, hand-stitch the three layers of fabric and batting together at one of the pinned points. Stab stitch several times, pulling the stitches as firmly as possible to ensure a luxurious padded effect.

6 Tie off each thread neatly and securely on the reverse side of the quilt. Repeat the tying process at each of the pinned points.

1 With the chalk, lightly draw a pinpoint grid in a criss cross design on the right side of the fabric that you have chosen for the top of the quilt.

2 Pin this fabric to the bottom fabric, with the right sides together. Stitch around the sides, allowing ⅝in/1.5cm seam allowance and being careful not to pucker the fabric. Leave a 27in/70cm gap on one of the short sides.

3 Cut the corners at a 45 degree angle. Turn out, then press, so that the seam is crisp and straight.

4 Insert the batting into the cover, ensuring it is flat and fits properly into the corners. Hand stitch the opening neatly.

variations

If you prefer, you can use a lighter weight batting and neatly machine stitch lines in a square or diamond pattern over your bed cover.

If you want to make a double bed cover, simply double the width of both fabric and batting — if the batting isn't wide enough, hand-sew two widths together first.

Ombré wrap

You will need

(To make a wrap measuring 15¼ x 58in/
38 x 144cm)

- Iron
- 16 x 64in/40 x 160cm lightweight
  iron-on interfacing
- Enough ombré silk to cut two pieces,
  measuring 16 x 64in/40 x 160cm and
  16 x 58¾in/40 x 146cm, both with a
  good variety of shading (this project
  used shades of gray)
- Scissors
- Measuring tape
- Tailor's chalk
- Pins
- Sewing machine
- Thread to match the silk
- 16 x 58¾in/40 x 146cm thin interlining
- Needle

This wrap is warm and comforting yet surprisingly light and delicate. The graphic ombré silk combines with the abstract stitched pattern for a contemporary take on more traditional quilting.

This wrap has been designed with energetic lines of stitching contained within pieced sections of ombré silk, an appealing juxtaposition of discipline and free-flowing lines. Simple to make, the project can be easily adapted to other sizes and colors, or even other fabrics — though the silk ombré is a particularly striking choice, and feels very luxurious next to the skin. In this muted shade it is easy to wear, and would look as good with a smart business suit as with an elegant evening dress.

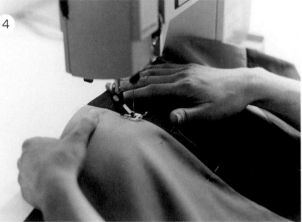

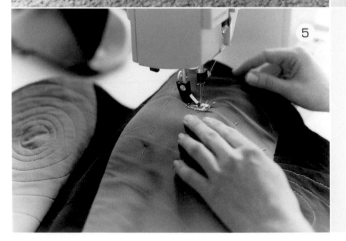

neat stitching

Make sure that the spiral machine stitching is as neat and fluid as possible, by keeping the action continuous and turning the fabric cleanly as you go. The finished effect will be tidy and very professional-looking.

how to make:
Ombré wrap

1 Press the interfacing to the wrong side of the 16 x 64in/40 x 160cm silk rectangle. Cut this piece into eight rectangles of 8 x 16in/20 x 40cm. On a large work surface or the floor, re-arrange the pieces into one big rectangle, but this time with the shading directions alternating.

2 With the chalk, lightly draw a design of curving lines onto the right side of each section. With right sides together, pin then stitch the rectangles together, allowing ⅜in/1cm seam allowance, and press the seams flat.

3 Lay the interlining flat on your work surface, and place the second piece of silk on top of it, with the right side up. Place the stitched silk on top, right side down. Pin together, then machine stitch around all four sides, allowing a ⅜in/1cm seam allowance, but leaving a gap the width of one stitched section. Turn out, press, and hand-stitch the opening.

4 Pin along the seam lines, working from the center outward, checking that both front and back are smooth. This will section off each area and make the piece more workable. Machine stitch along each seam line, through all three layers, to start to create a padded effect.

5 Pin along one of the chalk lines you drew in step 2, again working from the center outward to avoid puckering and checking that both front and back are smooth. Stitch through all three layers. Pin and stitch all the lines, changing the bobbin and top thread occasionally, to match roughly the changing shading on the top layer of ombré. Hold down the fabric and maneuver the quilt under the needle, taking care to regulate both stitch length and straightness. Remember that if you have drawn any tight curves you will have to remove the presser foot from the sewing machine, lower the teeth and the presser foot lever, and free machine embroider.

Appliqué

What better way to make the most of worn-out or leftover fabric than to turn it into another, perhaps more beautiful, textile? Appliqué does just that — its use is as old as cloth itself and its designs as varied as the different societies, ancient and modern, that have discovered its decorative power.

Whether for repair or decoration, the use of scraps of one fabric stitched on (or, rather, applied to) another is common to almost all cultures and probably stretches back to the very first items of clothing. The Eskimos of northern Alaska, for example, made coats from appliquéd skins, adorned with stitches and beadwork, while North American Indians made appliqué from birch bark sewn with spruce roots; the peasants of Persia created felt-work appliqué in bold designs, while leather appliqué in bright colors and intricate floral designs is typical of Hungary.

One of the oldest forms of appliqué is the *suradeq*, an Egyptian tent lined with exquisite, hand-stitched appliquéd forms in red, black, yellow, green and blue. Their patterns, based on ancient Pharonic art and Coptic and Islamic motifs, include lotus flowers, geometric shapes and calligraphy. The tents are made by men only, in designs passed down from generation to generation. Ancient Egyptian rulers used the suradeq as traveling palaces, transporting them on camels. Today new tents are still made for special celebrations.

In Central America, the women of the Cuna tribe, of the San Blas Islands in Panama, still make colorful *molas*, or blouses, from appliquéd cloth. Newer versions employ standard appliqué, embellished with decorative stitching, but traditional molas use complex reverse appliqué, where pieces of fabric are stitched together in layers, then patterns cut from them and hemmed back to reveal the colors beneath. The best examples are collectors' pieces, highly prized as works of art.

Examples of European appliqué can be found as far back as the Middle Ages. It was rich and colorful, used for wall hangings (the only way to keep out drafts in a medieval manor), clothing, clerical vestments and heraldry. It was also a good substitute for expensive solid embroidery and whole brocades or velvets. And, from the late-18th century, appliqué was used to make quilt covers; American settlers went on to develop this as a widely practiced domestic art form — thrifty and extraordinarily skilful.

Appliqué came to the fore again in late-19th-century Britain, thanks to the proponents of the Arts and Crafts movement, who urged a return to well-crafted, hand-made things. Appliqué was seen as particularly appropriate to their esthetic, and emphasis was placed on stylized designs and simple fabrics, rather than expensive cloth and intricate stitching. Such thinking has remained predominant today, as craftspeople working with appliqué continue to explore its versatility. It can be abstract or figurative, as simple or as complex as the maker desires, in plain or unexpected cloth, embellished with additional stitching or left for the fabrics to speak for themselves — a spontaneous craft that crosses all barriers.

Leaf placemats

You will need

(To make six placemats, 15 x 19in/
38 x 48cm)

- Six pieces of pale blue/gray linen, each
  measuring 16 x 20in/40 x 50cm
- Pins
- Iron
- Sewing machine
- Sewing thread to either match or
  contrast with the two colors of linen
- Scissors
- Small piece of green linen
- Beading, or very fine, needle
- 30 seed beads in a variety of
  coordinating colors

The striking simplicity of this appliquéd placemat is its strongest feature — a spare and elegantly stylized motif, two colors and some careful stitching make it an arresting home accessory.

A pattern of curving leaves lends itself beautifully to this straightforward project, though as you become more skilled in the art of appliqué you may wish to develop the design to incorporate more complex shapes, and maybe even further colors, too. Texture and color are very important here, and the delicately woven surface of the linen works with the appliquéd cut-outs and the tracery of stitching to create subtle interest. The beaded edging finishes things off with decorative flair.

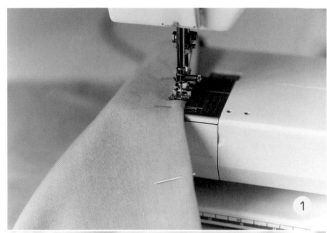

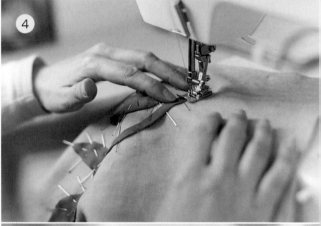

how to make:
Leaf placemats

1 Turn a narrow double hem along all sides of each linen rectangle, taking care that the corners are neat. Pin and press. Stitch the hem in either a complementary or contrasting color.

2 Cut a stem and leaves from the green linen (see diagram on page 420). Snip small cuts, about ³⁄₁₆in/5mm long, around the edges of the leaves.

3 Turn the edges of the leaves under and arrange in place, around the stem, on the placemat. Pin to secure in place, then press.

4 Straight stitch neatly down the middle of the stem, using either a complementary- or contrasting-color thread. Remove the pins as you go.

5 Then, straight stitch neatly around the edges of the leaves, as close to the edges as possible, again removing the pins as you go. Press the placemat on the wrong side.

6 To finish, sew the beads, about 1¼in/3cm apart, along the short edges of the placemat, using one continuous thread hidden in the hem.

turning a double hem
To turn a double hem, simply fold over the edge of the fabric and press, then fold over again, pin, press and stitch.

Kitchen tablecloth

You will need

(To make a tablecloth measuring about 60in/155cm square)

- Four pieces of coordinating linen, each cut to 31in/80cm square (this project uses lemon yellow, soft pink, gray/blue and soft turquoise/blue
- Pins
- Sewing machine
- Sewing threads to complement and contrast with the colors of linen
- Scissors
- Scraps of different-color linen
- Iron
- Needle

For a charming and stylish table setting, this appliquéd cloth is ideal. Although striking, it is understated enough to be a perfect complement to crockery, cutlery and glassware.

What makes this tablecloth special is the clever repetition of color and pattern, with motifs placed carefully in an apparently random pattern. Choose any colors you wish and experiment with different cut-out shapes (but keep them simple) and decorative overstitching. The size of the cloth can be varied according to your table. It could also be very effective to make matching placemats or napkins in coordinating colors and designs; or to use this technique to create a set of cushions or even a unique wall hanging.

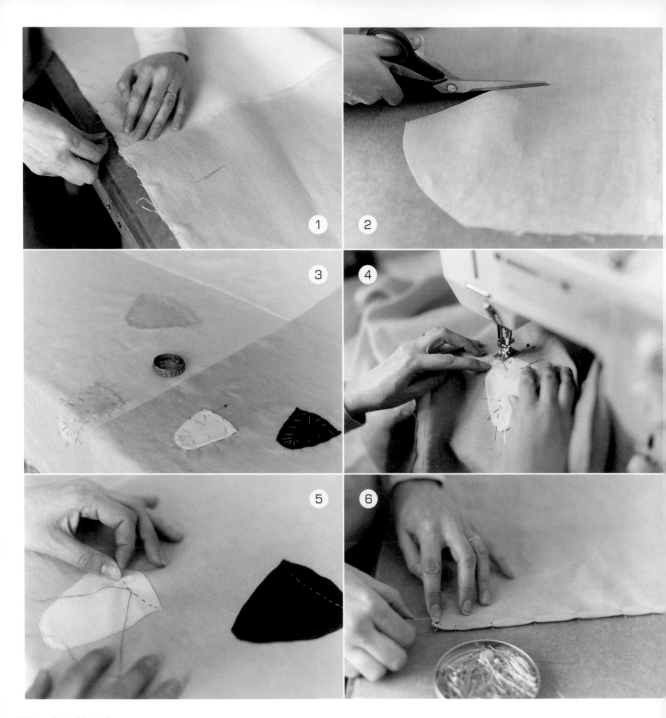

how to make:
Kitchen tablecloth

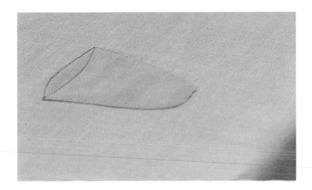

1 First, stitch the four linen squares together to make one large square. Pin two pieces right sides together and stitch one edge, allowing ⅛in/5mm seam allowance. Zigzag the raw edges to prevent fraying and press flat, pushing the seam to one side. Repeat with the other two pieces, then stitch the two larger pieces together in the same way. On the right side of the fabric, sew over the two seams, so the stitches show on the top of the tablecloth.

2 Cut the bowl, cups and leaves motifs from the different-color scraps of linen (see the diagrams on pages 420–1). Snip small cuts, about ⅛in/5mm long, around the edges of the curves.

3 Turn the edges of the motifs under and arrange in place on the tablecloth. Check the composition by standing well back. Pin, then press carefully.

4 Straight stitch neatly around the edges of the motifs, as close to the edges as possible, using either complementary- or contrasting color threads. Remove the pins as you go. Press.

5 Add lines of tiny hand stitching to emphasize the lines on the cups and bowls, using complementary-color thread.

6 Turn a narrow double hem all around the tablecloth, pin and then press. To finish, stitch the hem in either a complementary or contrasting color.

variations
You may wish to use other shapes of your own design to decorate your tablecloth. If so, keep the shapes as simple as possible. Make sure, too, that your designs are not too large, or they may overwhelm and give the tablecloth an imbalanced feel.

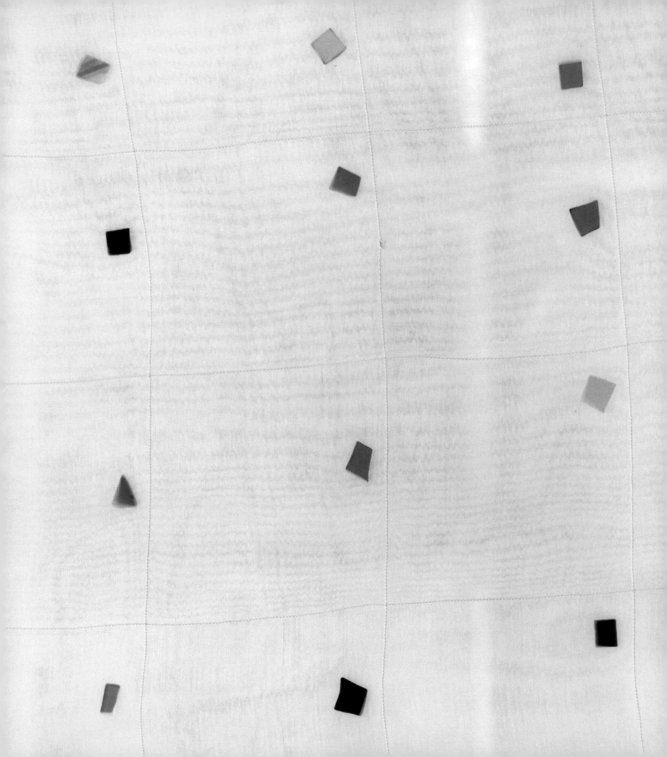

Complex textiles

For thousands of years we have embellished textiles, from dyeing and painting to stitching and ribbonwork. Each technique can be used alone, but the most dazzling results come about when they are combined, using modern techniques and materials to create a complex and impressive effect.

Once man had learned how to spin yarn and weave cloth, he soon developed ways of embellishing the fabric to make it even more decorative and desirable. Textile dyes were used in China well over 4,000 years ago, and by the Middle Ages the Japanese were combining sophisticated dyeing techniques with intricate hand embroidery and free brushwork to create gorgeous kimonos. In Medieval Europe, meanwhile, stitchery was a highly accomplished craft, and appliqué and embroidery were used together in fabulous wall hangings, clothing, clerical vestments and heraldry. From the late-18th century onward, appliqué and stitching were combined in quilted bed covers, which were made with extraordinarily high levels of skill in both Britain and America.

Quilting is now undergoing a revival. In fact, a wide range of traditional textile techniques, such as appliqué and beading, have been brought back to life in the last few decades, treasured for what previously made them so unfashionable — the fact that they are very time-consuming, more expensive than their machine-made counterparts and require meticulous attention to detail. When used together, all these techniques are highly effective; when used with cutting-edge techniques and materials, the results can often be truly stunning.

A contemporary branch of textile art that has sprung up only in the last decade is a fascination with the layering of sheer fabrics and the effects that can be achieved by combining those layers with other types of fabric, with dyed areas of cloth, with stitching and with three-dimensional objects trapped between the layers. One reason for this must be the new trend in simple, streamlined fashion and home decoration, where texture has overtaken color as a predominant consideration; another is the ease with which modern sewing machines can deal with new fabrics and threads and create all sorts of intricate effects easily and quickly.

Yet another is the ready availability of all sorts of intriguing new fabrics, man-made or natural, which offer the textile designer endless possibilities for experimentation. New forms of dye, too, give the craftsperson a host of innovative methods to try — not forgetting natural dyes, which have also experienced a renaissance in recent years. And, finally, there is the impetus of exploring and remembering the past through today's eyes, which is seen in the cycles of retro-chic fashion and in the work of craftspeople whose aim is to create a 21st century heirloom. By suspending beads, glass, pebbles or small mementos within delicately stitched pockets of fabric, made into wall hangings, pictures, cushions, bags, throws and even dresses, it is possible to capture memories, to stimulate the senses and to embody a variety of age-old techniques in a way that could not be more new and exciting.

Hanging tidy

You will need

(To make a tidy measuring 24 x 30in/
60 x 75cm)

- White cotton organdie, measuring
  42 x 48in/105 x 120cm
- Scissors
- Ruler
- Pins
- 6¾yds/6m white cotton bias tape
- Sewing machine
- White thread
- 'Invisible' embroidery pen
- Decorative inserts (such as buttons,
  small shells, glass beads or flat pebbles)
- Iron
- Pale green cold-water dye (optional)

While primarily a decorative object — perfect for a
bedroom, bathroom, hallway or even kitchen — this
hanging tidy would also be useful for storing and
displaying small, light, delicate items.

The sewing techniques necessary to make this tidy,
with its rows of different-size pockets, are pretty
straightforward. The project's clever touch is in its
incorporation of tiny inserts that are trapped between
the thin layers of organdie to provide shadowy decoration.
The choice of objects to enclose is all part of the
enjoyment, as is the selection of a pretty rod — be it
bamboo, wood, slender wrought iron or shiny stainless
steel — from which to hang the tidy.

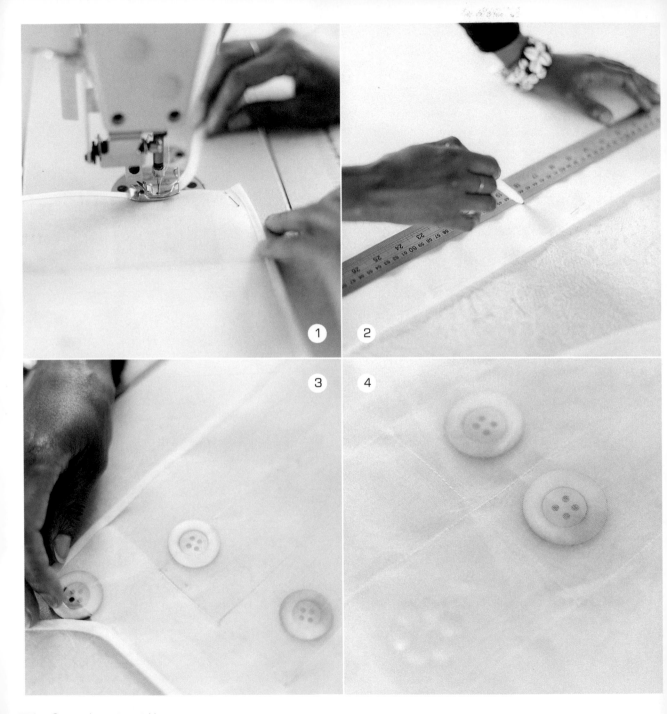

how to make:
Hanging tidy

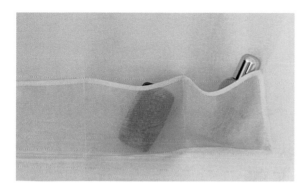

1 Fold your fabric in half crosswise and cut out two each of the following rectangles: 24 x 30in/ 60 x 70cm (A), 8 x 20in/20 x 50cm (B) and 4 x 20in/ 10 x 50cm (C). Pin the two layers of shape A together, wrong sides facing, and edge with bias tape, leaving a gap in the top edge large enough to slip your inserts in.

2 Using the embroidery pen, draw a 2in/5cm-deep border inside the bias tape, and stitch along this line, leaving a gap opposite the one in the bias tape of the same size.

3 Stitch another line, 4in/10cm below the top border line, and push the inserts in. Divide them in half, and stitch another line between them, 2in/5cm below the top border line.

4 Neatly stitch the two gaps closed. Separate each of the inserts into pairs by stitching vertically across the enclosure.

Hanging tidy

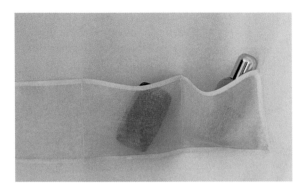

5 Take shape B and pin the layers together securely, with the wrong sides facing. Edge with bias tape. Repeat with shape C.

6 Take shape B and place it across the bottom of the border in shape A. Stretch it flat and pin in place. Attach with two lines of stitching (on the outer and inner edges of the bias tape) along both sides and the bottom.

7 Repeat step 6 with shape C, placing it about 4in/ 10cm above the top of shape B. Mark a vertical line at the mid point of each pocket and stitch along, creating two pockets in each. Mark two further vertical lines at the mid points of the two pockets in shape C and stitch along them, creating four pockets. Press, avoiding the inserts.

8 Take 20in/50cm of bias tape, fold in half lengthwise and stitch the edges together to form a long tape. Cut into five equal portions and fold in half to form loops. Mark points at even intervals on the reverse side of the tidy at the top edge. Sew a tape to each point. If you wish, you can dye the finished tidy with cold-water dye.

working with bias tape
When edging the fabric with bias tape, it is helpful to crease the tape in half along its length first, then stitch along both the right and the wrong sides to ensure that it is attached firmly.

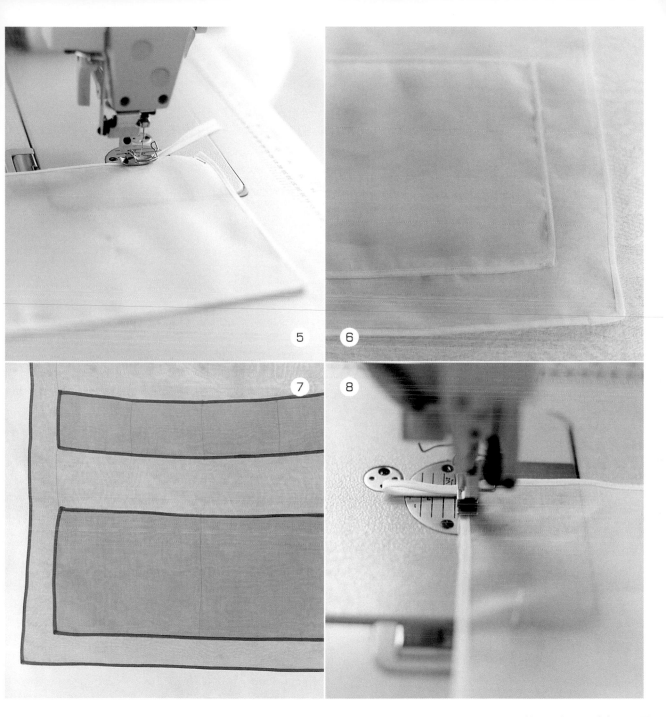

Flower cushion

You will need

(To make a cushion measuring about 14 x 14in/35 x 35cm)

- 2¼yds/2m white cotton organdie (at least 40in/102cm wide)
- Ruler
- Scissors
- Pins
- Iron
- 'Invisible' embroidery pen
- 3yds/2.7m of ⅝in-wide/1.5cm white cotton bias tape
- Sewing machine
- White thread
- Plate (about 10in/25cm diameter) or a compass
- Masking tape
- Bowl or box
- Paintbrush
- Small bottle blue silk paint or dye
- Decorative inserts (such as small glass buttons, shells or flat pebbles)
- White 14in/35cm square pillow form
- Cold-water dye (optional)

The frothy layers of this organdie are utterly delightful, and here they are brought into clever contrast with the solidity of a dyed motif and a variety of tiny objects trapped behind the sheer layers.

This project is relatively complicated as it contains a number of different processes — from cutting and stitching to layering and entrapment — but it is the combination of these various techniques that gives the finished cushion its precise sophistication and professional appearance. Take it slowly and carefully and you shouldn't run into any problems. In white, the cushion has a cloudy, ethereal look. You could easily, however, dye the fabric any color of your choice, or vary the color of the painted motif.

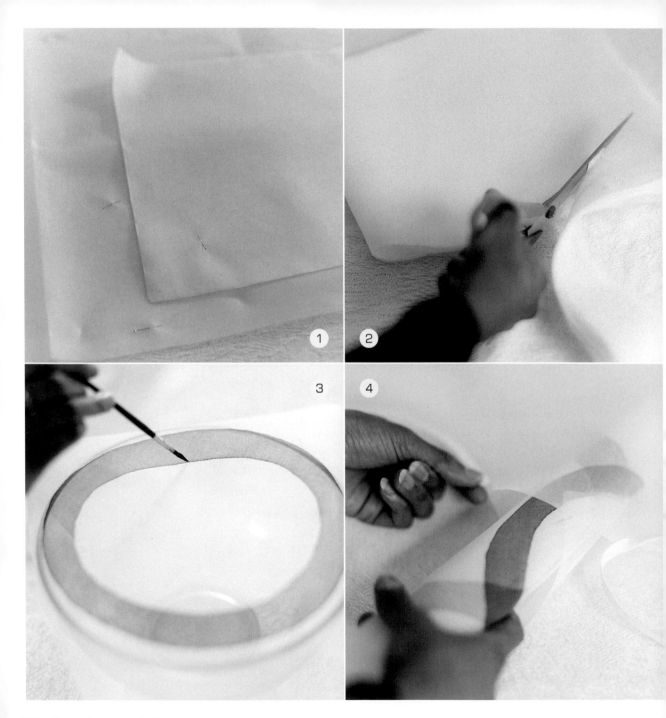

how to make:
Flower cushion

1 Take the organdie and cut out two shapes, 24 x 24in/60 x 60cm and pin securely, wrong sides together (A). Cut a square 16 x 16in/40 x 40cm (B). Cut two rectangles, each 16½ x 32½in/42 x 82cm and pin securely, right sides together (C). Press them with a hot iron.

2 Fold shape A into a flat quarter. With the embroidery pen, draw the shape of a petal (see template on page 422) ensuring that the starting and finishing points have the same depth. Cut along this line through the layers of fabric. Unfold and remove enough pins to press flat. Edge with bias tape, leaving a 4in/10cm gap for the inserts. Remove the pins.

3 Take square B and draw a circle with a diameter of around 10in/25cm in the center of the fabric, either around a plate or using a compass. Handling the fabric gently so as not to distort its shape, tape the corners onto a bowl or box to give you a flat surface on which to paint. Lightly paint around the edge of the circle with the silk dye, creating an irregularly shaped line about 1–1½in/3–4cm wide.

4 When the dye is dry, press the fabric to fix it (follow manufacturer's instructions). The fabric does not need hemming, but you can fray the edges for decorative effect. Roll the fabric into a sausage shape and insert it into the gap left in shape A. Unroll using a ruler and ease into the center of the flower shape. Press flat and pin into position.

continued:
Flower cushion

5 With the embroidery pen, draw the shape in which the inserts will be positioned. Insert them into the cushion cover above the painted shape B. Pin into position, then sew around them (through all the layers) to secure in place.

6 Stretch and fold a 12in/30cm length of bias tape and stitch the outside edges together to form a tie. Cut into two equal lengths. Attach one end of one of these lengths to the wrong side of A/B in the center, at the top of the design. Take shape C (the two rectangles you pinned together in step 1) and stitch around the edge of the rectangle ⅜in/1cm in, leaving about 4in/10cm unstitched. Ensure that the edge outside the stitching is neat; trim if necessary. Remove pins and turn out carefully. Press flat.

7 Make the cushion flap. Fold C in half crosswise and mark the halfway point at each side. Unfold and lightly draw a line joining the halfway points. Overstitch around one half of the fabric, along the line and around the three remaining edges (see diagram on page 422), as close to the edge as possible. Attach one end of the second piece of tape to center of fabric, laying it in the stitched half.

8 Take shape A/B and place it right side facing down. Place C on top, right-side up, with the unstitched half of shape C over A/B, aligning it with B. Make sure both ties align at the top of the cushion. Pin A/B and C together and stitch along three sides of the unstitched half of C, as close to the edge as possible. Remove all pins and insert the pillow form, tucking down the flap of C smoothly inside the sleeve. Tie the tapes. If you wish, dip the cushion cover in cold-water dye.

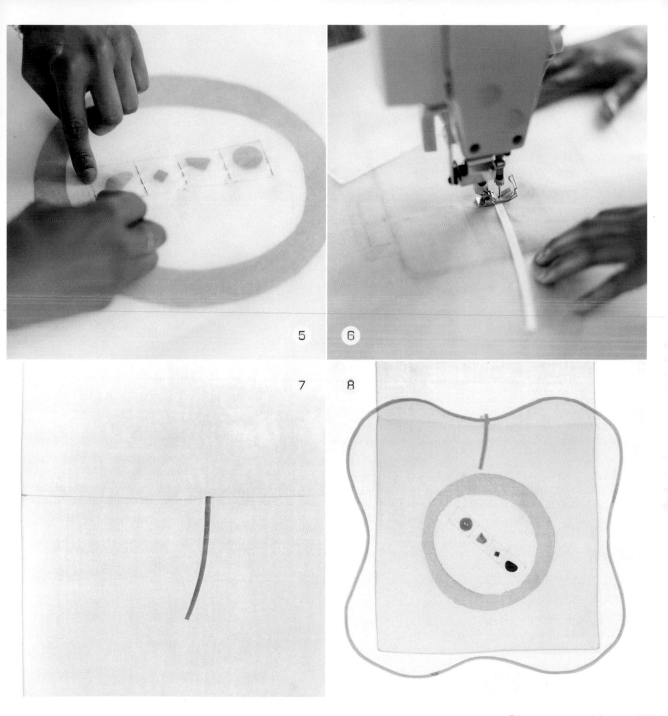

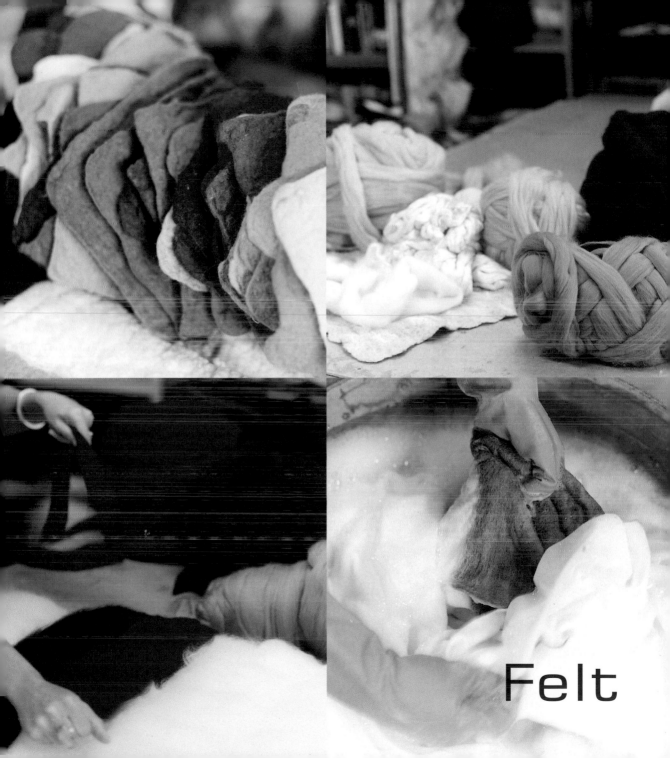

Felt

Felt making

Soft and warm, hand-made felt is also malleable and sculptural, combining all the advantages of beauty, versatility and practicality. Both ancient and modern, felt crosses all boundaries and is as appealing in a contemporary apartment as in its traditional home on the Central Asian plains.

Felt is the oldest form of textile on earth and one of the easiest to create — a simple combination of fleece, hot water and agitation will produce a unique fabric made of bonded fibers that will not unravel, even if cut. The first felt makers (probably around 8,500 years ago) were the nomadic people of Central Asia, who used felt as housing and clothing. Collapsible tents, called 'yurts', were covered with large pieces of felt, often decorated with colorful appliqué. Inside, flooring, cushions, storage and bedding were all made from felt, while their owners wore felt hats, boots, cloaks and gloves. Indeed, so important was felt to the nomads that by the fourth century BC their territory was known to the Chinese as 'the land of felt'.

Even today felt is still essential to the lives of the remaining nomadic communities of Turkmenistan, Uzbekistan, Kyrgyzstan and parts of Mongolia and China, who make their yurts, carpets, bags, saddles and cloaks from felt, in patterns and colors that have been handed down from one generation to the next. At the end of each summer, the women wash the fleece and beat it with willow sticks, dye it and layer the fibers onto a reed mat. After a sprinkling of hot water and soap, the mat is rolled up, ready to be kicked and rolled around, or dragged behind horses across the steppes.

From Central Asia, the practice of felt-making spread west towards Europe, Scandinavia and eventually South America. Felt's great protective properties made it a useful fabric for lining metal armor, and in the late Middle Ages the Cossack armies were known as the 'felt troops' because of the amount of felt that they wore. It was actually only in the 1950s that the Turkish military stopped wearing felt boots. Roman soldiers also wore felt, in the form of tunics, armor and boots, and at the preserved Italian city of Pompeii a wall painting is probably the oldest surviving illustration of felt making. The Icelandic sagas describe how felt was used to make saddles, while during the French revolution the Jacobeans wore a felt cap as a symbol of freedom and in the early-20th century Cornish tin miners protected their heads with stiffened felt helmets.

As industrialization became more prevalent, the practice of hand-making felt declined in most societies. In recent years, however, craftspeople around the world have developed it as a modern medium that combines both artistry and practicality, developing its potential by blending wool with other natural fibers, such as camel, alpaca, silk, cashmere and linen, and exploring the uses of natural and synthetic dyes for soft or vibrant effects. Today, hand-made felt makes a welcome appearance in 21st-century life in the form of rugs, cushions, wall hangings, blankets and throws, valued for its fluid, organic appearance, its wonderfully soft, warm texture and its dual qualities of function and beauty.

Table runner

You will need

(To make a runner measuring about 12 x 78in/30 x 200cm)

- Four pieces of nylon net, each 39 x 70in/1m x 1.8m
- Measuring tape or ruler
- Tailor's chalk or pencil
- 36oz/1kg natural wool fiber (tops), such as Blue Faced Leicester, Jacob or Merino
- 3½oz/100g of one or a mix of other natural fibers (tops) such as cashmere, silk, camel or alpaca
- Fine darning needle
- Strong, thin wool floss
- Laundry detergent
- Rubber gloves
- Sewing machine (or large needle)
- Thread to match your fibers

Table runners are increasingly fashionable, and there is no better way to add tactile appeal to a dining table than with a gorgeous runner made from the softest wool in subtle, sophisticated colors.

The process of making felt by hand may be thousands of years old, but the results can appear surprisingly modern — perhaps thanks to the fashion for all things natural and organic. Our table runner has a wonderfully natural look, with its uneven edges, silky surface and deliberately visible seams. If you prefer a neater style, however, just trim the edges and sew the seams invisibly. As another alternative, do not sew the rectangles together, but use them singly as placemats, or make smaller versions to use as coasters.

Table runner

1 Lay out one piece of nylon net on a flat surface and, using the tape or ruler and chalk, mark out a rectangle 18 x 30in/45 x 75cm. (This will make a finished piece of felt measuring 12 x 20in/30 x 50cm — to make a different size, add 50 percent to the measurements you require, to allow for shrinkage.) Start laying out the wool fibers within the rectangle. Pull fine handfuls of fibers from the end of the roll and lay them all running from left to right, close to each other and overlapping slightly, until the whole rectangle is covered with a fine layer of fibers.

2 Add another layer of wool fibers on top, this time laying them all running in the opposite direction, from top to bottom within the rectangle. This will begin to create a woven build-up of fibers.

3 Keep building up the layers, until you have about five layers, or a dense build-up of fibers. Then, on the top layer, work in the contrasting fibers. Add them across the top layer in long strips. You can create a very even or a more spontaneous and irregular design.

4 Fold the nylon net over the top to cover, containing the fibers inside.

Table runner

assist the felting process. After about 20 minutes, you will feel that the bundles have each started to form a dense, well-integrated piece of fabric. Remove the net — remembering that the felt may still be a little delicate — and continue to wash the pieces (they will still shrink and felt further). At this stage, you can pull the pieces into shape and control how well-felted their surfaces become. This process usually takes around 30–40 minutes (for all four pieces).

5 Baste the net into place with the strong woolen floss. Fold this into three so that it is more manageable to work with. Repeat from step 1 to make another three pieces to the same dimensions.

7 Rinse thoroughly in cool water and squeeze out as much excess water as you can. Place each piece on a flat surface and gently pull into an even rectangular shape. If a piece needs more work, wash it again for a little longer. Allow to dry (flat if possible) away from direct heat.

6 Run a few inches of very hot (but not boiling) water into a sink or large container and add a cup of laundry liquid or powder. If using powder, it must be well dissolved. Place the four bundles into the water and, wearing rubber gloves, beat and squeeze the bundles vigorously with your hands. At regular intervals, as the fibers absorb the water and the water cools, add a burst of very hot tap water to

8 Use a sewing machine or a large needle to stitch together the four pieces of felt. Sew along the short edges of the pieces, with the wrong sides facing. If you wish to make more of a feature of the seams — for a more rustic and textured look — you can overstitch by hand using colored floss and blanket stitch (see page 408).

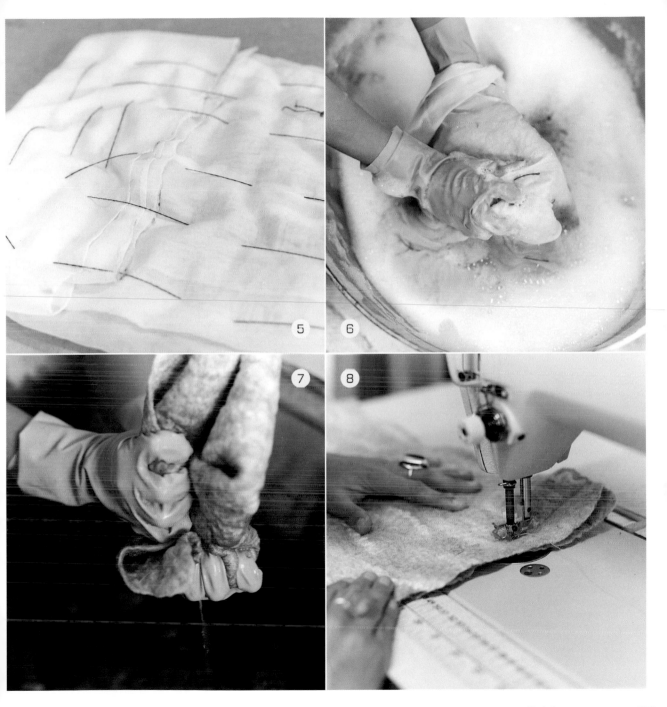

Striped rug

You will need

(To make a rug measuring about 28 x 39in/70 x 100cm)

- A piece of nylon net 78 x 98in/ 2 x 2.5m
- Measuring tape or ruler
- Tailor's chalk or pencil
- 3¼lb/1.5kg natural-color merino wool fiber (tops)
- 18oz/500g merino wool fiber (tops) in three different colors (this project used dusty pink, red and burgundy)
- Fine darning needle
- Strong, thin wool floss
- Laundry detergent
- Rubber gloves

This impressive rug would be ideal beside a bed or in front of a fire. Created from the softest, warmest materials, it feels immensely cozy and gives a welcoming touch of color and texture.

Although this rug is a fairly ambitious project, it is not as difficult as it looks. Get a feel for it by experimenting with simpler items such as the table runner on page 168, and you should have no problem at all. In fact, you will probably want to go on to increasingly complex versions. For a larger rug, make three more of the same size and stitch together; you may also want to try different fibers in order to produce a variety of surface patterns. The possibilities are endless, and enormously rewarding.

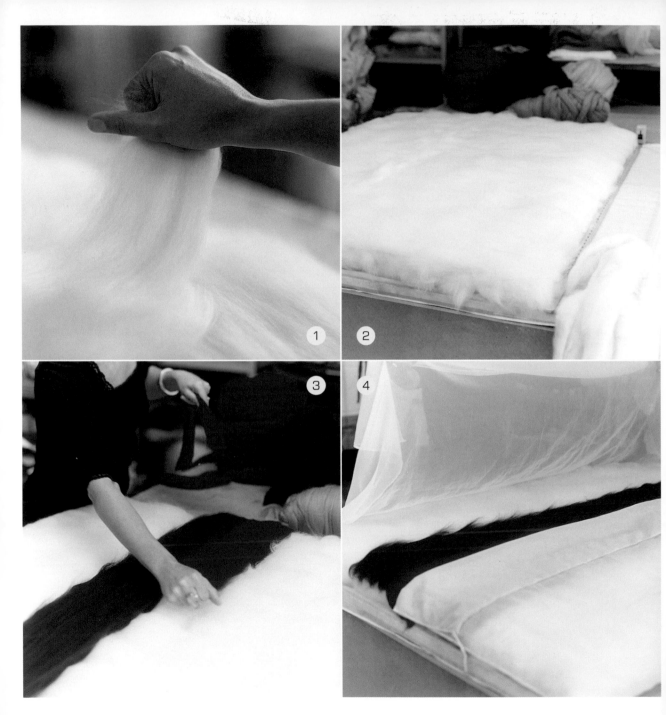

how to make:
Striped rug

2 Add another layer of merino fibers on top, this time laying them all running from top to bottom within the rectangle. Working in this manner, begin to create a woven build-up of fibers.

3 Build up the layers until you have at least eight layers or a very dense build-up of fibers. Then add the colored fibers, placing them across the top layer in long stripes, alternating the colors to create blocks in varying widths.

4 Fold the net carefully over the top to cover, containing the fibers inside

1 Lay out the net on a flat surface and mark out a rectangle 42 x 59in/105 x 150cm. (This will make a finished piece of felt measuring 28 x 39in/ 70 x 100cm — to make a different size, add 50 percent to the measurements you require, to allow for shrinkage.) Start laying out the merino fibers within the rectangle — pull fine handfuls of fibers from the end of the roll and lay them all running from left to right, close to each other and overlapping slightly, until the whole rectangle is covered with a fine layer of fibers.

working with fibers
To avoid holes or thin patches in your finished felt, layer the fibers as evenly and thoroughly as possible. The finer the fibers you use, the easier the felting process will be — and the more delicate the finished piece.

Striped rug

5 Baste the net into place using the strong woolen floss. Roll or fold the felt 'parcel' lengthwise so it is more manageable to work with.

6 Run a few inches of very hot (but not boiling) water into a sink or large container and add a cup of detergent. If using powder, it must be well dissolved. Place the roll into the water and, wearing rubber gloves, beat and squeeze it with your hands. At regular intervals, as the fibers absorb the water and the water cools, add a burst of very hot tap water to assist the process. After about 30 minutes, you will feel that the roll has started to form a dense, well-integrated piece of fabric. Remove the net and unroll the piece — the felt may still be delicate — then continue to wash it. At this stage, you can pull it into shape and control how well-felted the surface becomes. This entire process usually takes around 40–60 minutes (leave it in the water for a while if it becomes too tiring, and return to it later).

7 Rinse thoroughly in cool water and squeeze out as much excess water as you can.

8 Place the felted fabric onto a flat surface and pull into an even, rectangular shape. Allow to dry (flat if possible) naturally.

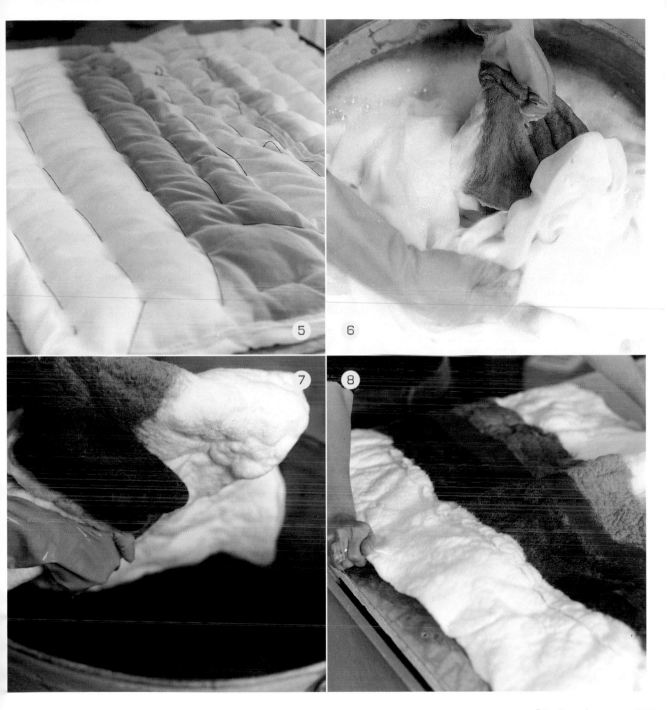

Using felt

In the 19th century it became possible to produce lengths of uniform felt by machine. The fabric has been used in thousands of ways ever since and, although many of its uses have been mundane, for some craftspeople it has become the vehicle for expression, innovation and experimentation.

The practicality and versatility of felt have been known to man since the seventh millennium BC, and making felt by hand, using woolen fibers, water, heat and agitation has been practiced ever since. Felt making was a cottage industry, however, until the arrival of industrialization in the 19th century. As wool manufacture became mechanized, so too did that of felt, initially as a means of using up waste wool, but later as a trade in its own right. By the middle of the 19th century, factories in the industrialized world were capable of producing large quantities of felt in long lengths of uniform quality, in different thicknesses and dyed (synthetically) in a rainbow of hues.

For the newly developed machine industry, felt was invaluable, and was used for shock and sound absorption, lining, sealing, air filtration, weather and dust shielding, heat and cold insulation, padding and packing. It was also used by hat makers, and went in and out of fashion as a garment fabric. It has periodically been made into coats, capes, jackets and skirts (its most recent incarnation being the duffel coat) as well as, in Finland, boots and socks.

The advantages of industrially produced felt did not stop there, however, and it soon came to be used all around the home, too. Its many applications — a great number of them still as relevant now as they were then — include roofing, carpet underlay and printed top carpets (a speciality of the late 19th century), piano dampeners, billiard tables, upholstery, table covers, cabinet linings, drapes and, of course, blankets and throws. Even from the mid-20th century, when synthetics such as nylon and rayon began to emerge as serious competitors for natural fabrics, felt never completely disappeared — it was simply too useful a fabric.

In the 1960s and '70s, craftspeople in Europe and America discovered the appeal of sheet felt for domestic hobbies. Here was a unique material that was tough and soft, strong and yet malleable. It was available in long lengths and small squares, in a range of thicknesses and an almost infinite number of vivid colors, and it could be cut without fraying, embossed, punched, stitched, glued, stuffed, sculpted and painted. Enthusiasm grew for making children's toys and games, in particular, from felt, and it was a favorite material for patterns in craft instruction books. The fashion waned in the 1980s and early '90s, but at the end of the 20th century, felt enjoyed a renaissance, re-entering the fashion arena as a fabric that offered huge potential for experimentation. In recent years, craftspeople have begun to see machine-made felt in a new light, as both environmentally friendly and avant-garde, and are using it in astonishing new ways — cutting, tearing, stretching, stitching and manipulating it into unexpected incarnations and giving a familiar fabric an exciting, modern twist.

Wall hanging

You will need

(To make a hanging measuring about
16 x 70in/40 x 180cm)

- 6 x 8in/15 x 45cm piece of ¼in-thick/
  6mm hard taupe felt
- Cutting mat
- Metal ruler
- Rotary cutter
- 18 x 74in/44 x 187cm semi-transparent
  ivory fabric (not too flimsy — nylon
  sailcloth is ideal)
- Iron
- Pins
- Sewing machine with a strong needle
- Thread to match the fabric
- Scissors
- Masking tape
- Pen
- Length of bamboo or wooden dowel
  (to fit the hanging) and hooks

Sometimes the simplest of projects can be the most effective, and what is so nice about this one is, indeed, its utter simplicity, resulting in work that has great subtlety but also quiet impact.

The qualities of manufactured felt are completely different to those of its hand-made counterpart. Available in a wide range of colors and thicknesses, it offers craftspeople plenty of possibilities — the trick is to make the most of its regularity without being hindered by it. Very simple to complete, this wall hanging has a subtle, tactile appeal, in neutral colors that would work with any style of décor. It could also easily be made larger or hung with several others to act as a striking door screen or a room divider.

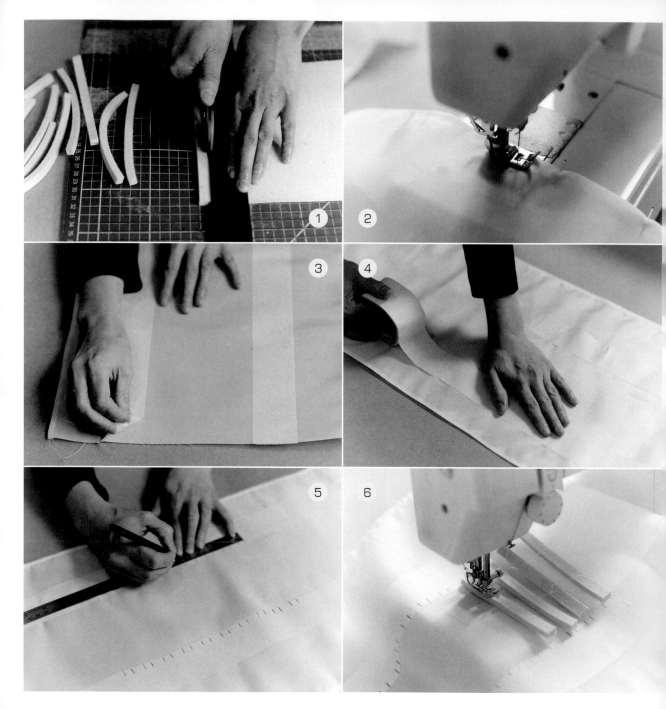

how to make:
Wall hanging

1 Place the felt on a cutting mat and use a metal ruler and a rotary cutter to cut 40 strips of felt measuring ⅜in by 6in/1cm x 15cm. Work with care when using the cutter.

2 Take the transparent fabric and turn the edges in by ⅜in/1cm, then another ⅜in/1cm. Press, pin, then stitch. Turn the top edge over by about 2in/5cm and stitch again, close to the edge

3 Stick the masking tape in two straight lines down the length of the fabric, about 4in/10cm from the left and 6in/15cm from the right, leaving a gap measuring 6in/15cm in the middle.

4 Make sure that you smooth down the masking tape firmly as you flatten it down the length of the fabric. Make certain also that there are no creases in the fabric beneath.

5 On the tape, mark the positions for your strips of felt, starting about 8in/20cm from the top edge and leaving a gap of about ⅝in/1.5cm between each one. Mark a group of 10, then leave a gap of 6in/15cm, then mark another group of 10, and so on.

6 Align your first strip with the top marking, and attach it to the fabric by stitching along its central line (2in/5cm each side hangs free from the fabric). Repeat until the fabric is covered with strips. Pull off the masking tape. Press, if necessary, then simply push the bamboo through the large hem at the top and hang.

> ### variations
> If you wish to vary the design of your wall hanging, you could dye the strips of felt in different colors using cold-water dyes, or cut them to different lengths, or stitch a large rectangle of contrasting fabric beneath the felt strips.

Funnel lampshade

You will need

(To make a lampshade 16in/40cm high
and about 6in/15.5cm diameter)

- Two rectangles of very pale mint green
  flame-retardant display felt, 16 x 20in/
  40 x 50cm
- Steam iron
- Scissors
- Sewing machine
- Thread to match the felt
- Pins
- Metal craft ring (6in/15.5cm diameter)
- Needle and thread (or a hot glue gun)
- Lampshade holder (6in/15.5cm diameter)

This unusual lampshade is made using a combination
of techniques, and while each is individually simple,
the end result is complex and intriguing. This is a
project with real character and impact.

Not only can felt be cut without fraying, but it can also be
stretched, stitched and layered with ease, allowing for
some really unusual effects. What is more, thin sheets of
machine-made felt are very slightly transparent, and so
lend themselves well to playing with light and shade. When
making this lampshade, remember that the same pattern
could also be put to use as a floor lamp or a pendant light;
you could also choose thread in a contrasting color for the
delicate stitching that emphasizes its unusual shape.

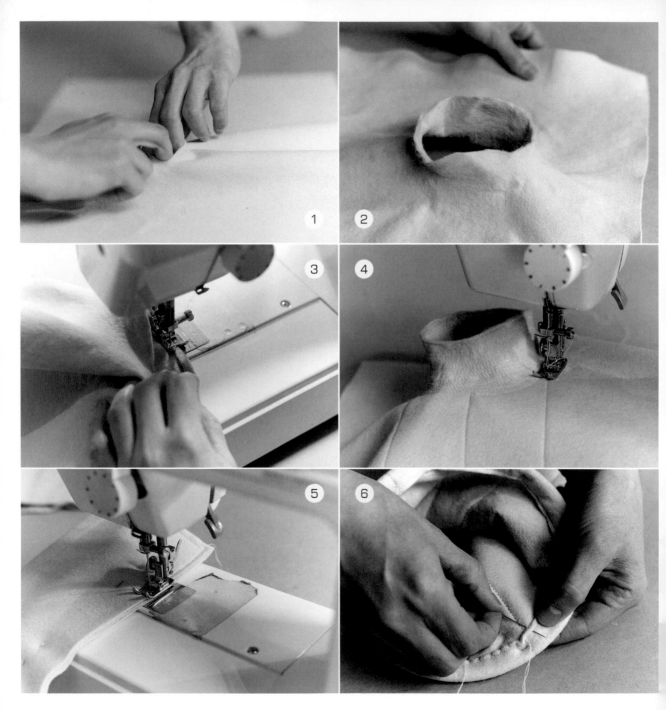

how to make:
Funnel lampshade

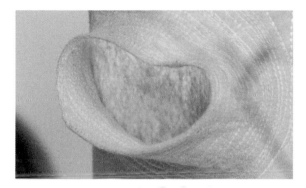

1 Press both pieces of felt with a steam iron. Take one piece and snip a hole in the center, about ¾in/2cm wide. Start to pull it out with your fingers, stretching the felt evenly to enlarge the hole a little. Be gentle or the felt may rip. Hold an edge of the fabric and pull on the central cylinder shape to make it protrude further. Every now and then, put the felt on a flat surface and flatten the edges.

2 Pull until the central cylinder is about 2¾in/7cm in diameter and about 2in/5cm high. Trim the top edge of the cylinder to even it out, and flatten the surrounding area.

3 Turn the top edge of the cylinder in about ⅜in/5mm and machine stitch a hem about ⅛in/3mm from the edge. Turn inside out and trim the hem close to the stitching. Turn out.

4 Align the sewing machine foot with the hem you have just sewn, and begin to stitch in a spiral shape around the cylinder. Do not worry about making this too neat. Keep going round and round until you have covered the 2in/5cm height of the cylinder or, if you wish to make it more elaborate, carry on stitching around the flat portion of felt. Lay the stitched felt on the other, plain piece, and pin together around the edges. Stitch two lines through both layers either side of the cylinder, and another two either side of the center of the cylinder. Stitch in a circle around the base of the cylinder. Press, avoiding the cylinder.

5 Stitch both layers together along the two long sides, very close to the edges. Fold the two short sides together, right sides together, to make a drum shape, and stitch along this seam through all four layers, close to the edge. Press, without flattening the cylinder, and turn out.

6 Insert the metal ring into the bottom of the shade and turn the edge of the felt over it by about ⅜in/1cm. Hand stitch invisibly or use a glue gun. Repeat with the lampshade holder, inserting it at the top of the shade. Place the shade on the base, making sure the felt is away from light source.

Weaving &
Beading

Weaving

From the simplest plain weave to twill, damask, satin, velvet and tapestry, weaving is one of our most ancient crafts — the means of producing textiles for warmth and clothing. However, it can also be a delightful way of exploring color, pattern and texture in two, or even three, dimensions.

When early man began to settle in primitive dwellings and to farm animals, it became possible to set up looms and weave cloth. It is even likely that weaving pre-dates spinning as it can be performed with natural materials, such as raffia. Although very simple weaving can be done with the fingers, the earliest type of loom was warp-weighted, where the vertical threads were hung from a horizontal beam and tied to weights of clay or stone. Illustrated on Greek vases from the sixth to fourth centuries BC, these looms were found all over Northern Europe before the Roman conquest, and were still used in Scandinavia until the 20th century.

As different looms were developed, so the art of weaving varied from place to place and time to time. In 4,500BC Egypt, very fine linen was woven on a horizontal loom for use as burial shrouds. Later, the Egyptians became adept at colorful tapestry weaving, for everyday clothing and for decoration. In India and South-East Asia the backstrap, or body-tension loom, became important, as it was able to produce a wide variety of complex patterns. It was the treadle loom, however, used for silk weaving in China as long ago as the third century BC, that took the art of weaving one step further. This made the technique faster and allowed longer pieces of cloth —

indeed, many hand weavers still use this type of loom today. The draw loom, which may also have originated in China but was developed in the Middle East in the sixth and seventh centuries, allowed even more complex and varied patterning. It was widely used until the early-19th century, when it was replaced by the mechanical Jacquard loom.

Over the centuries, various countries have been pre-eminent in the art of weaving. Beautiful fabrics were produced in Persia from the third century onward, and then in Spain and Southern Italy under Islamic rule. Later, Italian silks were most highly desired — those from Lucca were lavishly embellished with metallic thread, while Venetian and Florentine velvets were widely exported. When the silk industry established itself at Lyons, France, in the 16th century, it became the chief center for European silk weaving. England too, established a reputation for woven wool and silk, thanks especially to an influx of skilled Flemish and Huguenot refugees in the 16th and 17th centuries.

With the advent of mechanization in the 18th century, hand weaving virtually disappeared in many Western areas, until it was stimulated by a revival of interest in the late-1800s. Gradually, weaving workshops and guilds were set up, and the craft enjoyed a renaissance. No longer employed for widespread production of clothing and textiles, hand weaving is now an artistic medium in which the hand-made character can be enjoyed, traditional processes rediscovered and new methods explored.

Fringed lampshade

You will need

(To make 20in/50cm of braid, 6in/15cm deep, including tassels of about 4in/10cm)

- 2in-wide/5cm ribbon, long enough to wind around the base of your shade
- Plain white lampshade (fabric, paper or plastic)
- Frame — a square/rectangular tapestry frame from a craft supplier, a stretcher from a picture frame or even a chair back or ladder. It should measure at least 8in/20cm wide; the other length will determine how long you can weave each length of braid
- Reel of strong thread (the type used for beading is ideal)
- Scissors
- Masking tape
- 0.5mm diameter (25swg) silver-plated copper wire (wire A)
- Old scissors or pliers
- Ruler
- 40 skeins silver silk embroidery floss
- Letter-size/A4 card
- 0.25mm diameter (33swg) silver-plated copper wire (wire B)
- Needle and thread (or white glue, if the shade is made of paper or plastic)

Weaving need not involve only traditional threads — you can weave practically anything long and slender. This project employs silver-plated wire to unusual and extraordinary effect.

For a quirky contrast to a plain lampshade, this woven trim has the perfect note of glamorous eccentricity. It uses a mixture of wire and thread, achieving an effect that is ethereal and decorative but with an avant-garde edge. The weaving technique, however, is very straightforward — it is called 'plain weave'. This involves only working the weft inserts over and under the warp, backward and forward until you have created a trim to the depth you require.

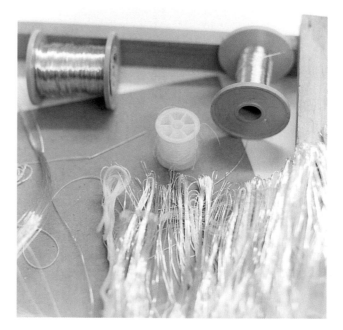

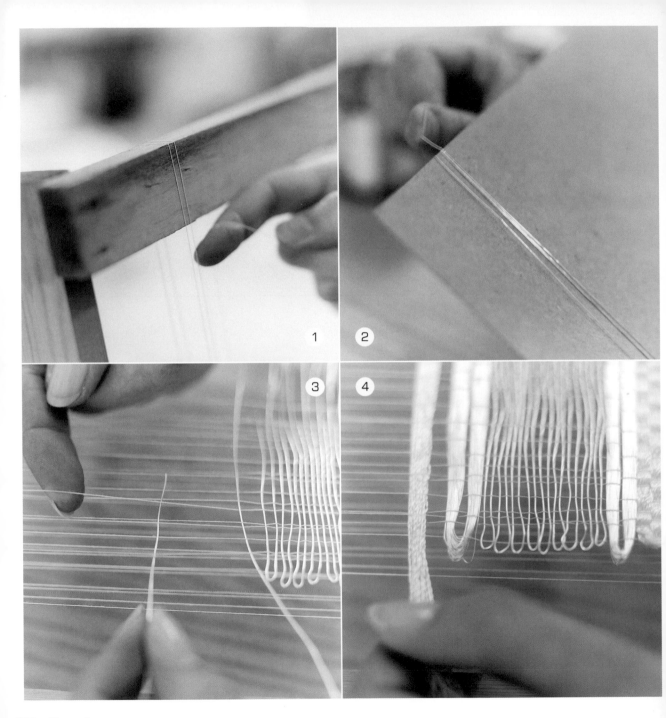

how to make:
Fringed lampshade

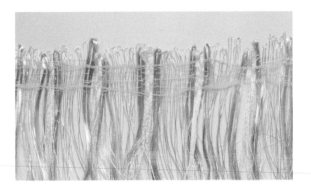

1 Wind a ribbon around the base of the lampshade in order to measure the length of braid you need to make. Then take the wooden frame and securely knot the strong thread (this is the warp) onto the bottom bar of the longest dimension of your frame. Take the warp up to the top bar and pass over it and back down behind the frame to the bottom bar, and again up over this bar, leaving spaces of about ⅛in/3mm between each strand. Continue doing this until you have passed the warp over the front 20 times — you will have 20 'ends' on the front and 20 on the back. Check that they are about ⅛in/3mm apart, and that the tension is taut, but not near breaking point — like a tambourine surface. Knot the thread onto the top bar and cut. Then repeat this process, 3in/8cm to the right of the warp you have just created, wrapping around only four times. This creates an 'extra warp' that will hold the tassels in place when weaving. Cover the threads with tape to hold them in place.

2 Prepare bundles of weft insertions (hanks). Cut wire A, using old scissors or pliers, into 14in/36cm lengths. You will need to cut 90 lengths in this way. Wind the embroidery floss around the long side of a piece of letter-size/A4 card 16 times, and slide it off the card, creating a tight bundle — prepare 10 hanks like this. Wind wire B around the card 16 times, and slide off — prepare 20 wire hanks in this way.

3 Take one end of wire A and insert it under the first warp thread on the left of your frame, then over the next warp thread, under the next and so on. Pull it through to your extra warp and go under and over the warp ends here, too. The wire will extend a little on the right hand side — this can be trimmed later. Bend the wire at the left-hand side, creating a hairpin effect, and take this under and over the opposite warps to the previous insertion. This is 'plain weave'. Repeat for nine 'hairpin'-type inserts.

4 Insert a hank of wire B, treating the bundle as if it were one thread and bending it back and through as for step 3. Next insert a hank of silk in the same way. Repeat steps 3 and 4, building up your stock of weft inserts until you reach the top of the frame.

Fringed lampshade

5 Carefully cut the warp at the back of the frame, leaving long ends, and repeat the entire process until you have made enough braid to go right around the base of the lampshade.

6 Lay two lengths of braid together, end to end. Join the warp ends by knotting like with like along the width of the braid. Repeat until you have joined all the lengths. Finish the two ends of the long braid by knotting pairs of adjoining warp ends together. Trim all weft ends to 4in/10cm, so that the total depth of the braid is 6in/15cm.

7 To attach the braid, place it on the base of the shade and make two stitches on top of each other through both layers at the top left-hand corner of the braid. Knot at the back. Wrap the braid around the shade, attaching with a single stitch at the top every 1–1½in/3–4cm. At the end, finish with a small, neat stitch. On plastic or paper lampshades, glue the braid with white glue.

weaving tension

In traditional weaving projects, the tension of the weft threads is enormously important. Here, however, you can afford to weave quite loosely in order to create a pretty, unstructured effect.

Trimmed shade

You will need

(To make 20in/50cm of braid, 5in/12cm deep, including 3in/7cm tassels)

- Measuring tape
- Plain fabric roller or roman shade
- Frame (see page 196)
- Reel of strong thread (will not break with a light tug — the type used for beading is ideal)
- Scissors
- Masking tape
- 24 skeins silk embroidery floss in ivory
- 24 skeins silk embroidery floss in silver
- 6 skeins silk embroidery floss in burnt orange
- Letter-size/A4 card
- Pins
- Needle and thread (or white glue)

This woven trimming adds texture, color and style to an otherwise plain and simple roller shade. Though designed according to the traditional principles of the craft, it is fun and frivolous, too.

Although it appears distinctly untraditional, this project involves techniques that would be recognized by weavers from centuries ago. How far you want to go is up to you. You could, as here, leave the weft ends long and uneven for an organic look, or cut them short and neat for a more ordered style. But crucial to the success of the project is the choice of colors — cool silver with burnt orange has the right mix of sophistication and surprise, though you could, of course, substitute any colors of your choice.

how to make:
Trimmed shade

1 Measure the width of the shade onto which you would like to attach your braid — this is the length of braid you need to create. Take the wooden frame and securely knot the strong thread (this is the warp) onto the bottom bar of the longest dimension of your frame. Take the warp up to the top bar and pass over it and back down the back of the frame to the bottom bar and again over this bar.

2 Continue doing this, leaving spaces of about ⅛in/ 3mm, until you have passed the warp over the front 20 times — you will have 20 'ends' on the front and 20 on the back. Check the ⅛in/3mm spacing and the tension — this should be taut but not near breaking point, like a tambourine surface. Knot the

thread onto the top bar and cut. Then repeat this process, 3in/8cm to the right of the warp you have just created, wrapping around only four times. This creates an 'extra warp' that will hold the tassels in place when weaving. Cover the threads with tape to hold them in place.

3 Prepare bundles of weft insertions (hanks). Take an end each of both the ivory and silver embroidery floss and, twisting them together as you go, wind the threads around the long side of a piece of letter-size/ A4 card 16 times. Slide the threads off the card. For one pattern repeat you will need to prepare 48 hanks like this. Wind the orange floss around the card 16 times, and slide off. For one repeat you will need to prepare six hanks like this.

4 Insert one end of a silver/ivory hank under the first warp thread on the left of your frame, then over the next warp thread, under the next and so on. Pull it through to your extra warp and go under and over the warp ends here, too. The silk will extend a little on the right-hand side — this can be trimmed later. Then turn the hank at the left-hand side and take this under and over the opposite warp threads to the previous insertion. This is 'plain weave'. Repeat for six hanks of silver/ivory.

Trimmed shade

5 The next step is to build up the pattern along with the six hanks above to create 6½in/16cm of braid. A: Insert a hank of the orange — weave one end through, then leave the other half dangling. B: Insert a hank of the silver/ivory — weave one end through and the other half back again. C: Insert another hank of the silver/ivory — weave one end through, then leave the other half dangling. D: Weave the dangling end of the orange hank from A. E: Insert six hanks of the silver/ivory and, one at a time, weave one end through and the other half back again. F: Insert an orange hank — weave one end through, then leave the other half dangling. G: Insert another hank of the silver/ivory — weave one end through, then leave the other half dangling.

H: Weave the dangling end of the orange hank from F. I: Weave the dangling end of the silver/ivory hank from G. J: Insert nine hanks of the silver/ivory and, one at a time, weave one end through and the other half back again. This is your repeat — now repeat steps 4 and 5, building up your weft inserts until you reach the top of the frame.

6 When you have finished weaving, carefully cut the warp at the back of the frame, leaving long ends, and repeat steps 1–5 until you have made enough braid for the width of your shade. To join your lengths of braids together, lay two lengths end to end. Join the warp ends by knotting like with like along the width of the braids. Repeat with each length of braid. Finish the two ends of the long braid by knotting pairs of adjoining warp ends together. Trim all weft ends to about 3in/7cm, so the total depth of the braid is 5in/12cm.

7 To attach the braid to the shade, place the shade flat on a large table and lay the braid on top of it. Pin. Starting on the left, make two small stitches on top of each other through both layers, about ⅜in/1cm in from the top edge of the braid. Sew with a small, neat running stitch along the length of the shade. Alternatively, glue on using white glue.

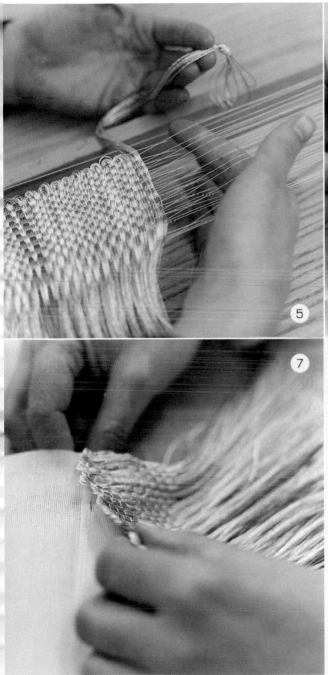

variations

Once you master the basic technique of plain weave, you can begin to experiment. Different colors and textures in both your warp and weft threads will give very different, and often surprising results.

Ribbonwork

Ribbons have always had symbolic meaning, representing love and friendship, remembrance or achievement, rank and status or military prowess. However, they also make unique decorations, pretty and precious, subtle or sumptuous, to adorn clothing and home furnishings of all types.

The intriguing art of *passementerie*, or decorative textile trimming, dates back to the very ancient civilizations of Greece, Rome, Egypt, China and South America — where decorative trimmings were placed in temples and the tombs of royalty and chiefs. In Medieval France it was highly esteemed and, as long ago as the 13th century, guilds had been established for the craftsmen who made embellishments for pillowcases, women's head dresses, tapestries, flags and church textiles. By the 17th century, as domestic textiles became more prevalent (in the form of drapes and upholstered furniture), passementerie was used increasingly around the home.

Decoration for its own sake was the fashion during the 18th century, and lavish adornments of all kinds were in vogue among royalty and the upper classes. Silk ribbons had by now become a favorite, as bows and ruching on bodices, robes, sleeves, hats, shoes and embroidery, and in both France and England they came to represent nobility. In fact, in England laws were passed that forbade the wearing of ribbons by anyone except the aristocracy. At first, ribbons were woven individually on hand looms, but mechanized weaving meant that advanced looms could weave any number of ribbons at once, and in all manner of beautifully intricate patterns.

The first American ribbon factory was set up in 1815, but it was some time before ribbons became widely popular with the settlers, as they were associated with their English rulers. Native Americans, on the other hand, had been introduced to ribbons by traders, and used them on shirts and skirts in colorful, abstract patterns.

The 19th century saw a resurgence of interest in ribbons in both America and Europe, and from the late 1800s numerous magazines offered instruction in ribbon embroidery and embellishments — for many purposes, including hair ornaments, belts, bags, parasols, hats, gloves, lingerie, ballgowns, pillows, firescreens and quilts. But as lifestyles changed, and both clothing and home décor became simpler, such extravagances were seen as outdated. By the First World War, the use of ribbons had declined, until eventually they were associated mainly with babies' clothing, lingerie and special-occasion dresses.

In recent years, however, the variety of ribbons has increased dramatically, and there has been a corresponding revival in ribbon trims and decoration. Craftspeople use them in projects ranging from cushions and throws to gift wrapping and Christmas decorations, often hand in hand with embroidery, appliqué and beading, but sometimes simply as an end in themselves. The techniques employed range from weaving and appliqué to making rosettes and tassels, adding a unique and attractive decorative esthetic and transforming the plain and ordinary into something utterly extraordinary.

Checkered cushion

You will need

(To make a 14in/35cm square cushion)

- Scissors
- 1¼yds/1m silk (at least 20in/49cm wide) in ivory/taupe
- Measuring tape or ruler
- 6yds/5.5m each of two organza ribbons in coordinating or contrasting colors (this project used ivory and mid-brown), 1⅛in/2.8cm wide
- Pins
- Needle
- Basting thread
- Sewing machine (a zipper foot is helpful but not essential)
- Sewing thread to match the silk
- Iron
- 1¾yds/1.45m fancy-edge tape, ³⁄₁₆in/4mm wide, to match the silk
- 1¾yds/1.45m piping cord
- Tailor's chalk
- 14in/35cm square pillow form

Unusual ribbons are available in all kinds of textures and colors, and this project makes good use of them to create a woven cushion cover with a simple tie closure that is both functional and decorative.

This attractive project is really feminine, yet its neat checked pattern gives it a bold look that is slightly plainer than some ribbonwork, while the crisp piped edging adds a clean, professional finish. Instead of fiddly zips or buttons, it features a simple overlap with a tie fastening made from matching ribbons. Sophisticated, muted colors have a contemporary appeal, though of course you could choose any hue to contrast with or complement your interior.

how to make:
Checkered cushion

1 Cut the silk into a 15½in/39cm square, and three rectangles measuring 10½ x 15½in/27 x 39cm, 10 x 15½in/26 x 39cm and 4 x 39in/10cm x 1m. Cut the organza ribbons to 13 lengths of 15½in/39cm in each color and two lengths of 8in/20cm in each color. Lay the 15½in/39cm square piece of silk flat. Place 13 ribbons on top, running from left to right, abutting each other, and alternating the colors. Pin, then baste them to the left edge of the silk.

2 Place 13 more ribbons on top of the fabric, over the previous set and this time running from top to bottom, again alternating the colors. Pin and then baste them to the top edge of the silk. Start to weave the ribbons one by one, under and over alternating ribbons, pulling them squarely into place as you go. When all the ribbons are woven, pin then baste them to the bottom and right edges of the silk.

3 For the piping, take the silk rectangle measuring 4 x 39in/10cm x 1m and cut it in half lengthwise. Place the right sides together and stitch down one short side with the sewing machine, leaving ⅜in/1cm seam allowance. Press open (on a low temperature). You should have a rectangle measuring 2 x 77in/5 x 198cm — now cut it down so it measures 2 x 57in/5 x 145cm. Pin and then stitch the fancy-edge tape to the right side of this piece, in the center. Fold the piece in half lengthwise, wrong sides together, and press. Then fold the piece around the piping cord and pin together, enclosing the piping. Stitch all the way along, as close to the piping cord inside as possible (a zipper foot is useful here, but not essential).

4 With the tailor's chalk, mark a 14in/35cm square in the center of your woven-ribbon panel, on the right side. Lay the piping around this, with its raw edges to the outside, and pin (clipping the seam allowance at the corners), then baste. Stitch it on (again, a zipper foot is useful), as close to the piping cord as possible.

Checkered cushion

5 To make the back of the cushion, take the two remaining silk rectangles. On both, take one of the edges that measures 15½in/39cm and turn it over by ⅜in/1cm, and then again by 1½in/4cm. Press, pin and stitch.

6 Place the woven-ribbon panel right-side up on a flat surface. Place the two other silk rectangles right side down on top of it, with their hemmed edges in the center, overlapping by 1½in/4cm. Pin and then baste together around the edges. Stitch together, ¹⁄₁₆in/1mm outside the piping. Turn out.

7 Press the cushion cover carefully, with the iron on a low temperature. Stitch the two pairs of 8in-long/20cm ribbons to either side of the opening, equidistant from the center, insert the pillow form and tie the ribbons together with simple knots or bows. (Smart, symmetrical bows will make the underside of the cushion look almost as beautiful as the woven top.)

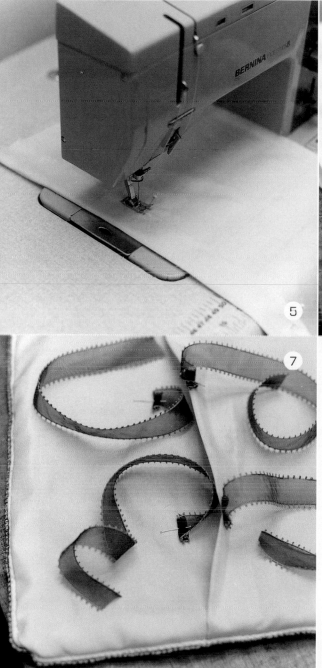

⑤ ⑥ ⑦

neat weaving

Make sure that you keep your weaving as tidy and flat as possible to prevent it bagging later. As you move across the cushion, check that the tension remains consistent and, if necessary, go back and tidy up at the end. The flatter the finish, the more professional the look.

Careful application of the piping will also add to the quality of the final cushion. Make sure your sewing is as neat as possible so that the piping creates an attractive border around the cushion.

Ribbon bag

You will need

(To make a bag measuring 8 x 12in/
20 x 30cm)

- Scissors
- 5⅔yds/5.2m organza ribbon in pale green, ⅝in/1.5cm wide (A)
- 4⅔yds/4.3m organza ribbon in mid-blue, ⅝in/1.5cm wide (B)
- 9¾yds/9m organza ribbon in mid-green, 1in/2.5cm wide (C)
- Measuring tape
- Four pieces of silk dupion, in citron green, two measuring 14½ x 20in/ 37 x 50cm, and two measuring 3 x 17in/8 x 43cm
- Pins
- Needle
- Basting thread
- 20–25 coordinating beads
- 20–25 coordinating sequins
- Iron
- Four pieces of iron-on interfacing measuring 14½ x 20in/37 x 50cm, 2½ x 14½in/6 x 37cm, and two of 1¼ x 16in/3 x 40cm
- Sewing machine
- Thread to match the silk
- 1¼yds/1m taffeta ribbon in dark green, 1in/2.5cm wide
- Button
- Thread to match the button

This gorgeous woven-ribbon bag, embellished with sparkly beads and sequins, is just the right size for a glamorous girls' night out.

The organza ribbons that are interwoven to create this project give it an air of delicacy and softness, but with its silk backing and iron-on interfacing the bag is robust enough to withstand a night on the town. When you are making it, simply ensure that the ribbons are straight and abutting each other neatly, and the rest of the project will be simplicity itself. If you wish, instead of the button-and-loop fastening, you could add a tie fastening with two ribbons, or an internal magnetic fastener.

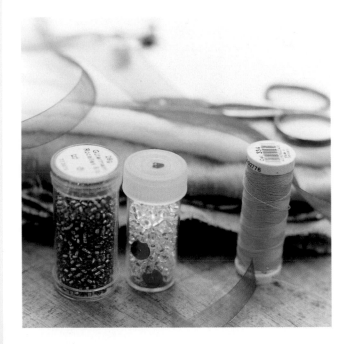

how to make:
Ribbon bag

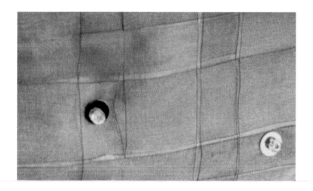

1 Cut the three organza ribbons into lengths — A into five lengths of 20in/50cm and seven lengths of 14½in/37cm; B into four lengths of 20in/50cm and six lengths of 14½in/37cm and C into nine lengths of 20in/50cm and twelve lengths of 14½in/37cm. Lay one silk dupion rectangle measuring 14½ x 20in/ 37 x 50cm on a flat surface. Place the 20in-long/ 50cm ribbons on top of it, abutting each other, alternating the colors as follows: ACBCACBC. Pin and then baste them to one edge of the silk.

2 Place the 14½in-long/37cm ribbons on top of the fabric, over the previous set and running in the opposite direction. Alternate colors as before. Pin and then baste them to one edge of the silk. Start to weave the ribbons one by one, under and over alternating ribbons, pulling them squarely into place as you go. When all the ribbons are woven, pin then baste them to the remaining two edges of the silk.

3 Neatly sew some beads and sequins to the surface of the woven ribbons, in a checkerboard pattern.

4 Press the 2½ x 14½in/6 x 37cm interfacing across the middle of the back of the woven-ribbon panel. Fold in half lengthwise with the right sides together; pin then stitch the two sides, leaving a ¾in/2cm seam allowance. Stitch diagonally across the two bottom corners, 1¼in/3cm from the corner points.

continued:

Ribbon bag

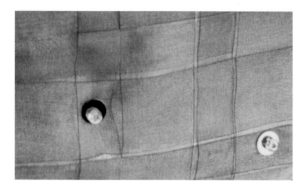

5 Cut, about ⅝in/1.5cm away from the stitching. Press the seams open and neatly turn out.

6 For the lining, press the 14½ x 20in/37 x 50cm interfacing to the other 14½ x 20in/37 x 50cm silk dupion rectangle. Fold in half (bringing the two short sides together), with the right sides together — pin then stitch the two sides, leaving a ¾in/2cm seam allowance. Stitch diagonally across the two bottom corners and cut (as before). Press the seams open. Put the lining inside the outer bag.

7 To make the handles, first cut the taffeta ribbon into two 20in/50cm lengths. Take one of the silk dupion rectangles measuring 3 x 17in/8 x 43cm. Fold in half along the length and press, then fold in ⅜in/1cm on each edge and press again. Press the interfacing to the inside of one half, and stitch the taffeta ribbon to the top of the other side. Stitch neatly along the two edges, on the right side.

8 Take a short length of the remaining ⅝in/1.5cm organza ribbon, fold it in half and stitch it together, making a loop large enough for your button. This will be the fastening for your bag, so check that it is positioned correctly. Insert the loop and baste it between the lining and the outer bag. Then baste the two handles between the lining and the outer bag. Turn in the top edges of the lining and outer bag by about ¾in/2cm each. Press, pin and baste. Stitch neatly around the rim of the bag, just below the top on the right side. To finish, sew on the button securely, opposite the loop.

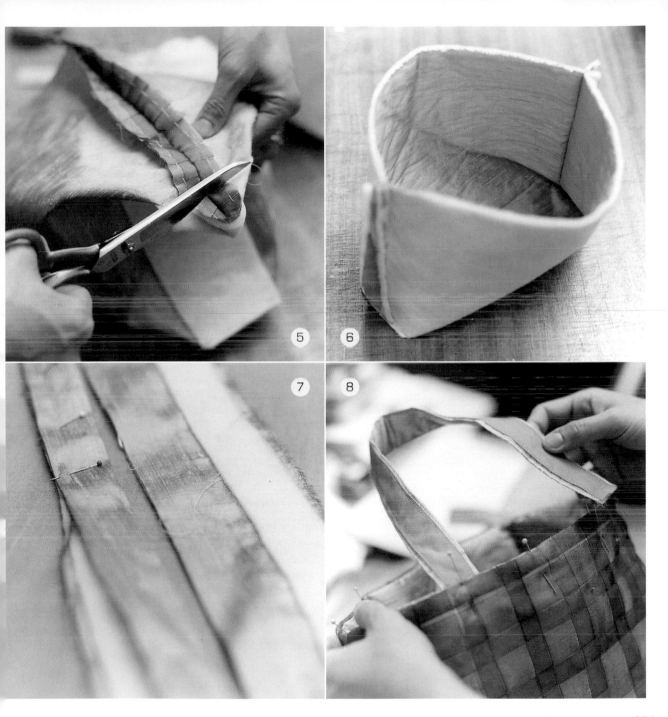

Beadwork

Beads have been made throughout human history, from a huge variety of materials — from bones to wood, glass to stones, shells to seeds. They have been used as trade goods, prayer aids, magical protectors, indicators of status and, of course, as adornment for clothing and other objects.

Beads have been around for as long as man: the earliest known examples, made from teeth and bone to be worn as pendants, date back to around 38,000BC.

Basic beads would have been fashioned from whatever materials were to hand, but even as long ago as the third or fourth century BC, a method of mass-producing glass beads was developed in South-East India, and later spread to Vietnam, Thailand, Malaysia, Indonesia and Sri Lanka. The resulting tiny, doughnut-shaped beads were probably strung as necklaces, woven or sewn onto cloth, and were traded all over the globe for 2,000 years.

Ancient Egypt was another center for beads, which were hand-made from stone and, later, glass, to adorn garments for everyday wear and funerary purposes. But beads were not only used for decoration. The name 'bead' comes from the old English 'bede', which means 'prayer', and the meditative nature of counting beads has for centuries given them a religious purpose. They have also had superstitious and symbolic meaning — to ward off evil or attract fertility, or imply purity, power, friendship or love. And, of course, they have been used for trade, by nomadic tribes who found them a convenient method of carrying wealth, and by Europeans who used them to deal with the peoples of Africa, Asia and America. Dutch traders, for example, bought the island of Manhattan with beads worth the equivalent of 24 dollars.

In the late 16th century, small glass beads were introduced to the Native Americans, who used them for necklaces and borders on clothing and other objects, in colorful, geometric patterns. This type of work is one of the predominant beadcraft forms today. African beadwork, too, is an important example of the craft. Stone, clay, shells, gems, coral, glass and metal were all used by African tribes to fashion beads. But it was the import of millions of glass beads from Venice and Bohemia in the late-15th century that transformed African beadwork, giving rise to traditions such as the beaded sculpture of the Grassfields region of Cameroon, the elaborate clothing and necklaces of the Maasai, and the abstract compositions of Ndebele garments.

In Europe, the use of beads reached its height during the Renaissance. The less well-off were forbidden to decorate themselves with beads and ribbons, but for wealthy people beaded clothing was a sign of status and good taste. Beadwork also boomed in Victorian times, when leisured ladies spent their time stitching samplers and other items. Since then people all around the world have continued to be fascinated by beads, using glass, stone, wood, china, pearls and other materials, small and large, plain or multi-colored, as an artistic, decorative and alluring way of embellishing clothing, home furnishings and all kinds of precious objects.

Sheer drape

You will need

- Scissors
- Length of organza cut to fit your window, allowing ¾in/2cm each side for seams, 4in/10cm at the top for hanging and 8in/20cm at the bottom for a hem
- Measuring tape
- Iron
- Pins
- Basting thread
- Needle
- Sewing machine
- Thread to match the organza
- Embroidery hoop
- Beading needle
- Nylon monofilament thread (clear)
- Imitation pearls in various sizes (this project required five strings each of ³⁄₁₆in/4mm and ¼in/6mm diameter, ten strings of ⁵⁄₁₆in/7mm and three strings each of ³⁄₈in/9mm and ½in/12mm)
- Polished rock crystal chips (this project required five strings)
- Dowel
- Hooks

This project needs nothing other than a length of organza as wide as your window, a scattering of imitation pearls in various sizes and a little sewing skill for fabulous results.

Sheer drapes are often a necessity, to prevent prying eyes from seeing in, or to disguise an unpleasant view. But sometimes they can be a delight as well; this example diffuses light softly with the added benefit of a glamorous beaded edging that shimmers gently and also gives the fabric extra weight. The stitching is straightforward — it is the skill in placing the random-size pearls that gives this project its beautiful, organic appearance. Never have net drapes been this good!

1

2

3

4

5

fine beading
Make sure that when you start to stitch,
you attach the thread to the fabric well,
so that it does not work loose. Always
keep the fabric taut, to avoid stitches
going baggy at the back.

how to make:
Sheer drape

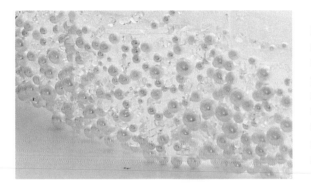

1 Cut a length of fabric to fit your window, plus seam allowances (see page 224). Turn over ⅜in/1cm at each side and press, then turn another ⅜in/1cm, press, pin, baste, then stitch.

2 At the top of the fabric, make a large hem by turning over ⅜in/1cm and pressing, then turning over 3½in/9cm and pressing. Pin, then baste and stitch to make a channel for a hanging rod. In the same way, make a hem at the bottom by turning the fabric over ⅜in/1cm and 7½in/19cm.

3 Insert a section of the fabric into the embroidery hoop so that it is as taut as possible. Using a beading needle threaded double with the monofilament, start to sew the beaded border, attaching the largest pearls first at random intervals. Ensure that your starting and finishing stitches, and the stitches at the back of the drape, are as neat as possible. Concentrate the larger beads towards the bottom of the drape, and sew some along the edge to create a modern, organic and naturally weighted feel.

4 Repeat with the medium and small pearls, building up a random pattern of different-size beads, and remembering to space the beads further apart at the top of the border to create a soft edge.

5 Finally, fill in the gaps between the beads with the rock crystal chips. To finish off neatly, bead only up to the stitch line of the side seams. Thread a piece of dowel through the hem at the top of the drape, distribute the fabric evenly into gathers and hang from hooks at either end.

Cuff bracelet

You will need

- Basting needle
- Basting thread
- Two 1in-wide/2.5cm ribbons (one black silk, one lime-green velvet), cut to the length of the circumference of your wrist, plus 1½in/4cm
- 12 x 12in/30 x 30cm piece of calico (or another fabric for a backing)
- Ruler
- Pencil
- Embroidery hoop
- Beading needle
- Nylon monofilament thread (smoke color)
- Approximately 100 ⅛ x ⅛in/3 x 3mm square pewter beads
- Approximately 3½oz/100g ¹⁄₁₆ x ¹⁄₁₆in/ 1 x 1mm square pewter beads
- Scissors
- Iron
- Needle
- Black thread
- Silk embroidery floss
- ¼in/6mm spherical button with a shank

The square, pewter-color beads of this supremely sophisticated beaded cuff catch the light elegantly without being either too glitzy or over formal — it is the perfect evening accessory.

The pleasure of this elegant cuff comes from its alluring combination of shimmering surface and a severe, plain pattern. Of course, you could choose any color beads you wish, though just one color on its own will provide the maximum impact. The tiny, square-profile beads are attached to the base fabric (which makes the bracelet wonderfully soft against the skin) by stringing several onto a needle at once — a time-honored craft method that makes this project both quick and easy to accomplish.

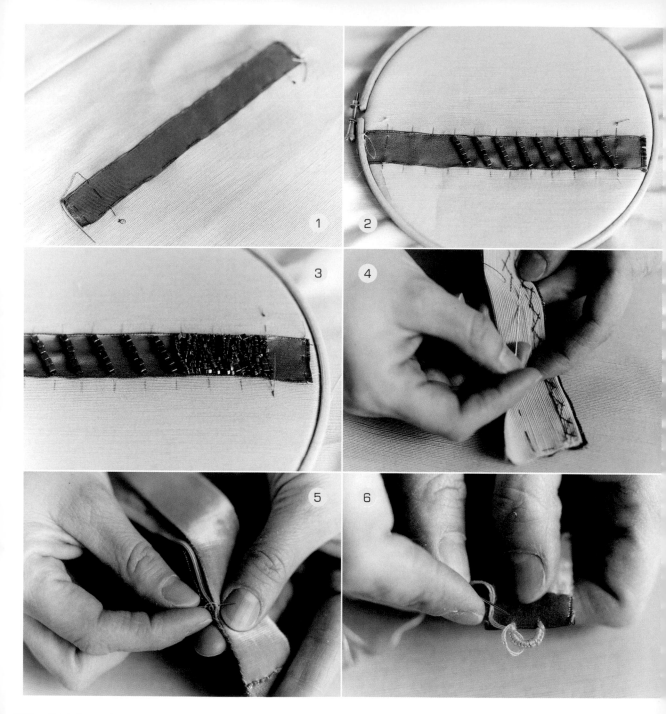

how to make:
Cuff bracelet

1 Baste the silk ribbon to the center of the calico. Measure ¾in/2cm in from each end of the ribbon and sew a line of basting across the ribbon at each of these points. You will only bead between them. Within these lines, use a pencil to mark every ⅝in/1.5cm on one edge of the ribbon and every ½in/1.25cm on the other edge.

2 Place the calico into the embroidery hoop. With the beading needle threaded double with the monofilament, cast on neatly to the back of the ribbon at the first ½in/1.25cm mark, and bring the needle up to the right side. Thread on approximately six of the larger beads. Take the stitch over to the first ⅝in/1.5cm mark on the opposite edge, making a slight diagonal, then sew underneath the calico, bringing the needle up on the first edge at the second ½in/1.25cm mark. Thread on six more large

beads and continue, sewing diagonally from pencil mark to pencil mark, until the entire ribbon (except for the ¾in/2cm at each end) is covered. Leave a little of the ribbon's selvage showing on both sides.

3 Fill in the gaps made by the first beading using the smaller beads (they will partially overlay the first ones and create a rounded effect). Work in a similar way, but this time sew the beads on two diagonals, creating a criss-cross effect. You will need about 13 of the smaller beads to cover a stitch that goes from edge to edge of the ribbon.

4 Allowing an extra ⅜in/1cm all round, cut the beaded ribbon off the backing fabric. Neatly cut the backing away from the unbeaded ends of the ribbon and turn in the remaining excess fabric. Press and hem neatly by hand.

5 Cover the back of the cuff with the velvet ribbon, and stitch into place. Turn each end over by ⅜in/1cm then another ⅜in/1cm, press and stitch neatly all around.

6 With the silk embroidery floss, make two loops in the center of one end of the cuff, large enough to go over the button. Blanket stitch (see page 408) over both loops to create a fastening. Sew the button onto the other end of the cuff.

Basketry

Since ancient times, basketry has been vital in every aspect of man's life — for work, play, shelter, clothing and culinary tasks. Baskets can also be incredibly beautiful and decorative, in traditional style or as a contemporary craft that pushes back the boundaries of techniques and materials.

Until recently one of the least appreciated of all crafts, basketry is also one of the oldest, dating back at least to between 10,000 and 8,000BC. What is likely is that as soon as man began to gather food, he needed something in which to carry and store it, and to interweave local materials into some sort of container would have been the natural response. Since then, in most societies around the world, baskets have been made in an enormous diversity of shapes, sizes and styles, their functions ranging from cooking and serving to hunting and fishing; from methods of transport and homes to clothing and toys; and from ceremonial gifts to coffins.

While beautiful basketry has been made by many civilizations, one of the most exquisite traditions is that of China and Japan, where the quality of a gift is traditionally expressed by the way in which it is wrapped, often involving intricate basketwork. Native American basketry is also world renowned, not only for its beauty, but also its range of techniques. Baskets were an indispensable part of the culture of these tribes from prehistoric times, and they used them in hundreds of ways, from daily chores to sacred rituals. Methods and styles varied, but notable examples include those of the Aleutian islanders who, until the mid-18th century, made delicately twined grass baskets that rivalled European linen for their fine texture, and those of the Pomo people, who produced baskets embellished with shell pendants or brightly colored feathers.

In Africa, baskets have also been important, often imbued with ceremonial or religious meanings. Many parts of Africa still produce baskets commercially today, though sometimes using new materials, such as the aid agency plastic rice sacks that are split and used for stitching in the Sahel area of Mali, and the colorful telephone-wire baskets coiled by the Zulu people of South Africa.

Basketry has a strong tradition in Europe, too. During the Roman empire, baskets decorated wealthy homes, and they were omnipresent in medieval households. The Industrial Revolution actually led to increased production of basketry, thanks to a huge demand for containers in which to transport materials and goods. In the 20th century, however, basketry declined, replaced by cardboard, plastic, plywood and fiberglass containers. In the 1970s, however, a new movement began in Europe and America, aimed at people who appreciated the hand-made and individual, who understood the 'green' nature of basket-making, or who wished to introduce new designs, pattern and materials. While traditional production is still diminishing, that artistic movement has gathered pace, so that now basketry is increasingly respected for its undeniable combination of beauty and function, and for its ancient methods married with new innovations.

Star decoration

You will need

(To make a decoration with a diameter of 10in/26cm)

- 30 lengths of white willow, each measuring 3ft/92cm
- Damp kitchen towel
- Pair of sharp pruning shears
- Bradawl or knitting needle

This simple star shape, propped up on a mantelpiece, window ledge or shelf, makes a lovely decorative accessory and brings a welcoming, natural element into any room.

The forms of basketweaving are at once ancient and modern. Many baskets are timeless in design and technique, and this star shape is no exception; it would fit well into a typical country cottage or add textural contrast to a sleek modern loft. The project uses white willow tied with white willow rods, though it would also be effective made in other colors, or perhaps with contrasting ties. You could also spray paint the finished form in silver, bronze, copper or gold for a beautiful Christmas decoration.

how to make:
Star decoration

3 Wrap the wet rod three times around the two bundles and slide the thick end (butt) up through the bind. It may help to use a bradawl to ease it through. Pull tightly to make it secure.

4 Trim the ends of the willow neatly with the pruning shears, so that the points of the star are even. Make sure that you do not trim too close to the binding, however, or you could weaken the joints. Take a third bundle and place over the other end of the second bundle. Hold at a 45 degree angle. Bind the ends together as before and trim them.

1 Soak 12 or 13 willow rods in a bath of cold water for an hour, then wrap them in a damp kitchen towel and set aside. With the pruning shears, cut the dry willow into 35 lengths, each 10in/26cm long. Divide these into five bundles, with seven sticks in each.

2 Take the first and second bundles, place the end of the first bundle on top of the end of the second bundle and hold at a 45 degree angle. Bind them together by taking a wet willow rod and sliding the thin end (tip) through both bundles about ¾in/2cm from the top.

5 Take a fourth bundle, and place over the other end of the third bundle — it should be placed across, over the first bundle and under the second bundle. Bind and trim as before. Bind the fifth bundle to the ends of bundles one and four, running over two and under three.

6 Arrange the star so it looks even. Then bind each of the cross sections — take a wet willow rod and slide the tip through the cross section so that it holds. Bring the butt up through the hole in the middle of the star and continue to wrap three times. Slide the butt through the bind and pull tight. Trim off all ends neatly.

Plant climber

You will need

(To make a climber about 39–58in/ 1–1.5m high)

- 12 straight willow or hazel rods, between 58in/1.5m and 78in/2m long (uprights)
- Pair of sharp pruning shears
- A piece of string, about 20in/ 50cm long
- 70–80 lengths of green willow, about 39in/1m long (weavers)

It looks impressive, but this plant climber is not terribly difficult to make. Use it for training sweet peas, runner beans or other fragile plants that would benefit from its sturdy support.

Like the most modern of buildings or items of furniture, the form and function of this pea climber are completely intrinsic to each other. With no decoration other than its own attractive, timeless shape, it appears solid and airy, strong and flexible, complex and simple. Even those who have never tried this ancient and appealing craft before, however, should have little difficulty with this project as it is very straightforward to make, and requires only patience, a little strength and just a touch of dexterity.

how to make:
Plant climber

1 On an area of grass or turf, cut the thick (butt) ends of the 12 uprights at a slant with the pruning shears. This will make it easier to push them into the ground.

2 Mark a 20in/50cm diameter circle on the ground with an upright (see page 242), then push the 12 uprights into the ground (butt end first) at even intervals like a clock face. Bring the thin ends (tips) together and tie them with a piece of string.

3 Take a weaver, bend it in half and wrap it around one of the uprights about 12in/30cm from the ground. Take the butt end of the weaver behind the next upright and bring it back to the front.

4 Now take the tip end in front of the second upright, behind the third upright and bring it back to the front. The tension of the weavers will hold them in place.

continued:

Plant climber

7 Remove the string. Take one thin weaver to bind the top: slide its butt end into the center of the uprights and, holding them together, bring the tip round 3–4 times, wrapping all the uprights and weavers together. Slide the tip up through the bind and pull it tight.

8 Finish by trimming all the ends of the uprights neatly. If there are any rogue splinters of willow sticking out of any part of the structure, snip them off with pruning shears.

5 Now join in another weaver. Slide its butt end alongside the butt end of the first weaver and work the two of them together in front of the fourth upright, then behind the fifth upright and back to the front.

6 Keep joining in more weavers at every upright until you are weaving with three or more to make a thick band. Weave three times around the structure, parallel to the ground, before spiralling up to the top, traveling around the uprights three times. Finish about 8in/20cm from the top.

marking a circle

To mark out your 20in/50cm circle, knock a stake into the ground and then tie a 10in/25cm piece of string to it. Tie a length of cane to the other end of the string and move it round the stake, scoring out the circle on the ground.

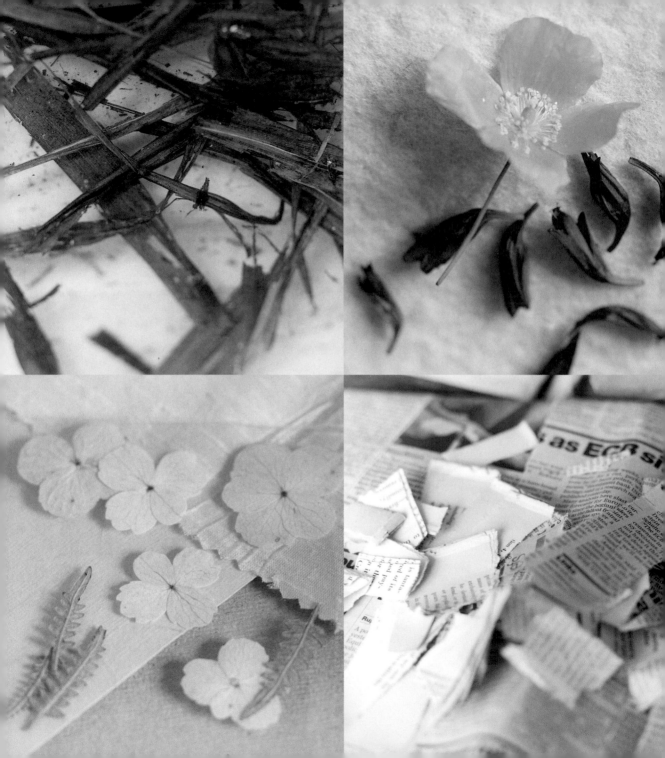

The International Criminal Tribunal
for the former Yugoslavia

The Verdict

Paper

Paper making

As books and money, packaging and clothing, leaflets and letters, wall coverings and paintings, paper affects the lives of each of us, every day. Yet mass-produced paper is significantly different to hand-made sheets, which have inherent character, a tactile quality and a unique artistic integrity.

Before paper, man used other materials on which to transcribe thoughts, records and important documents — engraved stone and metal, stamped clay, stripped bark, silk and parchment, for example. The closest to paper was papyrus, made from laminated strips of reed, first used in Egypt around four or five thousand years ago. But while some form of paper may have existed in China as long ago as 200BC, the first records of good-quality sheets of paper date to AD105, when the Chinese Imperial court official Ts'ai Lun documented experiments with beaten hemp, rags, fishing nets and tree bark. The practice of paper making, utilizing flax and silk fibers and linen rags, beaten and dried into sheets in the sun, became highly developed in China and then spread via artisans to Korea and Central Asia.

When the Arabian armies returned from raids on Chinese territories in the eighth century, they learned the secrets of paper making from their prisoners, and a paper mill was established in Baghdad in 794. The Arabic Muslims built more mills in Egypt, Morocco and Italy, and then Spain in 1144. They also standardized sizes and colors and introduced wire molds. Gradually, the craft became established in Europe, each country developing its own expertise and specialties. At the end of the 15th century there were mills in Italy, France, Germany, Poland and England. By the 17th century there was paper making in Scandinavia, and the first mill was built in America in 1690 (though paper-like beaten bark sheets were used by the Maya and Aztec civilizations long before the Spanish Conquistadors).

In the late-18th and 19th centuries, the demand for paper grew as printing developed. At the end of the 18th century came the first paper making machine, which could turn out endless rolls of paper quickly and easily. And by the late-19th century, processes for pulping wood had been introduced, giving the paper industry a readily available, seemingly endless, supply of its chief raw ingredient.

The making of paper by hand did not die out completely when industry took over, however. In Japan, although the practice is in decline, paper makers are still regarded as living treasures, and in China it is also a highly revered craft. Indian paper making was revived in the 1930s when Mahatma Ghandi encouraged traditional village crafts. In North America there are many small mills producing high-quality papers for artists and print-makers, while a handful of British hand-made paper companies sell their products to conservators, book restorers and painters. And craftspeople working at home continue to value the special qualities of hand-made paper — its textures and colors, the variety of additives that allow character and charm — and make paper for the sheer pleasure of the process and the beauty of the results.

Writing paper

You will need

(To make 10 sheets of letter-size/A4 paper)

- Newspapers (at least 10)
- Shallow plastic tray
- Paper-making mold (but not a deckle); the screen area should be about letter size/A4
- 11 smooth kitchen cloths
- Printers' offcuts or unbleached cartridge paper
- Food blender
- Seeds, dried leaves and grasses
- Plastic dishwashing bowl
- One tablespoon wheat starch
- Sponge
- Old book for recycling paper
- Newspapers for recycling paper
- Brown kraft paper
- Two wooden boards

They say that texture is the new color, and these elegant writing papers demonstrate just how attractive a combination of intriguing textures can be.

To make a stack of lovely writing paper all you need is to add a selection of seeds, leaves and grasses to the basic mix, as is done so well in many Indonesian papers. Ensure that the textural ingredients are not too lumpy, however, or it will be impossible to use the paper for its intended purpose; other than that you can have great fun with choosing which particular extras you like best. Irregular, uneven edges are another lovely touch that give this project a personal and organic look.

how to make:
Writing paper

2 If possible, soak the paper in water before you start (this makes it easier but is not essential). Take the printers' offcuts (or your palest color paper) and tear into 1in/2.5cm squares. Add a small quantity to a food blender two-thirds full of water, then add a small amount of the seeds, leaves and grasses. Blend for around 10 seconds and pour into a dishwashing bowl half full of water. Repeat three times. You should now have a full bowl of paper pulp. Stir in the wheat starch.

1 Prepare a couching mound. Fold up five newspapers so that they fit into the tray, stacked with the folded edges on alternate sides. Fill the tray with water until the newspapers are covered and leave until they are completely soaked. Drain off the excess water, then rock the mesh screen of the mold across the top of the newspaper mound so that it has a smooth surface, slightly higher in the middle than at the edges. Cover with a smooth kitchen cloth.

3 Stir the pulp with your hands and, with a sponge, wet the mesh screen of the mold. Holding the mold with the screen uppermost, lower it into the pulp at the back of the bowl. In one smooth, level movement, take the mold to the bottom of the bowl and up at the front, lifting the mold completely out of the water. Allow excess water to drain off.

4 Turn the mold over, placing its front edge at the front edge of the couching mound. Roll the mold onto the mound, pressing firmly, especially at the edges.

Writing paper

paper (you are working from the palest color paper to the darkest), to make a stack of writing paper (each sheet within two kitchen cloths) with a subtle color graduation. If you wish to make more than 10 sheets of paper, add another tablespoon of wheat starch to the pulp mix.

7 To press and dry the paper, lay a wooden board on the floor, covered with two dry newspapers. Carefully place the sheets of paper, still in the kitchen cloths, onto the newspaper. Lay two more dry newspapers on top, then another wooden board. Stand on the board for a minute or so.

5 Roll the mold back, holding down its near edge firmly. The wet paper will be transferred onto the kitchen cloth. Carefully cover with another cloth.

6 Repeat from step 2, this time using the old book to make pulp and adding to the pulp that is left over. Try adding different seeds or grasses, too. Then repeat using the old newspapers, then the kraft

8 Remove the newspapers and, with the paper still in the kitchen cloths, leave to dry either on flat, dry newspapers or by carefully pinning to a clothesline. When completely dry, carefully peel the paper away from the cloths.

Ornamental paper

You will need

(To make 10 sheets of letter-size/
A4 paper)

- Newspapers
- Shallow plastic tray
- Paper-making mold and deckle;
  the screen area should be about
  letter-size/A4
- Textured blanket or cloth, cut into
  11 letter-size/A4 pieces
- Two rolls of soft white toilet paper
- Food blender
- Plastic dishwashing bowl
- Sponge
- Collection of flower petals, thin plant
  stems and flat leaves
- Two wooden boards

The appeal of hand-made paper lies in its delightful surface texture and varied color. This project makes the most of both to create some impressive paper that is both useful and wonderfully good looking.

It is surprisingly easy to make your own paper, and attractive combinations of colors and textures are an intrinsic part of the process. To the basic mix of paper pulp one simply adds colorful flower petals, leaves, plants stems and so on; the results are gloriously individual and highly satisfying. Use the sheets as unusual wrapping paper, as a backing for photographs, sketches or prints, or simply mount one in a beautiful frame as a work of art in its own right.

how to make:
Ornamental paper

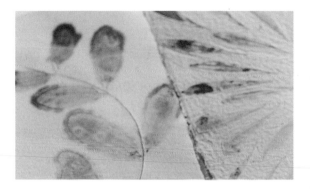

1 Prepare a couching mound. Fold up about five newspapers so that they fit into the tray, stacked with the folded edges on alternating sides. Fill the tray with water until the newspapers are covered and leave until they are completely soaked. Drain off the excess water, then rock the mesh screen of the mold across the top of the newspaper mound so that it has a smooth surface — slightly higher in the middle than at the edges. Cover with a textured cloth.

2 Take a handful of toilet paper, and tear it up into small pieces. Add a small amount to a food blender two-thirds full of water. Blend for around 10 seconds and pour into a dishwashing bowl two-thirds full of water. Repeat this three times.

3 Stir the pulp with your hands then, with a sponge, wet the mesh screen of the mold. Holding the mold with the screen uppermost and the deckle on top, lower it into the pulp at the back of the bowl. In one smooth, level movement, take the mold to the bottom of the bowl and up at the front, lifting the mold completely out of the water. Allow to drain.

4 Place the mold and deckle on a flat surface. Lift the deckle off the mold. Turn the mold over, placing its front edge at the front edge of the couching mound. Roll the mold onto the mound, pressing down firmly, especially at the edges.

continued:
Ornamental paper

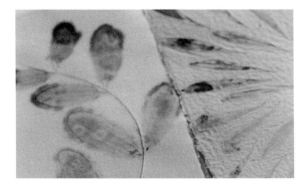

5 Roll the mold back, holding its near edge firmly down. The wet paper will be transferred onto the textured cloth. Lay the petals, leaves and stems onto the wet paper, until you are happy with the design.

6 Repeat the process from step 2, but this time do not use the deckle, (the paper should be a lot thinner). Place this sheet of paper on top of the other sheet that you have just made. This second sheet of paper should seal the flowers between the papers.

7 Carefully cover with another textured cloth. To press and dry the paper, lay a wooden board on the floor, covered with two dry newspapers. Carefully place the sheets of paper, still in the textured cloths, onto the newspaper. Lay more dry newspapers on top, then another wooden board. Stand on the board for a minute or so. This will help to squeeze all the excess water from the sheets of paper.

8 Remove the newspapers and, with the paper still in the cloths, leave to dry either on flat, dry pieces of newspaper or by carefully pinning to a clothesline. When dry, carefully peel the paper away from the cloths.

variations
You can use all sorts of flower petals for this project, but for the best results, make sure that you keep them bold in color.

Papier mâché

Literally meaning 'chewed-up paper', papier mâché is inexpensive and easy to work with, light yet strong and tough yet delicate. Its versatility has made it popular all over the world, for brightly colored folk art, detailed decorative moldings, furniture and, today, sophisticated accessories.

Paper was invented in China in the second century AD, and, of course, papier mâché inevitably followed soon after — being a good way of re-using a commodity that was limited and expensive. It was also exceptionally strong for its light weight and, toughened with lacquer, was used by the ancient Chinese for making war helmets, among other things. The craft eventually spread to Samarkand and Morocco, and from there, by the 10th century, to Spain, France, Germany, Italy, Persia and India.

The first Europeans to see the value of papier mâché were the French, who used it to make items such as snuff boxes and cups, and to imitate plaster and stucco, though only on a small scale. But it was enthusiastically taken up in England, where mashed paper or sheets of paper pasted together were molded, baked and often varnished ('japanned') to form light, inexpensive decorative moldings that could be sawed and screwed just like wood.

By the 1770s, papier mâché manufacturing was one of the most important trades in the midlands of Britain, producing not just moldings but trays, chairs, tables, lamp stands, sconces, coach panels, bookcases, screens, candlesticks, bedsteads and all sorts of other domestic items. These usually had a black background and intricately painted floral decoration, and were sometimes gilded and inlaid with mother-of-pearl. In France and Germany, too, papier mâché furniture had by now become popular, and makers were experimenting with the medium, creating extraordinary items, including a fully functioning watch and a village of ten prefabricated papier mâché houses. Papier mâché was also practiced in America, Russia and Scandinavia — in Norway in 1793, for example, an entire church was built from papier mâché and stood for 37 years.

Papier mâché's heyday in Europe lasted about a century, but by the 1870s its popularity was decreasing, its novelty having worn off and its designs no longer considered sophisticated, but garish and crude. Although mass production came to an end, there was, however, still a demand for hand-made papier mâché used for traditional folk craft, such as puppet shows (Punch and Judy in Britain, Pulcinella in Italy, for example) and figures or masks in processions. In fact, it is in such ancient, individual ways that papier mâché lives on around the world — in the form of Japanese toys, Indian painted vases, boxes, lampshades, bangles, cups and bowls; and Mexican dolls, *piñatas* (containers holding sweets and small toys), masks and figures. Such tradition and ancient symbolism, married with bright colors and intricate patterning, are often found in papier mâché. Modern craftspeople, however, are just as likely to use 21st-century imagery, subtle colors and sophisticated, minimal patterns to explore this medium's endless potential.

Leaf bowl

You will need

- Newspapers
- Protective gloves (if you are sensitive to glue)
- Wallpaper paste
- Mixing bowl
- Mixing spoon
- White glue
- Plastic wrap
- Glass bowl of the same shape and size as the one you wish to make
- At least 6 sheets letter-size/A4 recycled paper
- Paintbrush
- 3–4 sheets letter-size/A4 hand-made paper
- Skeletonized leaves (quantity will depend on the size of your bowl and your chosen design)

Making this project may bring back childhood memories of papier mâché, but this simple bowl with its delicate decoration is perfectly grown-up, very subtle and sophisticated.

While vivid shades and bold patterns can be highly effective, there is much to be gained from exploring a contemporary look that plays on form and texture rather than just color. The key to the charm of this project is to choose a mold in a lovely shape, then simply build up layers until you have a form that appears fragile, but is actually rather strong. Scatter on dried leaves, flowers, petals, ferns or similar, and use for whatever purpose you like, whether display, storage or simple ornament.

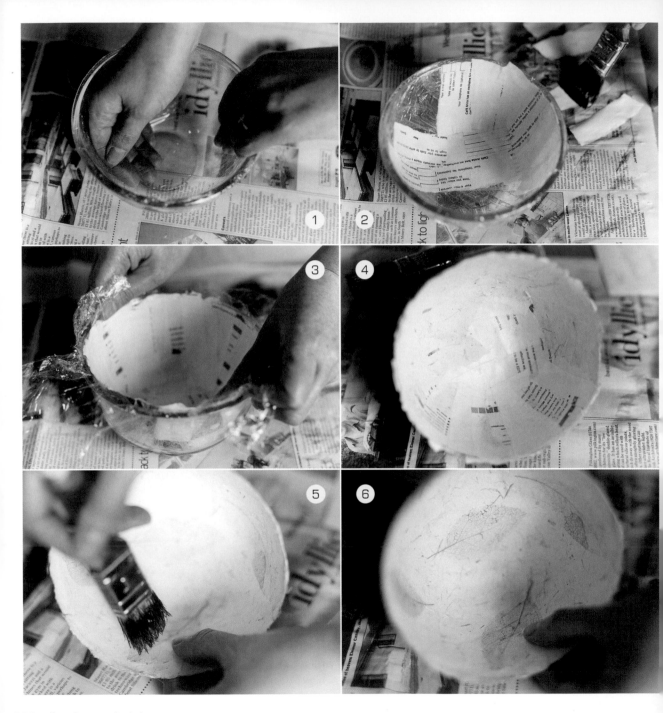

how to make:
Leaf bowl

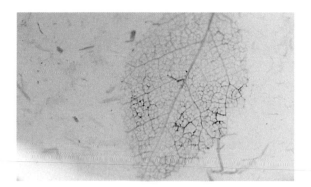

1 Cover your work surface with newspaper. Wearing the gloves (if necessary), mix up the wallpaper paste in a bowl, three parts paste to one part white glue. With the plastic wrap, carefully cover the entire bowl that you will use as a mold.

2 Tear the recycled paper into strips measuring ¾ x 2½in/2 x 6cm. Using the paintbrush, paste the strips in slightly overlapping rows on the inside of the bowl, smoothing down the strips as you go. Where the paper reaches the rim, leave the edge slightly rough and uneven to complement the natural look of this project. Allow to dry.

3 Paste a second layer of strips, this time in the opposite direction to the first. Allow to dry. Continue until you have applied at least six layers, leaving each layer to dry before adding the next. When the final layer is dry, carefully remove the papier mâché bowl from the mold.

4 Tear up the hand-made paper and, using the white glue, cover the inside and outside of the papier mâché bowl with a layer.

5 Using the white glue, decorate the inside of the bowl with skeletonized leaves, placed randomly.

6 Set the bowl aside, so that the glue has a chance to dry completely before use.

how many layers?
The more layers of paper you apply, the stronger the bowl will be. If you decide to make a bigger bowl, you will need to apply more layers, so that it is strong enough to support its own weight.

Jewelry box

You will need

(To make a box measuring about 2⅜ x 5⅛in/6 x 13cm, and 2⅜in/6cm high)

- Ruler
- Pencil
- 1 sheet tabloid-size/A3 card, at least ¹⁄₁₆in/1mm thick
- Craft knife
- Masking tape
- Newspapers
- Protective gloves (if you are sensitive to glue)
- Wallpaper paste
- Mixing bowl
- Mixing spoon
- White glue
- At least six sheets letter-size/A4 recycled paper
- Paintbrush
- Four sheets letter-size/A4 hand-made paper
- Pressed leaves/flowers to decorate
- Piece of batting or foam, about ¼in/5mm thick, measuring 2⅜ x 5⅛in/ 6 x 13cm
- Piece of silk measuring 4 x 6¾in/ 10 x 17cm

This simple box in soft colors is brought to life with the addition of subtle embellishments from nature — tiny ferns and a pressed flower. With its charming decoration, it is as pretty as it is useful.

This lidded box can be made to more or less any dimensions, and painted in any color you like — though to remain within a contemporary esthetic it is best to choose a pale, muted shade rather than anything too bright. The finishing touch is the subtle, three-dimensional effect of applied shapes and ferns, leaves or petals. If you wish, you could also add a handle by piercing two holes in the lid and threading through a length of ribbon or a leather strip, or create a knob by gluing on a small pebble.

how to make:
Jewelry box

1 Follow the template on page 423 and measure out onto the card. Cut and fold where shown, and tape together, to make a box shape.

2 Cover your work surface with newspaper. Wearing the gloves (if necessary), mix up the wallpaper paste in a bowl, three parts paste to one part white glue. Tear the recycled paper into strips measuring about 1¼ x 4in/3 x 10cm.

3 Paste the strips in slightly overlapping rows onto the inside and outside of the box, smoothing them down as you go. Allow to dry. Paste a second layer of strips, this time in the opposite direction to the first, and allow to dry. Finally, paste a third layer, in the same direction as the first. Allow to dry thoroughly.

4 If you wish, add a raised design by cutting out small squares and/or rectangles of card and gluing onto the box with the white glue. Cover these with a layer of pasted-on recycled paper and allow to dry.

variations
If you wish, you could use contrasting-colored papers for the inside and outside of the box. Ensure that the lining paper coordinates with the color of the silk pad for a really pretty effect.

Jewelry box

5 To make a lid, draw around the top of the box onto the card twice. Cut out both rectangles and glue them together. Measure the inside of the rim of the box and cut out three pieces of card about ⅛in/ 3mm smaller all around. Adjust to fit the box if necessary. Glue these three rectangles together, then glue them, centered, to the first rectangle. Allow to dry, then check for fit.

6 Tear up the hand-made paper and, using the white glue, cover the outside of the box, overlapping the rim by about ⅜in/1cm. Smooth the paper over the rim neatly so it does not look uneven. Then cover the inside of the box, taking the paper to about ¹⁄₁₆in/ 1mm below the rim. Using the white glue, decorate the outside of the box with the pressed leaves and/or flowers.

7 Carefully cover the lid of the box with one layer of recycled paper and one of hand-made paper.

8 Cut a piece of card to fit inside the base of the box. Glue the batting onto the card. Cover with the silk and tape neatly on the reverse. To finish, glue the pad to the bottom of the box on the inside.

Papercraft

An ordinary sheet of paper can be transformed by an artist or craftsperson into an extraordinary creation. For two millennia man has explored the potential of papercraft, punching and piercing, dyeing and printing, folding and weaving, in displays of invention that are dazzling and intriguing.

Since paper was invented in the second century, it has been possible to use the material in all sorts of ways. The first papercraft to develop was almost certainly origami, the art of paper folding, which began in China but was refined in Japan over the course of centuries. At first, paper was a rare commodity, and so early origami models were abstract figures with ritualistic meaning.

Origami was taken to Spain by the Moorish invaders, but their religion forbade them from making representational figures, so the craft there took the form of geometric studies. It was not until the early-1900s that the art of origami model-making traveled to Europe and America, where it was enthusiastically taken up. In 1935 a set of symbols for instructions was developed, and today master paper folders can be found all around the world, producing models of astounding technical skill and artistry.

Découpage, or the art of adorning surfaces with paper cut-outs, is thought to have originated in Italy in the 17th century, though it may have been a European folk craft long before that. Venetian craftsmen used découpage as a way of imitating expensive inlay, marquetry and Chinese lacquerwork and, at the height of its popularity, it spread to France, where it was given its name. It is reported that Marie Antoinette and her court became so enthusiastic about découpage that they cut up original works by Boucher and Watteau in order to make their scenes. Découpage was also practiced in Germany, Austria, Belgium, Scandinavia, Poland and North America, and in England it was deemed a suitable pastime for fashionable ladies. Although découpage gradually died out as a hobby, in the mid-20th century it was revived, particularly in America, Australia and South Africa.

In the early 20th century, the craft of collage came to the fore. Here, scraps of paper (or other flat material) are glued to a backing. Although the technique was ancient, it was not given a name until the Cubist artists Pablo Picasso and Georges Braque began to incorporate newspapers, cloth, sand, hair, feathers, string and even tickets into their abstract paintings. It was a revolution for traditional art, and was taken up, most notably, by Henri Matisse, and by various movements including the Dadaists, Surrealists, Futurists and Pop Artists. Today it is an accepted element in much modern art — free, direct, inventive and experimental.

The ways in which paper can be manipulated are almost endless, and as well as these main areas of papercraft, there are plenty of others, including construction, marbling, dyeing and printing, casting, piercing, stamping, punching, weaving and relief marking. Strong, yet malleable and light, paper can be transformed to create the most amazing items.

Translucent lamp

You will need

- Bulb and bulb fitting with flex, suitable for fitting into a bottle
- Small, heavy candlestick holder
- Scraps of translucent and opaque colored paper in green, blue and lilac
- Cutting mat
- Craft knife
- Swivel craft knife
- 1 sheet heavyweight (160–200gsm) translucent or tracing paper, suitable for the size of lamp you wish to make (for this project, the paper measured 14 x 25in/35 x 64cm)
- Small selection of sequins to match the scraps of paper
- Spray adhesive
- Clear adhesive squares (or double-sided tape, or staples)

This column of light creates a soft pool of brightness, glowing through a simple flower pattern. Although understated, it is an elegant and beautiful accessory to add to an interior.

While the people of China have long understood paper's marvelous potential, in the West it is only recently that working with paper has become a respected craft form. This project makes the most of the material's translucency and malleability, its colors and ability to be cut into intricate shapes. The result is a lamp that is not only decorative when unlit, but also just as attractive when softly illuminated, in a timeless shape that would suit a bedroom, living room or hallway in classic or contemporary style.

how to make:
Translucent lamp

1 Fit the bulb fitting into the candlestick holder — this will act as a simple lamp base. The shorter the candlestick holder, the better, as the bulb looks best if it is near the bottom of the lamp.

2 For the flowers, take one of the colored papers and roughly cut out about 10 circles, 1½in/4cm in diameter. Put the circles on the cutting mat and use the craft knife to cut out a series of triangular shapes from these circles, leaving daisy-like petals. When each flower shape is completed, cut out a small circle from the center.

3 To make the leaves, take another of the colored papers and use the swivel craft knife to cut out long teardrop shapes. Cut out tiny triangles along each edge to break up the line.

4 Trim the tracing paper until it is about 12in/30cm wide and 24in/60cm long. Coil the paper into a double coil — this will be the final shape and size of the lampshade. It is a good idea to check at this stage if it is a suitable height and width, and work out where to position the leaves and flowers.

5 Arrange the flowers and leaves over one half of the translucent paper, then scatter a few sequins between the 'sprigs'. Carefully fix them all down with spray adhesive.

6 Coil the paper again, ensuring that the leaves and flowers are between the layers of the double coil. Fix the edges of the coil together using clear adhesive squares. The edges could also be fixed with double-sided tape (although this can yellow with age) or staples (which are more visible). Cut a small, neat 'U' shape into the base of the lampshade, to allow the lamp flex to pass through the shade so that the lamp will stand flat. Place the shade over the bulb. The shade is light enough and sturdy enough to be lifted to allow access to the bulb switch. Keep on a flat surface and out of strong drafts.

Book covers

You will need

- Selection of different papers in a variety of colors, textures and weights (you will need about 9 different tabloid-size/A3 sheets to cover a letter-size/A4 book)
- Ruler
- Hardback notebook or photograph album
- Double-sided tape
- Spray adhesive
- Craft knife
- Clear self-adhesive vinyl

Bold stripes and intriguing colors give these fabulous covered books an air of utter sophistication. The look is modern yet classic, and the project itself combines practicality with decorative effect.

Bound blank paper is always useful, whether for albums or sketch books, recipe holders or notebooks. The next step is to create a cover that will protect the books and look appealing, too. This project takes simple stripes and gives them a clever twist by using different widths and unusual color combinations. The hand-torn edges of each stripe demonstrate the textural nature of the paper itself, and give the covers a fuss-free, hand-made look. The result is something that is almost too good to use.

how to make:
Book covers

1 Arrange your papers so that you can picture them as strips of varying widths, ensuring that the final selection is balanced and pleasing, with wide strips in pale or neutral colors and thinner strips of more intense color.

2 Tear the strips by holding a ruler level to the edge of the paper. You may wish to measure the strip first so that it is the same width all the way down. Holding it firmly with one hand, use the other to tear the paper down the line of the ruler carefully, creating a pleasing rough edge. Ensure that the strips are about 4in/10cm longer than your book, both at the top and the bottom.

3 Start by covering the book at the spine. Place a length of double-sided tape down the spine and spray a strip of paper, wide enough to overlap the front and back of the book, with spray adhesive. Fix the strip to the spine and, with the book closed, fold the paper round the sides. Do not worry if the paper starts to peel away a little — it can be secured later. Cut four incisions into the excess paper, two at the top and two at the bottom, where the spine and the covers meet. Open the book flat, fold over the paper and fix it to the inside covers of the book with double-sided tape. You should now be left with a 'tongue' the same width as the spine. Trim this until it is about 1½in/4cm long and carefully tuck it down into the gap where the pages and the cover separate when the book is opened.

4 Cover the rest of the book by slightly overlapping successive strips of paper, working from the spine to the edge. Ensure that each strip is straight. Fix strips of double-sided tape on the inside covers, along the top and bottom edges. Then fold over the ends of the strips and secure them neatly on the inside of the cover.

Book covers

5 For the last lengths on the outside edges of the book, position two wide strips on the front and back of the cover. Use a craft knife to cut across the corner of the excess paper, so that when it is folded over the edges, it makes neat, mitered corners.

6 Firmly fold over the edges of the paper and crease. Secure the edges on the inside cover with double-sided tape.

7 Cut a piece of clear self-adhesive vinyl large enough to wrap around the book and with enough excess to fold over the edges. Very carefully score a strip of the backing paper from the center, exposing the sticky vinyl. Leave the vinyl on a flat surface and place down the spine of the closed book so that it adheres. Cut and tuck the vinyl around the spine as with the paper in step 3.

8 Gently peel away the backing paper, smoothing the vinyl onto the book. When all the backing paper has been peeled off, cut a mitered corner and fold the vinyl over the edges. To tidy the inside cover of the book, cut a rectangle from one of the thicker papers, small enough to fit within the edges of the cover, but large enough to cover the rough edges of the paper and vinyl. Attach this using strips of double-sided tape along all four edges.

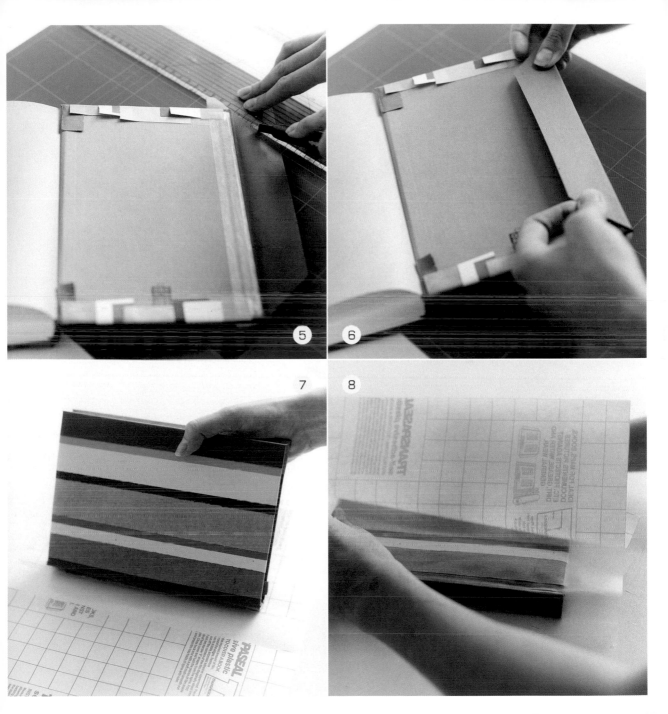

Ceramics & Glass

Ceramic painting

Since Iron Age man first shaped clay into small figures of animals, we have been fascinated by our ability to create pottery from the earth. And while function has frequently been the foremost consideration, surface decoration has been intrinsic to the craft, from ancient times to the present day.

The discovery of clay's potential occurred at various times around the world, from Africa to South America, from Europe to the Far East. One of the first civilizations to develop a sophisticated ceramic tradition was Ancient Greece, where elegant jars, urns, amphorae, bowls and pitchers were part of ceremonial and everyday life. Decoration was initially in geometric patterns, but later, narrative scenes were painted in a glossy black slip, sometimes scratched through with a pointed implement (*sgraffito*). The Romans inherited Greek techniques and spread them through the Empire, commonly embellishing red earthenware forms with raised patterns and a fine slip.

When the Roman Empire fell, ceramic techniques died away in Europe, but in China the industry had become highly sophisticated. High firing kilns allowed a wide range of glazes, with decoration going hand in hand with perfection of form. And when porcelain was discovered during the Tang dynasty (618–906), craftsmen were given a supremely fine material with which to show off their skill. The resulting use of sensuous glazes applied to simple shapes was subtle and utterly beautiful.

Throughout early Medieval Europe much pottery was utilitarian and decorated minimally, if at all. In the Near East, however, new skills of lead and tin glazing and luster decoration had evolved, which reached a peak in 13th-century Spain. The Italian nobility loved this work, which featured bright, clear colors on a white background, and Italian potters took it up to such an extent that by the 15th century their *majolica* ware dominated the European market.

Trade with the Far East in the 17th century introduced Europeans to the finesse of Chinese ceramics, which now featured a new style — blue and white paintings of naturalistic scenes. It became enormously popular in the West and helped raise the quality of European ceramics in general as German, French and English makers realized just how great the demand could be for good-quality work. Thus were established the great factories of Meissen, Sèvres, Limoges, Wedgwood and Spode.

Despite the high standards set by all of these manufacturers, the production of ceramics became increasingly industrialized, and it was not until the middle of the 19th century that the Arts and Crafts movement urged a return to the craftsman who made and decorated his own work. Thereafter, the studio movement spread through Europe and America, and individual potters explored (again) the influences of the Far East, considered form versus function and began to regard pottery as sculpture. Studio pottery grew and grew, gaining influence and experimenting ever more daringly, so that the styles we see today, which build on the techniques of the past but also break new ground, could scarcely be more diverse and intriguing.

Painted vase

You will need

- White vase with a smooth (either matte or shiny) glazed surface
- Dishwashing detergent
- Newspapers
- Overalls, apron or an old shirt
- White tile or an old piece of white ceramic
- Flat, soft watercolor paintbrushes
- Ceramic paints in your choice of colors (this project used blue and turquoise)
- Old plate to mix colors on
- Scissors
- Masking tape
- Ruler
- White (mineral) spirit
- Cotton swabs
- Large sheet of watercolor paper and acrylic paints (optional)
- Paper towels (optional)
- Ceramic painting pens (optional)

Flowers look beautiful in a sleek-looking modern white vase, and the fresh simplicity of this design would offset any floral arrangement wonderfully.

Painted pottery can be crude and unsophisticated, but with care it can just as easily be delicate and subtle, as shown by this project, which takes as its starting point a plain vase in a delightfully considered shape. Don't be taken in by the apparent simplicity of the painting, however — though it is not overly difficult to achieve this look, it really is well worth practicing first on some unwanted pieces of white china in order to perfect exactly the watery, brushed-on effect that makes this design so appealing.

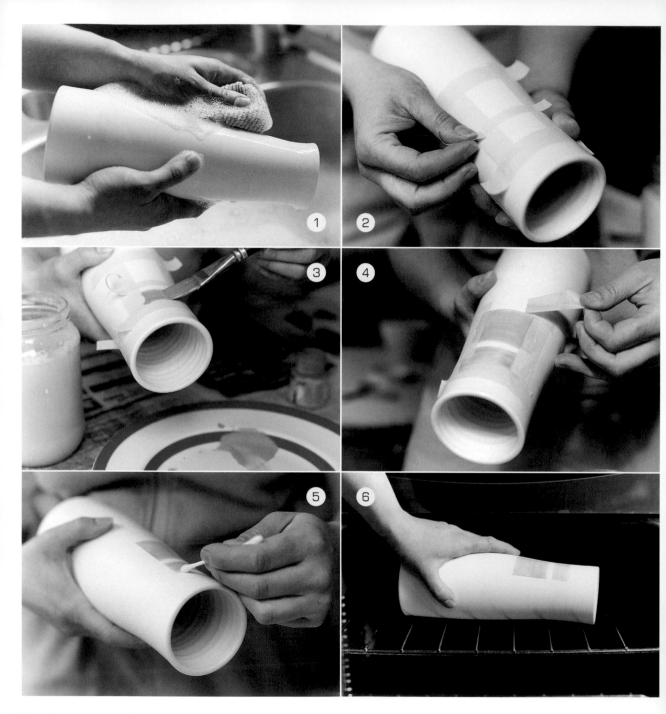

how to make:
Painted vase

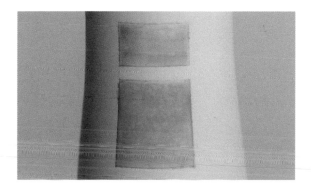

1 Wash the vase in hot soapy water. Dry thoroughly. Cover your working area with newspapers. Wearing overalls, an apron or an old shirt, practice painting on a tile or old piece of ceramic (mixing the colors on an old plate).

2 Cut five strips of masking tape, each one approximately 4in/10cm long, and apply two strips vertically and three strips horizontally to the vase, to form two rectangles in its center. Rub over the tape so the paint cannot seep underneath.

3 Stir the ceramic paints (do not shake, as this can create air bubbles). Paint onto the vase, inside the masked-off areas, with as few strokes as possible. Aim to create flat blocks of color with just one layer, working quickly and covering the area with one or two brushes of paint. After painting, wash the brush immediately in hot, soapy water.

4 Leave to dry for a few minutes until the paint is tacky, then carefully remove the masking tape.

5 Clean untidy edges with white spirit and a cotton swab. Leave to dry for 24 hours in a dust-free place.

6 Follow the manufacturer's instructions to finish the pot in the oven. Ensure the room is ventilated and that no children or pets are around. (Before washing the vase in a dishwasher, check the paint manufacturer's guidelines.)

professional painting

Before painting, you may wish to practice on a sheet of watercolor paper, using ordinary acrylic paint. On three-dimensional objects, paint can seep to the bottom. Collect it with the tip of a dry, clean, flat brush.

To apply watery washes, contain the paint within a masked-off area and apply a small amount at a time. If the color looks thin, apply another layer; if it is too thick, dab with a paper towel. You could experiment with freehand painting and ceramic painting pens.

Cup and saucer

You will need

- White cup and saucer with a smooth (either matte or shiny) glazed surface
- Dishwashing detergent
- Newspapers
- Overalls, apron or an old shirt
- White tile or an old piece of white ceramic
- Flat, soft watercolor paintbrushes
- Non-toxic ceramic paints in your choice of colors (this project used two shades of blue and one of green)
- Old plate to mix colors on
- Scissors
- Masking tape
- Ruler
- White (mineral) spirit
- Cotton swabs

Take your time over a cup of tea or coffee with a set of adorable cups and saucers hand-painted in shades that perfectly complement your interior décor.

This project explores the pleasant possibilities of soft, easy-going colors that are layered onto each other for an unusual effect. Strong squares and rectangles create a graphic, dynamic pattern that is contemporary without being harsh, and the watered-down paints soften the look to create a painterly effect that nicely complements the crisp, clean forms of the cup and saucer themselves. This is ceramic decoration at its most mature and subtle, though the process could hardly be more straightforward.

how to make:
Cup and saucer

1 Ensure that the surface of the cup you wish to paint is clean and grease-free by washing in hot, soapy water. Dry thoroughly. Cover your working area with a layer of newspaper.

2 Wearing overalls, an apron or an old shirt, practice painting on a tile or old piece of ceramic (see page 295), mixing your colors on an old plate. The more familiar you become with the paint at this stage, the better the effect will be later, especially if you practice layering one color on top of another, as this can be tricky.

3 Cut five strips of masking tape, each about 4in/ 10cm long, and apply two strips vertically and three strips horizontally to your chosen cup, to form two rectangles in its center — if possible at least 1¼in/ 3cm down from the rim. (Although the paints are non-toxic, it is best to avoid contact with food and drink.) If space does not permit, simply drink from the other side of the cup. Rub over the tape to ensure that the paint cannot seep underneath.

4 Choose a pale-colored ceramic paint (or mix several on the old plate to create the desired color) and stir thoroughly (do not shake as this can create air bubbles, which may be hard to get rid of). Paint onto the cup, inside the masked-off areas, with as few strokes as possible — your aim is to create a flat block of color. It is better to try to achieve this with just one layer, working quickly and covering the area with just one or two brushes of paint. When you have finished painting, wash the brush immediately in hot, soapy water.

Cup and saucer

5 Leave to dry for a few minutes until tacky, then carefully remove the masking tape. Clean any untidy edges with white spirit and a cotton swab. Leave to dry completely for 24 hours in a dust-free place.

6 Carefully follow the manufacturer's instructions to finish the cup in the oven, ensuring that the room is well ventilated and there are no children or pets in the room when firing.

7 When the cup has completely cooled, mask off another area, slightly overlapping the painted rectangles, and overpaint with a darker shade, to create a layered effect.

8 When the paint is dry enough, remove the masking tape and carefully clean up untidy edges with a cotton swab. Leave to dry completely for 24 hours, then finish the cup again in the oven. You may also wish to paint a small part of the same design onto the saucer. (A small rectangle of color will reflect the design of the cup without overwhelming it.) If so, simply follow the same instructions as for the cup. Before washing your cup and saucer in a dishwasher, check the paint manufacturer's guidelines.

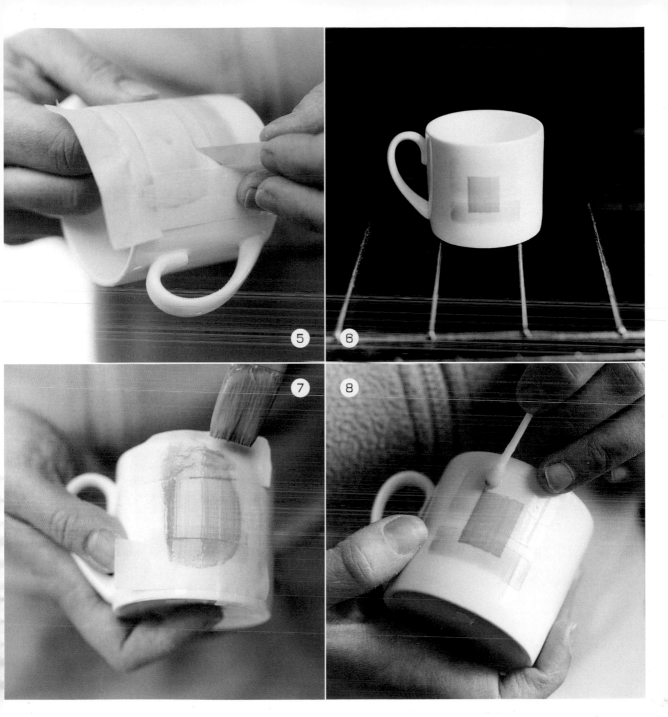

Glass painting

Sandblasted or stained, acid-etched or relief-molded, engraved or enameled, glass can be decorated in innumerable ways. Most of these techniques date back to the days of the ancient Romans, but modern interpretations give new life to a traditional and timelessly beautiful craft.

The identity of the people who first discovered how to work glass is a mystery, but we do know that the ancient Egyptians became adept at producing brightly colored, molded glass items that were considered a great luxury. The Romans used glass extensively, too, and when the technique of glassblowing was discovered (in the first or second century BC), the art flourished. Glassworks were established from Syria to Brittany for objects ordinary and ornate, many of which were cut, engraved, painted, molded or gilded.

When the Roman Empire collapsed, the glass industry declined, but Byzantine and then Islamic glass continued to flourish, with gilding and enameling the favorite methods of decoration. In Japan, too, there were skilled glass craftsmen, producing blown glass and delicate pieces in a technique called *cloisonné*, where colored glass fills tiny gaps between flattened wires.

The idea of using colored glass to make church window panels appears to have originated in sixth century Constantinople. At first, the glass was stained by adding metallic oxides to the molten glass, but later the stain was painted onto the surface of the glass, and from then on the two techniques were often combined to awe-inspiring effect. Many large and elaborate church and cathedral windows were produced in the 13th and 14th centuries. At around the same time, Venice emerged as the pre-eminent center for secular glasswork. In 1291 the Venetian glassworks were moved to the island of Murano, partly as a fire precaution but mostly to control the movement of highly skilled craftsmen. The penalty for revealing their secrets or for leaving the island was death.

Glass decoration — enameling, gilding and engraving — reached new heights, and Venetian glass was widely exported and imitated. By 1600, Venetian techniques were common all over Europe, and a glassworks was set up in America in 1609, claiming to be the first industry of the 'New World'.

In the late 17th century an Englishman discovered that adding lead to glass made it softer and easier to engrave. This established the lead-crystal glass industry in Britain and then Ireland. The 19th century Art Nouveau movement was a catalyst for another major style of glass decoration, popularized by the creations of Louis Comfort Tiffany, Émile Gallé and René Lalique.

Glasswork of the early 20th century was more restrained, but a flowering of individualism came with the studio glass movement that began in the 1960s, in which artists worldwide have pioneered interest in glass as a stimulating medium. Often vigorous and daring, contemporary glass — functional or ornamental — experiments with a variety of decorative techniques, both old and new.

Etched tumbler

You will need

- A clear glass tumbler
- Dishwashing detergent
- Newspapers
- Long thin strips of masking tape or stickers
- Overalls, apron or an old shirt
- Rubber or surgical gloves
- Small sponge
- 1fl oz/20ml etching paste
- Plastic bucket
- Half a teaspoon of washing soda crystals (for safe disposal of etching paste)

Frosted tumblers make a marvelous point of the contrast between clear and opaque. In this project the pattern is almost like a bar code — strongly linear and appealingly contemporary.

Glass etching paste is a wonderfully versatile material, and can be used to paint with either directly or with the aid of a mask or stencil. The trick is to create a pattern that is clear and clean. Here the long, thin lines have a graphic look that contrasts with the curving form of the glass itself. Of course, you could use all sorts of other stickers as a basis for your design, on tumblers, wine glasses, cups, bowls, plates, vases or any other glass objects you wish. To make several tumblers, simply increase the quantities.

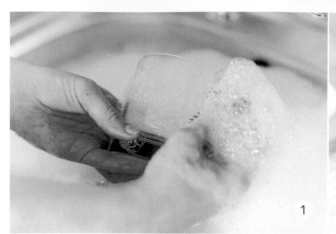

1

2

3

4

5

safe disposal

You cannot empty the bucket of paste-water down the drain as it is — first you must neutralize it properly by adding half a teaspoon of washing soda crystals. It is then safe to dispose of it.

how to make:
Etched tumbler

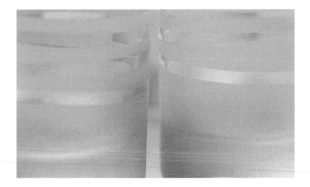

1 Ensure that the surface of the tumbler you wish to paint is clean and grease-free by washing in hot, soapy water. Dry thoroughly. If you wish, cover your working area with newspaper.

2 Stick the masking tape or stickers in lines curving around the tumbler. Rub over the tape to ensure that the paste cannot seep underneath.

3 Wearing overalls and the rubber or surgical gloves, use a sponge to cover the tumbler with the etching paste. If you want a completely frosted look, cover it evenly all over. Alternatively, you could create a textural look by dabbing it unevenly and even leaving some areas completely free of paste.

4 Once the tumbler is covered in paste, leave for two minutes, then wash off. To do this you will need to fill a plastic bucket with warm water. Keeping the gloves on, immerse the glass in the water and rinse the paste into the bowl. Use the sponge to wipe off the paste around the stickers.

5 Peel the tape or stickers off the tumbler and wash it thoroughly again, ensuring that you remove all traces of the paste. Leave to dry. (The etched glass is now non-toxic and dishwasher-safe.)

Window hanging

You will need

(To make a hanging measuring 6in/15cm square)

- Piece of ³⁄₁₆in/4mm thick float glass, with a sandblasted surface on one side, cut to 6 x 6in/15 x 15cm and with two small holes drilled in the top left and right corners. Ask your supplier to take off the sharp edges
- White (mineral) spirit
- Cloth
- Newspapers
- Overalls, apron or an old shirt
- A small piece of glass offcut
- Glass paints in a variety of colors (this project used navy, turquoise, gray-blue, emerald green, rose pink, purple, orange and crimson)
- Small, flat paintbrush
- Paper
- Colored pencils or crayons
- Masking tape in a selection of widths
- Cotton swab
- Piece of aluminum foil (if your paints require firing)
- Length of clear nylon monofilament (fishing line) for hanging

This striking window hanging is like a piece of modern sculpture — both bold and refined, it is sophisticated in color, dynamic in pattern and, in its minimalist way, totally eye-catching in appearance.

Colored glass sometimes has rather unfortunate, dated connotations, but glass paints can be used in ways that are as contemporary as you like. Choose abstract patterns and modern shades and, as here, the results will be anything but old fashioned. You can hang this project in a window in any room in the house, as a single piece or with several strung together, to create an arresting, irresistible 'mobile' that will catch the light and add flickering dashes of lively color.

how to make:
Window hanging

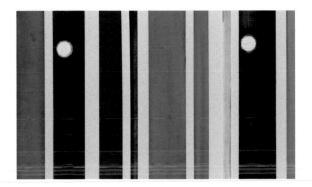

1 Ensure that the sandblasted surface of the glass you wish to paint is clean and grease-free by wiping over the surface with white spirit. Dry thoroughly. If you wish, cover your working area with newspapers.

2 Wearing overalls, an apron or an old shirt, take the glass offcut and put a dab of each paint color onto its sandblasted side. (The paint color appears very different once it is on the glass.) If you wish you can practice painting on the offcut. At this stage it is also a good idea to sketch out how wide you would like your stripes to be and in what order you will eventually paint the colors.

3 Working from your sketch, take the masking tape and stretch it vertically across the glass, on the sandblasted side, keeping the holes at the top of the panel. Use different widths of masking tape to create different widths of stripe. Try not to cut through the holes with the tape — cover them or leave them to be painted over. Rub over the tape to ensure that the paint cannot seep underneath.

4 Stir the glass paints thoroughly (do not shake as this can create air bubbles). Apply to the glass with the small, flat brush, starting from one side and working across. Your aim is to create flat blocks of color. It is better to try to achieve this with just one layer, working quickly and covering the area with one or two brushes of paint. Wash the brush immediately after use in hot, soapy water.

5 Leave to dry for a few minutes until the paint is tacky, then carefully remove the masking tape. Clean untidy edges with white spirit and a cotton swab. Leave to dry for 24 hours in a dust-free place. If your paints require firing, place the glass (painted side up) on a piece of aluminum foil and put in the oven. Follow the paint manufacturer's instructions for firing, ensuring that the room is well ventilated and that there are no children or pets in the room.

6 When the glass has cooled down, thread the monofilament through both holes and tie in a knot.

Mosaic

Combining design, expression and form, mosaics have scarcely changed over the centuries. Floors, walls and furnishings in patterns of stone and glass have the same appealing beauty and practicality for us today as they did for the ancient people of Greece, Rome and the Byzantine Empire.

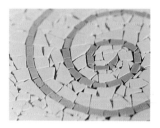 The direct roots of mosaic extend back to Ancient Greece, where floors were made from uncut pebbles laid in simple geometric patterns and, later, figurative and floral designs. As its decorative potential became apparent, mosaic became more elaborate, using small cubes of stone, marble and sometimes glass. The gaps between the tesserae were filled with a 'grout' of lime and powdered marble. By the time of the Roman Empire, mosaics had become detailed and realistic, made to such a high standard that they resembled paintings, complete with shadows, highlights and even brushstrokes. They were the usual choice of flooring, and were also used for walls, pavements, vaults and fountains.

During the Byzantine era, from around the fourth century AD, mosaic developed as a truly extraordinary craft. In time, glass tesserae came to replace marble and stone almost entirely — their many colors and glittery effect making them an impressive medium with which the early Christian church could depict religious scenes. For about a thousand years, mosaic-making was the supreme art form of the Byzantine Empire. Technique and artistry combined to create works that were rhythmic and dynamic, their style sparse and flowing, yet powerful in intensity.

Ironically, it was the Renaissance that heralded a decline in mosaic making, as frescos and oil painting came to the fore and attention turned to more realistic ways of depicting man. In Europe, mosaic came to be used for little more than copies of paintings, though in Central America the Conquistadors used natural stones to cover ritual objects in colored mosaic patterns.

It was not until the early 20th century that mosaic enjoyed a revival, when the Art Nouveau movement rediscovered its potential. It was used by Gustave Klimt for murals in a Brussels house and used extensively by the Spanish designer/architect Antonio Gaudí, whose outdoor mosaic work was hugely imaginative and exuberant, creating sculptural, three-dimensional forms that were entirely unique. Modern artists, including Léger and Bazaine, made use of the medium's strong colors and abstract shapes, while in the 1950s the Mexican muralists Rivera, Siqueiros, Morado and O'Gorman took mosaic into the realm of socialism, covering public buildings with mosaics that told the various stories of Mexican history.

Both decorative and functional, mosaic is ideally suited to eye-catching patterning and to stylized, powerful imagery. Modern craftspeople revel in its versatility and experiment with its dynamism, using materials that range from 'found' objects to precisely cut smalti. Mosaic is a craft that has changed surprisingly little over the course of centuries, and is still very much alive today.

Colored shelf

You will need

(To make a shelf measuring 8 x 30in/ 19 x 75cm)

- Plywood or fiberboard, 7½ x 29½in/ 18.5 x 74cm and ¾in/2cm thick
- Sandpaper and block
- Surgical gloves
- Overalls, apron or an old shirt
- White glue
- Paintbrush
- Dust sheet
- Safety glasses
- Protective mouth and nose filter mask
- One 1lb/500g bag each of 16 graduating colors of smalti mosaic tesserae
- Hammer and hardie
- 11lb/5kg white cement-based powder adhesive (such as Ardurit X7)
- 4½lb/2kg mortar additive (such as Ardion 90)
- Bucket (or bowl) for mixing
- Notched trowel, ⅛in/3mm
- Bradawl or prodding tool
- Sponge
- Soft, dry cloth
- Brackets to fit the shelf

In a range of jewel-bright, watery colors, this simple mosaic shelf in an abstract pattern is a stunning base for displaying elegant bathroom accessories.

While its effects look impressive, the basic principles of mosaic are very straightforward, and once you have mastered them, you can quickly build up exciting pieces in glorious colors and patterns. Sometimes, however, it is the simplest ideas that work best, and this project utilizes a basic (but beautiful) color graduation to make a gorgeous bathroom shelf. Decorative in itself, it is also very practical, and the beauty of this design is that you can adapt it to any size to make a shelf — or even a table top — that perfectly fits your requirements.

how to make:
Colored shelf

1 Sand the piece of plywood or fiberboard with the sandpaper and block until all the rough edges are smooth and even. This will provide the perfect surface for priming.

2 Wearing surgical gloves and overalls, and working in a well-ventilated area, prime the top and three sides of the board by painting them with the white glue (wash the paintbrush immediately afterwards). Leave to dry.

3 Lay down a dust sheet and, wearing safety glasses and a protective mask, cut about a quarter of each color of the smalti into halves. Hold a tessera with your thumb and finger and place it with the part you want to cut over the blade of the hardie. Bring the hammer down lightly but firmly onto the center of the tessera. Avoid inhaling dust by not cutting directly under your nose.

4 Still wearing the surgical gloves and overalls, mix the adhesive with the additive and water in a bucket or bowl, following the manufacturer's instructions, then place a small amount onto a trowel and apply to one end of the board. Stick down the tesserae one band of color at a time, mixing the cut and uncut tiles for interest, but ensuring that they are evenly spaced. Each band is four whole tesserae wide and 12 long.

Colored shelf

6 Remove any protruding adhesive from between the tesserae with a bradawl or prodding tool. Go carefully, so as not to damage the surrounding tesserae. Clean with a damp sponge. When dry, polish with a soft, dry cloth to achieve a shine.

7 Hang the shelf on the wall, using the brackets, taking care that it is straight.

5 When the top is complete, stick the tesserae around the edges, in corresponding colors to the design on the top. Leave to dry for 24 hours.

storing materials

When storing tesserae, it is best to make them easily identifiable, so use glass or transparent containers for loose cubes and clearly labeled boxes for flat sheets. All adhesives, cements and additives are best stored in a cool, dark place.

Decorative bowl

You will need

- Dust sheet
- Safety glasses
- 12 x 12in/30 x 30cm sheets porcelain mosaic tesserae (1 x 1in/2.5 x 2.5cm) in four colors
- Mosaic nippers
- Tracing paper and soft pencil
- Shallow ceramic bowl
- Surgical gloves
- Overalls, apron or an old shirt
- White glue and paintbrush
- 11lb/5kg white cement-based powder adhesive (such as Ardurit X7)
- 4½lb/2kg mortar additive (such as Ardion 90)
- Two buckets (or bowls) for mixing
- Palette knife
- Bradawl or prodding tool
- Sponge
- Rubber gloves
- 11lb/5kg white powder grout (such as Ardurit C2)
- 2¼lb/1kg grout additive (such as Ardion 101)
- Grouting float
- Soft, dry cloth
- Paint to match the mosaic or grout color (optional)

This mosaic bowl, with its soft coloring and stylized design, has a vaguely oriental look and a zen-like, calm quality. You could use it to hold fruit or, perhaps, favorite items of jewelry.

The delicate pattern of this bowl makes use of rectangular, circular and randomly shaped tesserae, and the first art of this ancient craft is to cut the shapes precisely. The next step is to arrange them in a way that brings out the design to its best advantage. Neither skill is difficult to learn, and once you have made your first piece of patterned mosaic, you will find that you simply cannot resist trying more and more. This project uses white, pink, chocolate brown and beige tesserae but you can use whatever colors you like.

how to make:
Decorative bowl

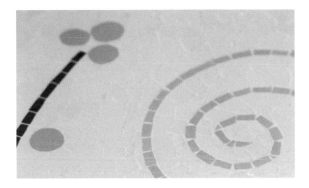

2 Trace the design on page 424 onto a piece of tracing paper, turn over and draw the outlines again, then place the paper into the bowl and trace the design onto it (you may need to enlarge or reduce it on a photocopier).

3 Wearing the surgical gloves and overalls, and working in a well-ventilated area, apply a coat of white glue to the bowl (wash the paintbrush immediately afterwards) to prime it. Allow to dry. Mix the adhesive with the additive and water in a bucket according to the manufacturer's instructions.

4 Place a small amount of adhesive onto a palette knife and apply to the small circles of the design. Stick the circle-shaped tesserae down, then repeat for the stem.

1 Lay down a dust sheet and, wearing safety glasses, start to cut the mosaic tesserae using the nippers (cut a few at this stage and then more as you need them). Hold the nippers in one hand, towards the bottom of the handle, and a tessera in the other. Place the tessera face up between the cutting edges of the nippers and apply firm pressure. Cut a few of the chocolate brown and beige tesserae into eighths for the outlines, a few of the white tesserae into random shapes for the background, and a few of the pink and chocolate brown tesserae into circles. To do this, nip off the corners and slowly 'nibble' all the way around the tile in order to produce a smooth, round shape.

> ### useful equipment
> Nippers that have spring-action handles make cutting less arduous. Also, you may find it helpful to use a pair of tweezers to position small tesserae.

Decorative bowl

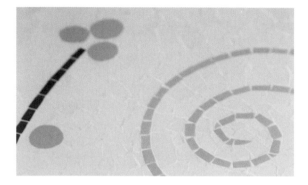

5 Complete the background of the design by applying the adhesive to the bowl, then sticking down the randomly shaped tesserae, ensuring that they are evenly spaced. Start by outlining the details you have already completed, then fill in the rest of the background. Leave to dry for 24 hours.

6 Remove any protruding adhesive from between the tesserae using the bradawl. Clean with a sponge.

7 Wearing rubber gloves, mix up the grout with the additive and water, according to the manufacturer's instructions, then smooth on all over the bowl with the float, starting from the center.

8 Spread the grout outward and up to the brim of the bowl. Remove any excess with a damp sponge, then clean and polish with a soft, dry cloth. Leave to dry for 24 hours. You may wish to paint the outside of the bowl to match your mosaic or grout color.

Metalwork

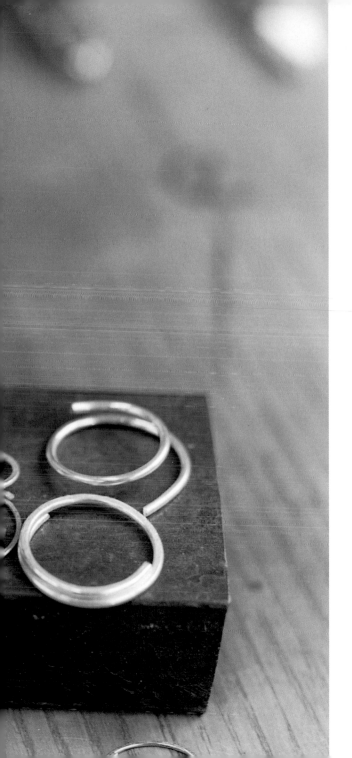

Gilding

The glitter of gold has entranced man since ancient times, and gold leaf has been employed to decorate objects with religious purpose or simply as a means of displaying power or wealth. Gilding can be subtle and delicate or excessively lavish, but it is always fascinating and alluring.

While traces of gold have been found in some caves used by early Paleolithic man around 40,000BC, the date it was first put to use is still open to speculation. It is thought that Egyptian pharaohs and priests began to use gold as an adornment around 3,000BC, linking it to their sun god, Ra. Eventually they discovered that it was possible to beat the precious metal into very thin sheets and apply it to surfaces as a decoration for religious artefacts. In time, the technique of gilding spread to China and the Greek and Roman Empires, with stunning results — ornaments, items of furniture and even religious buildings shone with the luster of applied gold.

In the early Middle Ages, gilding was practiced in Asia and the Middle East, but it did not return to Europe until the 14th century, when it became prized for use on icons and other religious works. In 1437, Italian artisan Cennino Cennini published *Il Libro Dell'Arte* (*The Craftsman's Handbook*), which included detailed instructions for carrying out gilding on wood and glass. Not long afterwards, the technique was perfected when artists, including Giotto, Duccio and Masaccio, realized that layers of gesso and a clay solution would seal the wood, prevent the gilding from flaking away and enhance its depth and color.

By the 17th century, gilding had reached a peak in Europe. It was an essential element in the baroque style, which began as an attempt by the Church to reinforce its authority, but developed into an extravagant means for the upper classes to flaunt their secular wealth. Dazzling and theatrical, baroque furniture and accessories (many imported from the Far East) featured heavy carving and gilding, marquetry and inlays. In the 18th century, a less decadent look prevailed, but gilding continued to be popular, used for architectural emphasis on columns, moldings and other details, and delicate inlays on furniture, light fittings and picture frames. It was at this time that the term *verre eglomisé* was coined for gilding on glass, after the 18th-century painter and frame maker Jean Baptiste Glomy. Other popular *verre eglomisé* items included mirrors, table tops, clocks and even whole pictures. In America, a folk art version arose — using imitation gold and metal foil, it was known as 'tinsel painting'.

Complex, time-consuming and expensive, today traditional leaf gilding is usually carried out in order to restore antiques, by expert craftsmen who painstakingly recreate its sumptuous effect. But other methods, including creams, pastes and paints, have been developed, and though their appearance is different, the results can be just as effective. The art of gilding may not be widely practiced, but it has not died out, and it is possible to use either the centuries-old technique or its newer counterparts to create modern pieces that are vibrant and impressive.

Table centerpiece

You will need

(To make a 16in/40cm square panel with a central image approximately 10 x 14in/ 25 x 35cm)

- 16 x 16in/40 x 40cm Optiwhite glass panel, ¼in/6mm thick
- 2fl oz/60ml rubbing alcohol (plus extra for cleaning)
- Soft cloth
- Masking tape
- Two gelatin capsules
- 6fl oz/180ml distilled water
- Two bowls
- Measuring cup
- Glass jar
- Mixing spoon
- Paintbrush
- Booklet loose silver leaf (thin)
- Gilder's tip
- Small jar petroleum jelly
- Cotton balls
- Soft brush (or gilder's mop)
- Ruler
- 1fl oz/25ml (approx) silver lettering enamel

This table centerpiece employs the delightful technique of verre eglomisé. You could use the same process to make a runner for a dining table, a small top for a bedside table, or even a set of coasters.

In verre eglomisé, silver leaf is applied to the underside of glass to beautiful effect — its lustrous, ethereal sheen looks as attractive today as it did hundreds of years ago. To give this ancient technique a modern twist, this project uses a sheet of plain glass combined with a bold pattern. Copy this pattern or devise your own; as an alternative you could even use gold, brass or copper leaf. Although applying the delicate leaf can be fiddly, it becomes easier with practice, and the end result is truly satisfying.

how to make:
Table centerpiece

1 Thoroughly clean the glass with rubbing alcohol and use a soft cloth to remove any smears. With masking tape, outline the area of the glass to be silvered. Turn the glass over.

2 To make the size, dissolve the gelatin capsules in a small amount of warmed distilled water. In the cup, measure out the rubbing alcohol and distilled water. Pour into the glass jar and stand it in a bowl of hot water to warm the mixture, then stir in the dissolved gelatin. Start at a corner of the outlined area of glass and paint on size covering an area slightly larger than a leaf. Mask the outer edges of the sized area to keep the shape.

3 For the gilding, work in a draft-free room with the silver leaf, size and gilder's tip near at hand — the technique requires fairly fast work. Touch the gilder's tip to the silver leaf and raise the square (if the tip fails to lift the leaf, smear a thin layer of petroleum jelly onto your arm and wipe the tip across it). Place the tip parallel to the glass and lay off the leaf smoothly. If it tears or folds, remove it with a cotton ball damped with size and start again.

4 Cover the entire area, laying the leaf in slightly overlapping rows. Small cracks are inevitable and add character — but if you wish, you can repair them by carefully applying size in the spaces (avoid wetting the leaf already laid) and laying on small pieces of leaf. Leave to dry for two days. Once the front and back of the silver leaf have a high shine and there is no cloudiness, use a soft brush (or gilder's mop) to dust away the loose leaf. Remove the masking tape.

5 To neaten the edges, gently lay a ruler onto the gilding, aligned near one edge. Holding down the ruler, use a cotton ball dampened in rubbing alcohol to rub away the silver up to the ruler's edge. Lift the ruler carefully and repeat on the remaining three sides.

6 To protect against tarnishing, paint over the gilding (on the reverse of the glass) with silver lettering enamel.

Tealight sleeves

You will need

(To make 3–4 sleeves, depending on the size of the tealight holder)

- Tabloid-size/A3 sheet heavy (112gsm) tracing paper
- Ruler
- Pencil
- Glass tealight holder
- Newsprint (or other clean paper)
- Adhesive film
- Small, flat brush
- 1oz/25g wax gilt (copper, gold or silver)
- Small piece of muslin
- Soft brush
- Scalpel or fine craft knife
- Cutting mat
- Spray adhesive

Wax gilt can be used for decorating almost any surface, and comes in various metallic colors. Here it is used on heavyweight tracing paper to make pretty sleeves for glass tealight holders.

Wax gilt is easy to use and creates immediate and impressive results. While familiar in traditional designs, there is no reason why it should not be used in more modern ways. This project makes the most of the interplay between the semi-transparent tracing paper and the opacity of gilded patterning; flickering candlelight not only emphasizes the contrast, but also enhances the soft sheen of the metal. Create infinite variations on this theme simply by cutting a variety of stencil patterns.

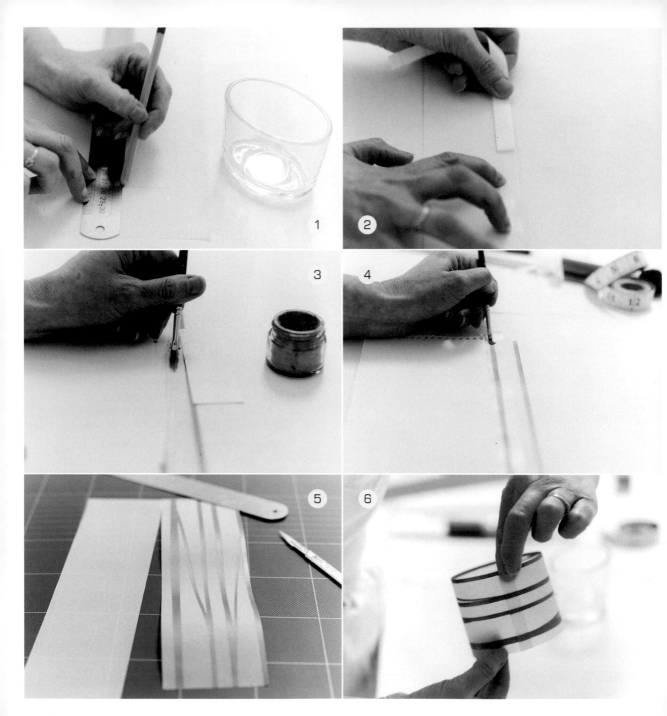

how to make:
Tealight sleeves

4 Decide where the next strip should be and lay down two strips of fresh adhesive film. Gild between them in the same manner as before. The space between the width of film decides the width of each stripe. Ensure that the stripes will meet up neatly when wrapped round the holder.

5 Continue making more stripes. To add interest, place random diagonal stripes between some of the horizontal stripes. Make sure any previous stripe is protected (by laying small pieces of paper over the relevant areas), as you do not want the adhesive film to lift the gilt off previous stripes. When the design is complete, leave to dry completely. If a slight smudge of gilt has occurred where it is not wanted, use a tiny piece of adhesive film to lift it up, or gently scrape off with a scalpel.

6 Using a scalpel and cutting mat, cut out the shape you marked on the tracing paper in step 1. Cover with a piece of newsprint for protection, leaving ⅜in/1cm showing at one end. Spray with adhesive. Fold around, press to the other end to form a sleeve, and slip over the glass holder.

1 On tracing paper, measure and mark out the area required to make a wraparound sleeve for your chosen glass tealight holder. Allow ⅜in/1cm extra on the width and about ⅛in/3mm on the depth. Place the tracing paper on a sheet of newsprint to collect any excess gilt particles.

2 Working from top to bottom, place a strip of adhesive film about ⅛in/3mm below the top edge of the tracing paper, and smooth down gently.

3 Working in a well-ventilated room, dip a small, flat brush into the wax gilt and brush it onto the tracing paper along the exposed top edge. It is best to protect the rest of the sleeve with a piece of paper, as the wax can easily mark areas that must remain pristine. Leave the wax to dry for one minute (or following manufacturer's instructions) then buff with a piece of muslin. Blow or whisk away excess gilt with the soft brush. Peel off the adhesive film to reveal the first stripe.

Silverwork

Silver comes second only to gold in terms of the degree to which we treasure it — its color and brilliance, light weight, resistance to tarnishing and malleability, coupled with its relative scarcity, have made it a prime choice for precious jewelry, ornaments and coins since earliest times.

It is thought that silver was discovered around 6,000 years ago, soon after gold and copper, and that by around 2,000BC the actual process of smelting to extract the metal from lead was being carried out. The first people to take advantage of silver's special qualities were Mycenean craftsmen, who produced large quantities of dishes and drinking vessels, using techniques that would still be familiar today. Silver has been used for jewelry, decorative objects and coins ever since, and in Medieval Europe it was essential in the creation of chalices, gospel covers and other decorative artefacts for the Christian church. Silver workshops were established in monasteries, and gradually the craft developed in the outside world. Guilds of goldsmiths (the term covered people working in both gold and silver) were set up, and in time the practice of hallmarking was introduced in order to control the purity of the metals. Interestingly, the metalworking techniques described in the 12th century working manual *De Diversis Artibus* have hardly changed at all in the intervening 900 years.

The practice of tea-drinking, which became popular in polite society in the late 17th century, gave new impetus to silver designers, who created entire tea sets in elaborate and sumptuous designs.

Silver was highly fashionable, not just for eating and drinking utensils, but also for chandeliers, fireplace accessories, candlesticks and even silver-plated chairs and chests. The abundant use of silver in the Baroque period gave way, in the 18th century, to a more sophisticated look, with designs that were simple, spare and elegant.

It was around this time, however, that the plating trade developed. This, coupled with increased mechanization, eventually led to a deterioration in quality and in the 19th century the most desirable silverwork was antique, or copies of antiques. This was a phenomenon that some silver designers attempted to redress, among them Christopher Dresser, whose minimal design style was a precursor of Modernism, and C.R. Ashbee, an Arts and Crafts designer whose Guild of Handicraft produced austere but beautiful silverware that was also to become influential for 20th century silver designers.

Contemporary craftspeople working in silver still battle against the tide of mass-produced, inexpensive products and the desire for cutlery and other utensils that do not require polishing and that can be washed in a dishwasher. Some beautiful work, however, both functional and sculptural, proves how much impact silver can make in the home. And silver jewelry remains as popular as it ever was — whether in the form of solid, cast silver, flat, beaten work or wire, modern silver jewelry is both innovative and wearable, demonstrating the enduring desirability of this timeless precious metal.

Coil earrings

You will need

- 7in/16cm soft silver 18 gauge/1.02mm wire, plated or real (it is advisable, however, to buy more wire to allow for experimentation and mistakes)
- Wire cutters
- File
- Round-nose pliers
- Flat-nose pliers
- Metal block or surface (textured if possible)
- Hammer (textured if possible)
- Earring backs to fit 18 gauge/1.02mm wire (if you cannot find these, buy a standard pair of backs and file down the ends of the wire)

Silver has been fashionable since ancient times, and when it is used to create a simple, modern design it has a timeless quality that is as desirable now as it was thousands of years ago.

Making your own jewelry is hugely satisfying, especially when you can work with a precious metal without needing to buy expensive and difficult-to-use equipment. These silver earrings, which could be worn either with a casual outfit or as a smart accessory, are intricate and delicate in style, yet not at all fussy or fiddly. With a little practice, making the spirals will become second-nature. The hammered surface on the shiny silver wire is a clever touch that adds textural interest to the dynamic form.

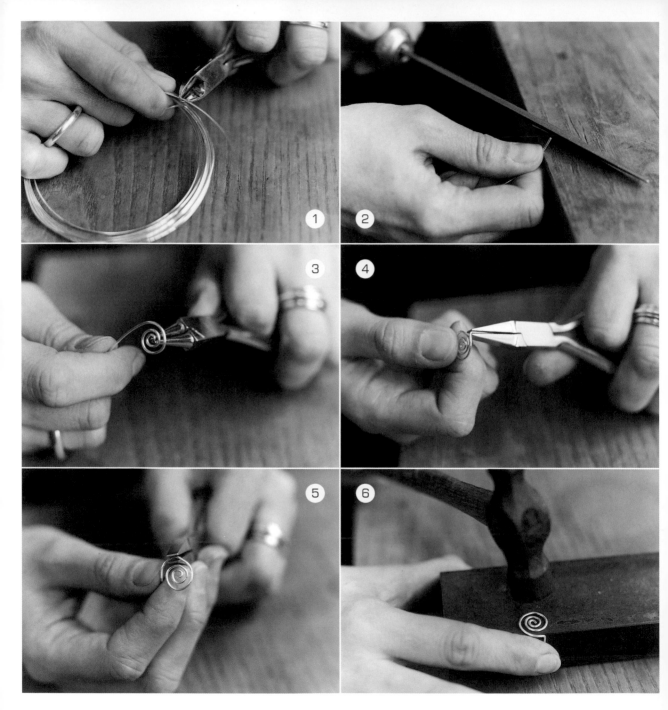

how to make:
Coil earrings

6 Lay the earring flat, post pointing down, on the edge of a metal block or surface (a rough surface is good because it adds texture), making sure that the spiral is not overlapping at any point. Hammer (again, a textured hammer is good) until the wire is flat and textured. Be careful not to over-hammer — experiment and allow for one or two mistakes. Make another so that you have a pair, and fit the earring backs onto them. (You may want to sterilize the earring posts by dipping them in disinfectant before you wear them.)

1 From the soft silver wire, cut a length of wire about 3¼in/8cm long.

2 File the ends, resting on a solid surface, to remove any sharp edges and neaten them.

3 Make a coil shape by gripping the end of the wire with the round-nose pliers and wrapping it around the tip several times.

4 To make the earring post, bend about ⅜in/1cm wire straight back, at right angles to the spiral.

5 Adjust the coil into a spiral shape by pushing some of the wire in and pulling some out, using your fingers if necessary. If the metal bends in unwanted places, straighten with the flat-nose pliers.

practicing your technique
Silver-plated wire is cheaper than silver wire. If you wish, practice with this before making the finished piece in the precious metal.

protecting the wire
If you don't have a pair of flat-nose pliers, wrap masking tape around the end of the pair you have. This will protect the wire from marking or damage.

Linked necklace

You will need

- Two reels of soft silver wire (plated or real), one 18 gauge/1.02mm and the other 14 gauge/1.63mm
- Round marker pen
- Wire cutters
- File
- Flat-nose pliers
- Metal block or surface (textured if possible)
- Hammer (textured if possible)
- Needle-nose pliers
- Masking tape
- One pack each of gold, brass and steel headpins, with the heads snipped off (or a reel of 18 gauge/1.02mm gold-plated and/or brass wire)
- Round ballpoint pen
- Small, silver (plated or real) circular connecting rings (without a gap)

This necklace uses varied repetition of a simple coil shape to great effect. Loose spirals link up to create a pattern that looks light and pretty against either bare skin or a simple shirt.

While this project is simple in concept, it can be adapted to be as complex and varied as you wish. Once you have mastered the basic technique, you can make spirals in different diameters and thicknesses, and join them to make different lengths. You may wish to use silver for the whole necklace or intersperse the silver coils with different colored metals such as gold and brass. For added impact, you may even want to wear several necklaces at the same time — they look especially effective over a dark top.

how to make:
Linked necklace

1 Make a coil shape by wrapping the 14 gauge/ 1.63mm silver wire around the marker pen at least one and a half times. Cut, then file the ends to remove any sharp edges and neaten them.

2 Adjust the coil into a spiral shape by pushing some of the wire in and pulling some out, using your fingers if necessary. If the metal bends in unwanted places, straighten with the flat-nose pliers.

3 Lay the spiral flat on a metal block or surface (a rough surface is good because it adds texture), making sure that the wire is not overlapping itself at any point. Hammer (again, a textured hammer is good) until it is flat and textured. Be careful not to over-hammer — leave time to experiment and allow for one or two mistakes.

4 If necessary, reshape the spiral, using the needle-nose pliers with masking tape wrapped around the ends to protect the wire. Then gently push one end of the spiral behind the other until they are creating resistance and tension between themselves (rather like a paperclip). The ends should now be touching.

5 Repeat steps 1–4, making as many spirals as you would like (the length of the necklace is dictated by the number used) in different colors and sizes. Use both thicknesses of wire, plus the headpins, and wrap around both the marker and the ballpoint pens. You may also wish to wrap some around more than one and a half times to create larger, more intricate spirals.

6 Once you have made a few spirals, start to slot them together to get a feel for how the necklace will look. The small connecting rings can be added randomly at any point. Either make the chain long enough to go over your head, or use any one of the rings as a clasp.

Wirework

A flair for form and an eye for decorative style can transform the most basic of materials into a beautiful object. Such is the case with wirework, which began as a rudimentary means of 17th-century repair and eventually became a highly skilled, timeless and attractive craft.

Wirework must surely be one of the least recognized — and certainly among the least formal — of all crafts. It first arose in the Slovakian region of Europe in the 17th century, with the repair of broken pottery using slender strands of iron. Repairing and restoring were a fact of life for peasant folk in those times, and sometimes people would not only repair their own possessions, but also those of other people in exchange for goods or food. They became known as tinkers, and, gradually, their wirework developed into a trade, not only for repairs, but also for the household objects that they made, which included spoons and ladles, colanders, baskets and animal traps.

By the end of the 18th century, Slovakian wireworkers had traveled further afield and spread their craft to Russia, Germany, France and America. The objects they made became more advanced — vases, fruit stands, cake platters, teapot stands, bottle carriers and toys were among the most popular. At the beginning of the 19th century it had become a custom in some areas to commission a head-turning piece of wirework to celebrate a special occasion. But the real flowering of the craft was at the end of the century, by which time, it is believed, 10,000 tinkers were practicing their craft in Europe and America. Some were itinerant, selling their wares from door to door or at markets; others established themselves in workshops, mass-producing wirework for catalogues and department stores, which offered an astonishing variety of objects. Each piece was carefully crafted from various thicknesses of wire — the thickest forming the main framework, then thinner and thinner lengths added. If necessary, the thinnest wires were wound around the armature for strength, or sometimes added for decoration in the form of spirals, twists, coils, tassels and braids. All the coiling and bending was done manually and without heat, and nothing was ever soldered, though eventually the whole piece was tinned to prevent it rusting. The pieces ranged from utilitarian items, such as egg holders, to the most amazingly ornate and fanciful works of art, including chandeliers, fire screens, candle holders and plant stands.

The fashion for wirework did not last; when more convenient and long-lasting materials, such as enamel, stainless steel and plastic, became available it disappeared almost instantly. By the Second World War it had all but died out. A new appreciation of the hand-made, however, has led us today to enjoy the charming individualism of wirework objects, and a few makers continue to work with wire. Traditional methods are still used, but most contemporary wireworkers more often take advantage of newer styles and materials to produce objects that may be practical or whimsical, heavy or light, simple or lavish, and suitable for use indoors or out.

Napkin holder

You will need

(To make one napkin holder)

- About 65 assorted beads (new or taken from old jewelry)
- Small container for holding beads, preferably with compartments
- 20in/50cm length of 18 gauge/1.02mm galvanized tying wire
- Toilet paper tube or similar
- Small pliers (with a cutting edge)
- Reel of florist's or beading wire

Utterly delicate and delightfully pretty, this gorgeous napkin ring, made from slender wire and colored beads, requires minimal outlay and only a very little patience to make.

While the spider's web structure of this napkin ring gives it a fragile appearance, it will hold its shape well if not treated roughly. The trick is to wind the wire in such a way that the pattern develops organically, yet still fairly evenly. Use beads in coordinating pastel colors and in slightly varying sizes, then tuck in a rolled white linen napkin for an upmarket and glamorous place setting. It helps to have an idea of the design before you start, but you may find that the natural curves of the wire dictate a different 'route'.

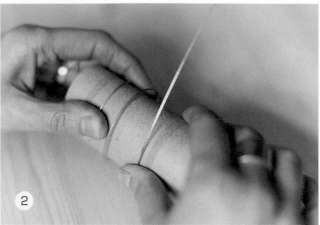

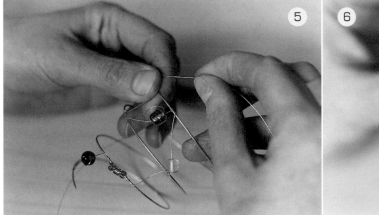

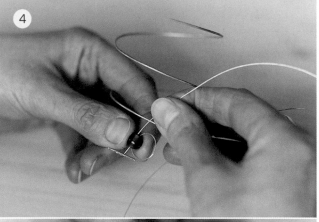

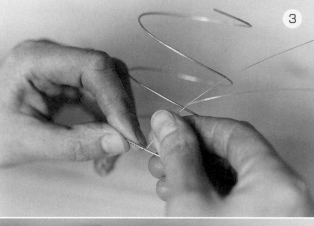

how to make:
Napkin holder

1 Choose a pretty selection of color-coordinated beads in various sizes, and set aside in a container.

2 Wind the 18 gauge/1.02mm wire tightly around the cardboard tube two and a half times. Remove the tube and tease out the coil to the required width.

3 Using the pliers, cut a length of the florist's wire (about 16–24in/40–60cm is comfortable to work with) and attach one end to the coil, about ¾in/2cm from one of the coil ends, by winding it tightly around four or five times. Pinch in the end neatly with the pliers. Florist's wire is very fine and kinks easily, so treat it delicately and be very careful that it does not flick into your eyes.

4 Select a bead and thread it onto the florist's wire. To fix it in a specific place, carry the wire round and through the bead again and then, holding the bead firmly, pull the wire tight. Anchor the wire to the next coil by winding it around tightly twice (adding another bead if you wish). Maintain a tension, but do not pull the florist's wire so tightly that the basic coil loses shape.

5 Continue weaving the florist's wire (like a spider's web), adding beads as you choose, always anchoring the wire when passing over the thicker wire of the coil. When you run out of florist's wire, finish by winding around four or five times and squeezing in the end with the pliers. Then attach a new length and continue.

6 When you are happy with your design and the coil is strong enough to maintain its shape, finish by protecting the two sharp ends of the thicker wire. Travel up to each one in turn with the florist's wire, and bind it around the end once. Thread a medium-size bead onto the florist's wire. Pull the bead halfway over the end of the coil and then double the florist's wire back through it to hold it in place. Wind the florist's wire around four or five times and travel back down. Cut the wire close to the coil, then pinch in with pliers.

Hanging heart

You will need

(To make the triple heart hanging in the center of the picture, right)

- About 300 assorted beads, approximately 275 tiny ones and 25 medium-size ones (new or taken from old jewelry)
- Small container for holding beads, preferably with compartments
- 40in/100cm of 18 gauge/1.02mm galvanized tying wire
- Small pliers (with a cutting edge)
- Reel of florist's or beading wire
- One silver headpin
- Heart-shaped bead (or a pear-drop, or any pretty hanging bead)
- Silver thread or coordinating ribbon for hanging

For a Christmas decoration — or indeed any other time of the year — this lovely hanging heart will add a dainty touch to a mantelpiece, window, door frame or shelf and, of course, a Christmas tree.

Although Slovakian tinkers may not have recognized this modern version of wirework, this project is undoubtedly highly decorative and appealing. While most obviously a Christmas decoration, it could equally well be used as an informal hanging anywhere in the house, throughout the year. Once you have mastered the heart shape, try your hand at creating circles, ovals, squares and even stars — the basic technique is the same and it would be wonderful to make a series of hangings in different shapes and sizes.

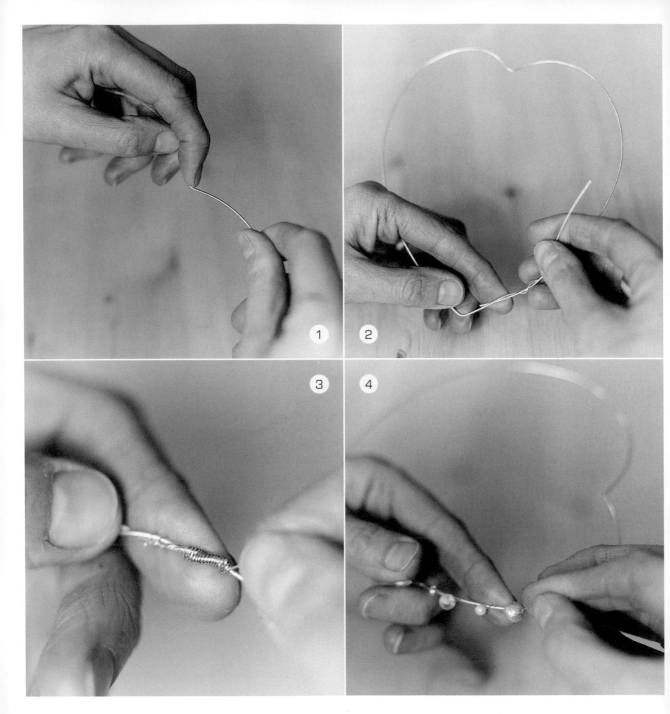

how to make:
Hanging heart

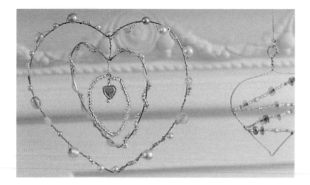

2 Holding firmly, and being very careful, curve both ends down to form a heart. Be firm, but do not make kinks as they will be very difficult to smooth out. When you are happy with the shape, sharply bend the longer end of wire upwards to form the bottom point of the heart. Twist it around the shorter end two or three times to fix in place. Cut the ends and pinch in with pliers. You may need to tease the heart into shape.

3 Cut a length of the florist's wire (about 16–24in/ 40–60cm is comfortable to work with) and anchor it by winding tightly around the joining twist of the heart base shape as many times as needed, until the ends are covered.

1 Choose a selection of color-coordinated beads and set aside in a container. Begin by making the largest heart. Cut 20in/50cm of the 18 gauge/1.02mm wire with the pliers and, using the natural curve of the wire, bend it (with the middle about 1¼in/3cm from the center of the length of wire) to form the two arcs that are the top of a heart.

4 Wind the florist's wire around the heart shape and add the beads, alternating sizes and colors, at intervals by threading them on.

Hanging heart

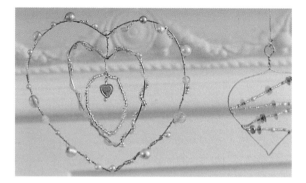

5 Every time you add a bead, anchor it in place by winding the wire around the base shape twice. When you run out of florist's wire, wind round four or five times and squeeze in the end with pliers. Attach a new length at the same point and continue. When you reach the top of the heart, form a tiny arch with the florist's wire then continue down the other side. Finish by winding the wire around tightly four or five times, then cutting off as close as possible to the base shape and using the pliers to pinch in the end neatly.

6 Make the second heart base shape as in steps 1 and 2, using about 14in/35cm of the 18 gauge/ 1.02mm wire. Thread a selection of small beads continuously onto lengths of florist's wire and wind them around the heart shape, attaching and finishing as in steps 3 and 5. Remember to make a small arch at the top with the florist's wire.

7 For the third heart, use 10in/25cm of the florist's wire, threading small beads onto it and then bending it into a heart shape. Make a small loop at the top with a twist of wire.

8 Thread a bead onto the headpin, then the heart-shaped bead, then another bead. Bend the top of the pin with pliers to form a loop and hang this from the loop at the top of the smallest heart. Use a short length of wire to twist around the center of all three hearts so that they are loosely linked together. To hang the decoration, loop a silver thread or ribbon through the largest heart.

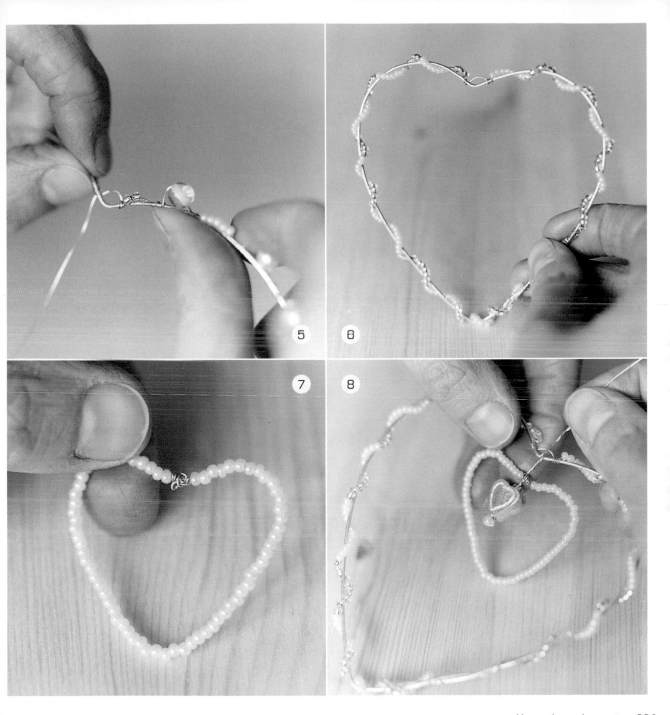

Casting &
Molding

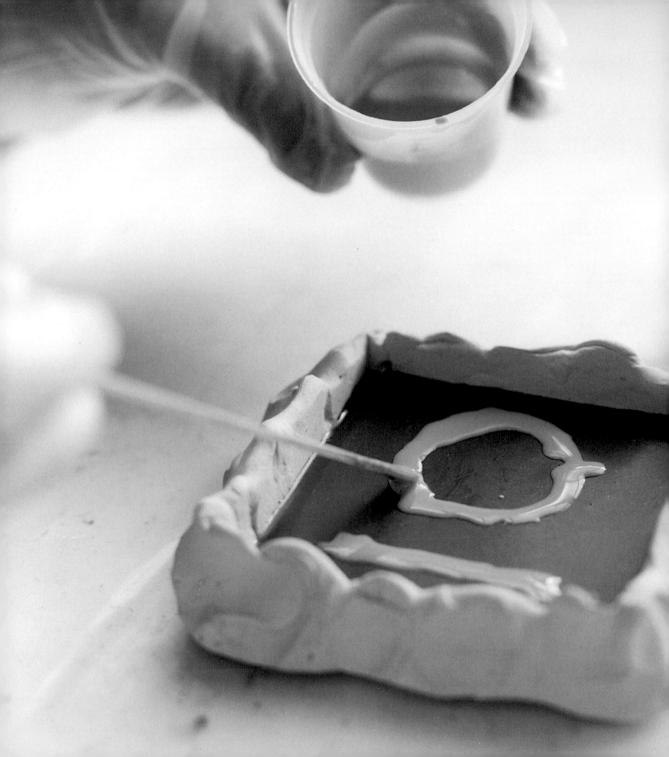

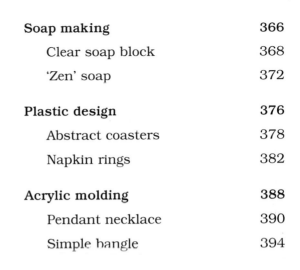

Soap making

The benefits of soap have been known to man for many thousands of years. Essential for hygiene and cleanliness, it is also a luxury, valued for its color, scent and texture — and modern hand-made soaps, in all sorts of styles and designs, are as attractive to look at as they are a pleasure to use.

Far from being a modern invention, soap has been around since at least the days of the Babylonians in the third millennium BC, where it was used for washing textiles. The Phoenicians and Egyptians, the Vikings and the Celts are thought to have known about soap, too, but the first evidence of soap making comes from ancient Rome, where the writer Pliny described a soap made from goat's tallow and wood ashes. Pompeii even had a soap factory, and it was Roman legend that gave soap its name. It was said that women washing clothes at the foot of Mount Sapo, where animals were sacrificed, discovered that the mixture of melted animal fat and ashes that ran down into the river made their cloth much cleaner.

In later Roman times, soap became popular for personal washing, widely used in the baths for which the Roman civilization is renowned. When the empire ended, however, soap fell into disuse in Europe — though the Byzantine and Arab people continued bathing — and the resulting squalor contributed to the plagues of the Dark and Middle Ages.

Soap was revived in Italy and Spain in the eighth century, and guilds of craftsmen guarded the secrets of how it was made. In the 13th century, the trade spread from Italy to France, and then to England a hundred years or so later — though the Southern European varieties, made from olive oil, were preferable to those made from animal fats in the North. But soap was heavily taxed, and therefore only available to the rich few; when the English tax was repealed in 1853 it led to a boom in hygiene. Early American colonists went to great lengths to make soap, using woodash boiled with waste fats to make a soft product. It was hard work, and not always successful, and eventually professional makers appeared, who made hard bars (by adding salt), sometimes scented with oils.

Scientific discoveries from 1791 onwards made soap production dramatically easier; it became cheaper and more widely available (in many different, desirable varieties), and bathing became the height of fashion. By 1850, soap making was one of America's fastest-growing industries. Small, wrapped bars of toilet soap were popular, and then, after the invention of the washing machine, synthetic detergents were developed by the giant soap companies that were, by then, well established.

Mass-produced soap making had come of age, but from the 1970s it came to be recognized as a domestic activity once again, especially in the United States, where it is now a thriving and innovative craft area. Modern soap-makers explore the visual, tactile and cosmetic potentials of both traditional soaps and newer, glycerin-based melt and pour soaps, experimenting with casting, sculpting, embedding, coloring and scenting, creating beautiful objects that combine artistry with practicality.

Clear soap block

You will need

(To make one block of soap)

- Mold (a large margarine container is ideal, as long as it is sturdy enough to withstand the heat of the melted soap)
- Petroleum jelly
- 2lb 10oz/1.2kg clear melt-and-pour soap base
- Kitchen knife
- Double boiler (or saucepan and heatproof bowl)
- Mixing spoon
- Candy thermometer (optional)
- Mixing bowl
- 2 teaspoons/8ml liquid soap colorant (this project used orange)
- Measuring spoons
- 2½ teaspoons/12ml essential oil (this project used Sweet Orange)
- Small spray bottle containing rubbing alcohol (optional)
- Knife, vegetable peeler or damp sponge
- Cheese wire or herb chopper
- Plastic wrap

How nice it is to make a joy of something as utilitarian as a bar of soap! These tempting, colorful examples can — just like a block of cheese — be cut into lovely thick slabs when required.

If you can bake a cake, you can make soap. This easy method, known as melt-and-pour, involves nothing more complex than heating gently and pouring the softened mixture into a greased mold. The possibilities of gorgeous color and delicious scent, however, are endless, and once you have tried once or twice you're sure to want to keep going. Make your soaps in different shapes and sizes, and display them on a window ledge in the bathroom or kitchen so that the light enhances their jewel-like qualities.

how to make:
Clear soap block

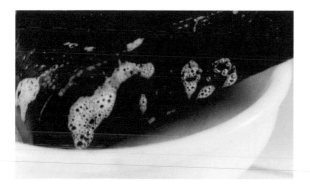

1 Lightly grease the mold with a small amount of petroleum jelly.

2 Cut the soap base into small pieces with a kitchen knife and melt over a gentle heat in the top half of a double boiler (or in a heatproof bowl over a saucepan containing a few inches/centimeters of water). Cover the pan while the soap melts, to keep moisture in. Do not stir, but occasionally lift the lid and give the soap a gentle nudge with the spoon. The ideal melting temperature of the soap is about 140°F/ 60°C — if it overheats, the texture will suffer. Using a candy thermometer to monitor is helpful.

3 When the soap has become fully liquid, remove from the heat. Pour a small amount into a separate bowl and add a little colorant, following the manufacturer's recommendations as to quantity. Use a measuring spoon to add this back to the melted base gradually until you reach the desired shade. Then add the essential oil. (For citrus or mint essential oils, do not exceed a 1 percent dilution, but for gentle essential oils, such as lavender, use up to 3 percent.) Stir gently.

4 Pour the soap gently and slowly into the mold. If you wish, spray the surface with rubbing alcohol to remove surface bubbles. Leave to set (this can take several hours). You can use the refrigerator for speed, but avoid using the freezer, as the texture of the soap can be spoiled.

5 When the soap has set, remove from the mold. It should come out quite easily, but if not, try flexing the mold gently or leaving it upside down in a warm room. To remove surface bubbles, slice off a thin layer with a knife or vegetable peeler or wipe with a damp sponge.

6 Slice into chunks with a cheese wire or herb chopper. Store in plastic wrap to avoid moisture loss.

'Zen' soap

You will need

(To make one bar of soap)

- Mold (a small Tupperware box is ideal, about 4in/10cm square)
- Petroleum jelly
- 7oz/200g clear melt-and-pour soap base
- Kitchen knife
- Double boiler (or saucepan with heatproof bowl)
- Mixing spoon
- Candy thermometer (optional)
- ½ teaspoon shea butter (optional)
- Mixing bowl
- ½ teaspoon water-soluble titanium dioxide (cosmetic whitener)
- 40 drops ylang ylang essential oil
- Small spray bottle containing rubbing alcohol (optional)
- Skewer or pointed kitchen knife
- ¼ teaspoon powdered black oxide (black cosmetic coloring)
- Small spoon
- Knife, vegetable peeler or damp sponge
- Plastic wrap

These striking soaps are soft and deliciously scented. Inlaid with a Chinese calligraphic symbol, they make a wonderful and unusual present for a friend, or a lovely treat for yourself.

Even soaps that appear quite complicated, such as these, are actually very simple to make. A graphic and simple combination of black and white works best for our Chinese calligraphy, but there is nothing to stop you carving your own, different patterns or symbols and employing other color combinations — maybe even three or more, once you have mastered the processes involved. Use shea butter to make a soap that's beautifully rich and soft on the hands, and ylang ylang as a delicate, suitably exotic fragrance.

how to make:
'Zen' soap

1 Grease the mold with petroleum jelly. Cut the soap base into pieces and melt over a gentle heat in the top half of a double boiler (or heatproof bowl over a saucepan containing a few inches/centimeters of water). Cover the pan while the soap melts (see page 371.) For a moisturizing bar, add shea butter to the soap as it melts.

2 When the soap has become liquid, remove from the heat. Pour a small amount into a mixing bowl and mix in the titanium dioxide until it is dissolved. Add back to the melted base (if the soap begins to set, return to the heat). When the color is incorporated, add the essential oil (see page 371) and stir.

3 Pour the soap slowly into the mold. Spray the surface with rubbing alcohol to help remove bubbles. Leave to set (this may take up to an hour, depending on the size of the mold). You could refrigerate, but avoid using the freezer, as the texture of the soap can spoil.

4 When the soap has set, remove it from the mold. If it gets stuck, try flexing the mold gently or leave it upside down in a warm room for a little while.

5 With the tip of the skewer or knife, score the outline for the template on page 425 onto the soap surface. Then carve right through the bar, removing the soap from the center. Keep these pieces to one side.

6 Replace the soap in the mold, if necessary adding petroleum jelly to help the soap stick. Collect the soap you removed from the center of the bar and re-melt in the double boiler (you may need to add extra soap base). When the soap is melted, remove from the heat and stir in a little powdered black oxide until the soap base has turned black. Spoon the black soap into the center of the white bar and leave to set. (If you overpour, simply slice off the excess later.) Once set, remove from the mold. Remove any surface bubbles by slicing off a thin layer with a knife or vegetable peeler, or wipe with a damp sponge. Store in plastic wrap.

Plastic design

Since they were first developed in the 19th century, plastics have transformed our lives, surrounding us at home and at work, indoors and out. Essential for industry, plastics have also become adapted for craft use, and today they are valued for the properties that give them unique creative potential.

A plastic is simply a material that in itself is inherently formless, but that can also be shaped under heat and pressure — from the Greek word *plastikos*, meaning 'to mold or form'. Natural plastics include amber resin and *gutta percha*, a rubber-like substance from a tropical tree, but today we generally use the word to denote man-made materials such as polythene, acrylic and polyester.

The earliest semi-synthetic plastic was Vulcanite, created in the late-1830s by Charles Goodyear, used for matchstick holders and (among other things) false teeth. As the 19th century progressed, however, mechanization increased and new materials had to be found to replace expensive, hand-crafted ones, such as ivory and horn. Plastics were the answer. In the 1860s, celluloid became the first mass-produced plastic, made into all sorts of items, from dressing table sets to jewelry and cigarette cases. Three decades later casein plastic was invented and then, in 1907, came the biggest breakthrough of all — Bakelite, the first truly synthetic plastic, invented by American Leo Baekeland.

Best-known for its use in radios, Bakelite was actually employed in the manufacture of all sorts of domestic products, and it was at this time that designers really began to appreciate the versatility, cheapness and creative potential of plastics. In the 1920s and '30s, polythene, nylon, acrylic, polystyrene and polyurethane were invented, and these materials were used more and more widely, for everyday necessities and luxury items. In the 1940s and '50s, unfortunately, plastic design was not always of the highest quality. Products were often made in huge volume at very low prices, and so developed the common opinion that plastic was cheap and nasty — a poor imitator of other, natural materials.

Plastic came back into favor in the 1960s, when vivid colors, organic shapes and disposable objects were all the rage. But it was in the 1970s that plastics were taken up by craftspeople, as a material that could compete with wood, textiles, and even precious metals, in its own right rather than as a poor imitator. Some jewelers, in particular, chose plastic above other materials precisely because it embodied qualities that were the opposite of those associated with gold, silver or gemstones. In Britain, Holland and America in particular, plastic was essential to what has been dubbed 'the new jewelry'. This focused on ideas rather than material values, and emphasized plastic's individual qualities — its ability to be molded or cast into many different shapes, its light weight, its coloring (either subtle or vivid), and its light-transmitting capabilities. From those experimental beginnings, the use of plastic in craft is now accepted and appreciated — its unique properties ideal for the modern craftsperson who wishes to explore all sorts of unusual possibilities.

Abstract coasters

You will need

(To make six coasters)

- Ceramic tile
- Block of modeling clay or Plasticine (or a ready-made mold)
- Protective mask
- PVC gloves
- 1lb/500g general-purpose resin and catalyst
- Small plastic graded cups (similar to measuring cups) for mixing colors
- Resin paste colors in white, brown and pale blue (in 1oz/25g pots)
- Popsicle sticks
- Small amount of detergent
- Old kitchen or craft knife
- Wet and dry sandpaper
- Self-adhesive felt the same size as the tile (optional)

These simple but hardy coasters with their naïve, free design are sharp and modern-looking as well as practical. They will not only protect your furniture from stains but also add contemporary class to your table.

Craftspeople — especially jewelers — discovered the delights of plastic in the 1970s, and since then it has become increasingly popular as a craft material. Resin casting is particularly satisfying as it is relatively straightforward, yet the results can be truly stunning and extremely professional. These coasters are an easy introduction to the process. Master the basics, then experiment with different colors and patterns, or make your own modeling clay molds in order to create any shape you wish.

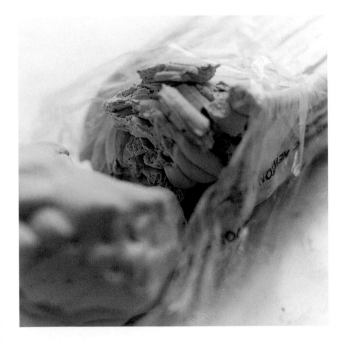

how to make:
Abstract coasters

1 Choose a ceramic tile in a size and shape you wish to copy, and press the modeling clay up evenly around it to create a cavity. Alternatively, you could use a ready bought mold made of polypropylene. This will be the mold for your coaster. If you wish to make more than one coaster, you will need to make a mold for each one.

2 Wearing a mask and gloves, and working in a very well-ventilated room (a good-sized workshop or garage is best), mix around 5 teaspoons of resin and 15 drops of catalyst in a plastic graded cup, and add small quantities of one color of paste. Pour into the clay mold so that it is half full and leave to set (this will take around 3–5 hours).

3 Mix the same amount of resin and catalyst again, this time adding a different color paste. Using a popsicle stick, carefully paint a raised pattern of resin onto the set bottom layer of the tile. Leave to set.

4 Once the raised surface has set, mix another color and pour in order to fill in the remaining area of the coaster. Leave to set completely for 24 hours.

5 Once hard, remove the coaster from the mold — do not worry if it feels slightly tacky. Soak it in water and detergent.

6 Remove the white layer from the coaster by scraping with an old knife. To finish off, place the coaster on a hard, flat surface and use wet and dry sandpaper on both sides until it is smooth. To protect surfaces, you may wish to stick self-adhesive felt to the back of the coaster.

catalyst quantities
Do not add more catalyst than stated to try to speed things up. This could be dangerous as the catalyst could cause overheating and smoking, and may also result in the piece cracking.

Napkin rings

You will need

(To make six napkin rings)

- Paper towel tube
- Scissors
- Epoxy putty
- Hot glue gun
- Square of thick, flat card
- Cereal box
- Sharp craft knife
- Metal ruler
- Masking tape
- Protective mask
- PVC gloves
- 1lb/500g silicone rubber
- Electronic scales
- 2¼lb/1kg clear or AM resin and catalyst
- Graded plastic cups (similar to measuring cups) for mixing
- About 30 small silver beads (large ones will break the surface of the resin)
- Plastic tweezers
- Wet and dry sandpaper
- Metal polish
- Soft cloth

These napkin rings look so professional it is hard to believe they are hand made. The combination of clear resin and silver beads is modern and elegant, and would work with almost any table setting.

It is difficult to find napkin rings that are eye-catching without being garish, and this project provides the perfect solution. The trickiest part is making the mold — once you've done that, the rest is plain sailing. You could vary the color of resin or the type of bead for different effects, or even try casting other objects, such as glitter, tiny silk flowers or colorful candies. Simply ensure that whatever you choose is perfectly dry, non-greasy and not too fragile, then experiment to produce unusual and impressive results.

how to make:
Napkin rings

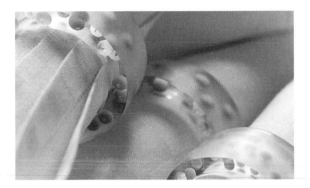

1 Make your ring shape by cutting the desired length from the paper towel tube and coating it in epoxy putty until it is about ⅜in/1cm thick. Using a hot glue gun, stick the coated ring to a square of card to form a flat base.

2 With an old cereal box, build a square wall around the tube and tape it together (use a knife and a metal ruler to score the card so that it folds easily). Stick it to the base card with a hot glue gun. Seal the edges with the glue, so that the mold does not leak.

3 Wearing a mask and gloves, and working in a very well ventilated room, mix about 9oz/250g silicone rubber according to the manufacturer's instructions (you will need accurate weighing scales). Pour the rubber into the mold, so that it is ⅜in/1cm higher than the top of the ring, and tap gently to release any air bubbles. Leave for at least 24 hours until set.

4 Ease away all the cardboard and the epoxy putty ring — you will be left with a square of rubber with a ring-shaped cavity in the center. This is the mold for your napkin ring; it can be re-used many times. (To save time, however, you could make more than one mold at once.)

Napkin rings

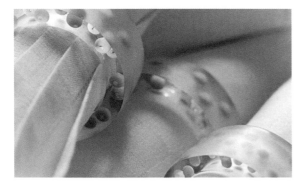

7 Remove the napkin ring from the mold — rubber is flexible so you can be quite forceful if necessary. Finish with wet and dry sandpaper to give a smooth finish (see box, below).

8 Polish the ring by dipping it in a pool of metal polish and rubbing with a soft cloth to achieve a high shine.

5 Mix up 5 teaspoons/25ml of clear resin with 15 drops of catalyst in a graded plastic cup and pour into the mold to a height of about ¼in/6mm. Leave to set for 3–5 hours.

6 Have your beads ready and mix more clear resin. Using plastic tweezers, dip a few beads into the resin to coat them, then carefully place in the mold and add a little more resin so that they are just covered. Leave to set again. Repeat as many times as you wish, until the resin is about ¼in/6mm from the top of the mold. Finish with a final layer of resin and leave to set completely for 24 hours.

creating a perfect finish
To give a smooth finish on your epoxy putty 'master' ring (and, therefore, the resin rings themselves), smooth it all over with a damp sponge before use and between moldings.

sanding the rings
When you are sanding your finished rings, wrap the wet and dry paper around a length of dowel — this will give you more control when you are working on their curved surfaces.

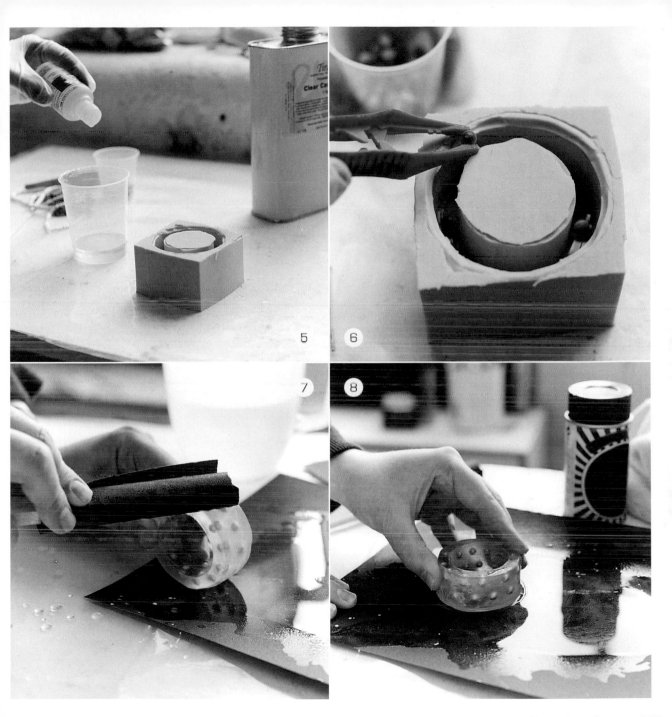

Acrylic molding

First used in the First World War as a material for aeroplane windscreens, acrylic has since found many uses both at work and at home. Light, clear, colorful and easy to work with, it has recently become highly appreciated by craftspeople who combine skilled workmanship with innovation.

The development of plastics in the late-19th century had quite far-reaching repercussions. No longer were we obliged to use the expensive natural materials that were sometimes in scarce supply, or required time-consuming hand-crafting processes that made them prohibitively expensive. Here was a material that could be used for both everyday and upmarket items, which could be molded, dyed, vacuum-formed, extruded, cut, ground, drilled, polished and cast, made to look like other materials or simply allowed to be itself. Its uses were myriad, from false teeth and dressing table sets in the early days to computer casing and boat hulls today.

Of all the types of plastic in existence, one of the most important is acrylic or, to give it its full name, polymethyl methacrylate, which was produced by the British company ICI in 1936. It is a fully synthetic thermoplastic, which means that it will soften every time heat is applied and can therefore be reformed over and over again. (The other type of plastic is thermosetting, which will soften when heated and then set permanently into its molded shape when cooled.) Due to its light weight, clarity and shatter-resistant properties, acrylic was first put to use in the form of protective screens, and especially aircraft canopies, during the First World War. It was later used for light fittings, and then signage — where its ability to take different colors made it an ideal material in the growing corporate identity industry. It was not long before it had become a sophisticated product with a variety of uses, often replacing glass, wood or metal in domestic or commercial environments, and available in a range of thicknesses, colors, tints and surface effects.

In craft work, acrylic figures most predominantly in jewelry, a field that has accepted the use of plastics since the 1920s, when manufacturers first began to make beads, pins and bangles in cast synthetic resins. Something of a novelty at first, plastic gained ground when fashion designer Coco Chanel produced a range of costume jewelry, and thrived during the American depression of the 1930s. In the early 1940s, 'lucky' bracelets were made from the scraps of acrylic left over from the making of fighter plane windscreens, and carved acrylic was used instead of rock crystal, wartime shortages having given costume jewelry another boost.

More creative, rather than imitative, work with acrylic began in the early 1970s, when jewelers discovered how suitable it could be for their work. Among the acrylic pioneers were Claus Bury, Gijs Bakker, Caroline Broadhead and Susanna Heron. Their work paved the way for a new generation of craftspeople who have also found that acrylic is an ideal material with which to introduce innovative ideas, break with past traditions and combine practicality with refinement and vigor with flair.

Pendant necklace

You will need

(To make one pendant)

- Piece of wet and dry emery paper, 320 (fine) grade
- Piece of plate glass or other suitable flat surface
- One piece ³⁄₁₆in-thick/4mm clear acrylic sheet, measuring 2in/5cm square. Do not remove the protective paper
- One piece ⅛in-thick/3mm red fluorescent acrylic sheet, measuring 1½ x 1¾in/4 x 4.5cm. Do not remove the protective paper
- File
- Ruler
- Pen
- Upright drill with a sharp, ³⁄₁₆in/4mm bit
- Vise
- Protective goggles
- Liquid paraffin
- Fine paintbrush
- Spare ⅛in-thick/3mm acrylic sheet (any color) to practice on
- Length of satin or elastic cord, or suede or leather strip

(If you wish to dye your pendant, see page 392 for equipment)

It is surprising that acrylic is so rarely used as a medium for popular craft. It is light, colorful and easy to work with, and — as can be seen here – wonderfully striking.

What could be more satisfying than to transform something that appears to be little more than a waste product into a beautiful pendant necklace? Small scraps of sheet acrylic, in a variety of colors or dyed to a shade of your choice, are easily cut into interesting shapes and drilled (with an ordinary household drill) to produce lovely patterns. The effect of two or more pieces layered onto each other adds another dimension of interest, while the finishing touch is the textural contrast of a satin ribbon or, if you prefer, a suede strip.

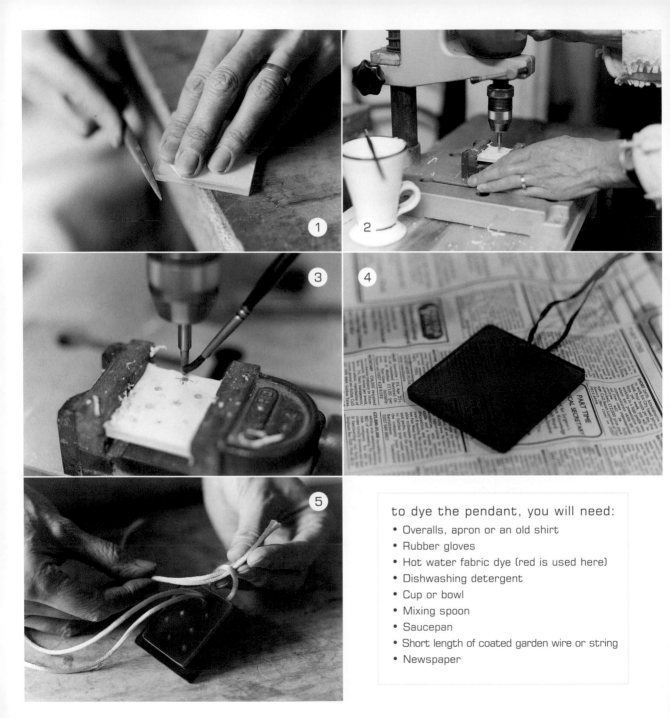

to dye the pendant, you will need:
- Overalls, apron or an old shirt
- Rubber gloves
- Hot water fabric dye (red is used here)
- Dishwashing detergent
- Cup or bowl
- Mixing spoon
- Saucepan
- Short length of coated garden wire or string
- Newspaper

how to make:
Pendant necklace

1 Wet the emery paper and place it on the glass (on a flat surface). Rub one edge of one of the pieces of acrylic up and down on the emery paper until it is smooth and matte. Repeat for all edges, then sand the other piece of acrylic, too. File the sharp corners off both pieces.

2 For each of the pieces of acrylic, find the center of the top edge, and mark ¼in/6mm down from this, on the protective paper. Place the bit in the drill and one piece of acrylic in the vise. Wearing protective goggles, and using the liquid paraffin (painted onto the bit) as a lubricant to stop the drill getting too hot, drill on a medium speed all the way through the acrylic at the marked point. Repeat for the other piece of acrylic.

3 On the smaller piece, mark a pattern of random dots. Put a spare piece of acrylic in the vise and practice drilling halfway through. Discard. When you feel confident, place the marked acrylic in the vise and drill halfway through each dot. Remove the protective paper from both pieces.

4 If you wish, you can now dye the clear acrylic. Wearing overalls and rubber gloves, dilute the dye as little as possible in a cup, adding a little dishwashing detergent, and bring to the boil in a pan. Hook the wire or string through the hole in the acrylic and immerse in the water. Agitate for five minutes; longer if you want a stronger color. Remove and, still wearing the overalls and rubber gloves, rinse in warm, soapy water and leave to dry on newspaper.

5 Thread the two pieces of acrylic together with the cord or strip, making sure that you keep the drilled pattern on the inside of the top piece. Then tie the ends together securely at the length you require for your necklace.

Simple bangle

You will need

(To make one bangle)

- Piece of wet and dry emery paper, 320 (fine) grade
- Piece of plate glass or other suitable flat surface
- Piece of ³⁄₁₆in-thick/4mm clear acrylic sheet measuring 1 x 8¾in/2.5 x 22cm. Do not remove the protective paper
- File
- Pen
- Ruler
- Upright drill with a sharp, ³⁄₁₆in/ 4mm bit
- Vise
- Protective goggles
- Liquid paraffin
- Fine paintbrush
- Some spare pieces of scrap acrylic
- Baking sheet
- Baking parchment
- Heatproof gloves (old, thick leather gloves are ideal)
- Glass jar, approx 2½in/6cm in diameter
- One or two 20in/50cm lengths of ribbon or leather strip

(If you wish to dye your bangle, see page 396 for equipment)

Because acrylic can be molded so easily, it is perfect for making colorful bangles. Wear just one for subtle impact, or several in a variety of colors.

Acrylic has been a medium of experimentation for cutting-edge professional jewelry makers since the 1970s. It is less often used in a domestic context, however, despite its versatility, practicality and attractive appearance. But now it is time to discover the many wonderful qualities of this modern material. These acrylic bangles really could not be simpler to make — in a variety of colors, widths and thicknesses. You could keep them completely plain and simple, or drill them in several places so as to thread a ribbon through for added decorative interest.

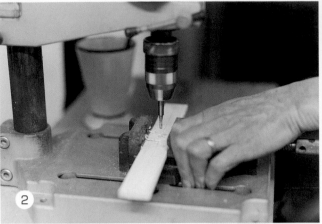

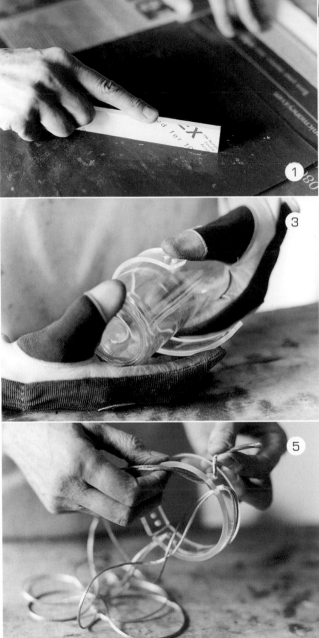

to dye the bangle, you will need:

- Overalls, apron or an old shirt
- Rubber gloves
- Hot water fabric dye (red is used here)
- Dishwashing detergent
- Cup or bowl
- Mixing spoon
- Saucepan
- Coated garden wire or string
- Newspaper

how to make:
Simple bangle

Preheat your oven to 280–350°F/140–180°C/ gas mark 1–4

1 Wet the emery paper and place it on the glass (on a flat surface). Rub one edge of the acrylic on the emery paper until it is smooth and matte. Repeat for all edges. File the corners.

2 Find the center of the acrylic and, with a pen, mark ¼in/6mm either side of it (in the center of the width) on the protective paper. Then mark ¼in/6mm either side of those points, and ¼in/6mm and ½in/12mm in from each end. Place the bit in the drill and the acrylic in the vise. Wearing protective goggles, and using the liquid paraffin (painted onto the bit) as a lubricant, drill on a medium speed right through the acrylic at the marked points. Carefully remove the protective paper from both sides.

3 To test the oven temperature, remove the protective paper from a piece of scrap acrylic and place on a baking sheet lined with parchment, then leave in the oven for 10–15 minutes. Remove, with the leather gloves — it should have become floppy. When you have found the correct temperature, place your drilled acrylic on the tray (remove the paper first) and leave in the oven for 10–15 minutes. Remove and, wearing the gloves, wrap it around the glass jar and hold it there to cool. Repeat this process if necessary.

4 To dye the bangle, wear overalls and gloves and dilute the dye in a mixing cup, adding a little dishwashing detergent. Bring to the boil in a pan. Hook the wire or string through a hole in the bangle and immerse in the water. Agitate for about five minutes. Remove, rinse in warm, soapy water and leave to dry on newspaper. If the bangle opens, return to the oven and repeat the bending process.

5 Finally, thread the ribbon or leather through the holes in the bangle and tie securely.

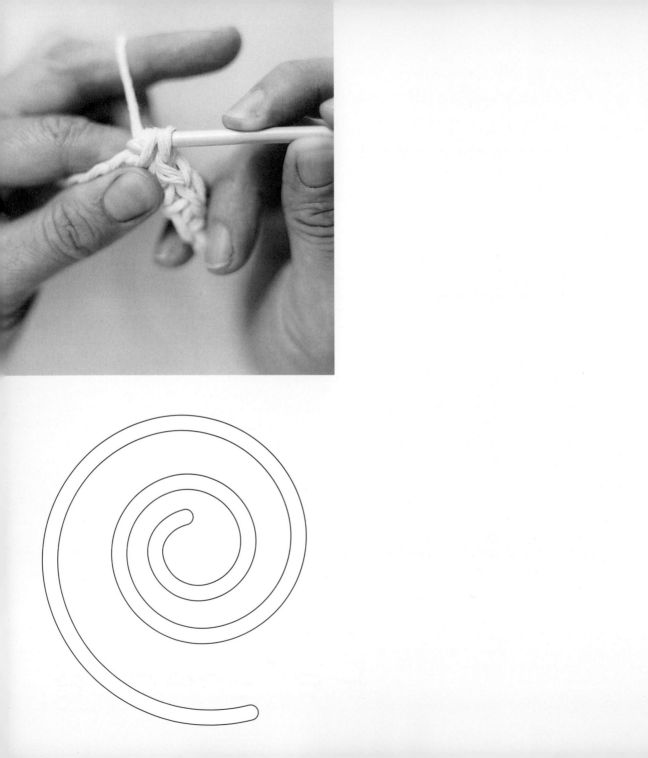

Reference

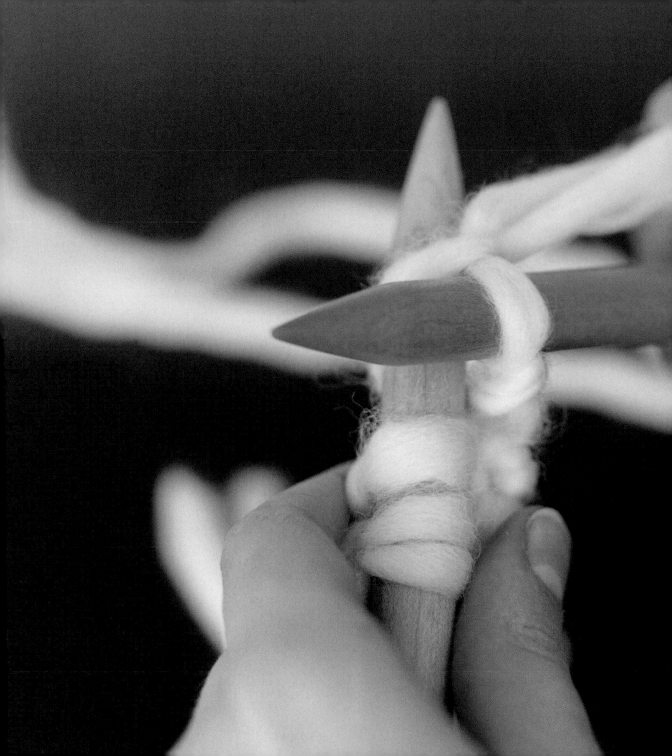

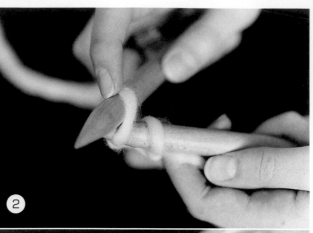

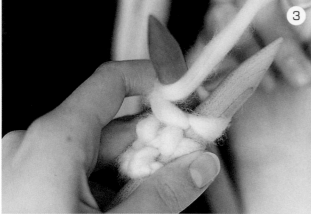

gauge/tension

Always knit a 4in/10cm swatch and change your needle size if your gauge/tension does not match that of your pattern.

how to: Knit

Slipknot

This makes the very first stitch, before you cast on. Leaving a long end, wind the yarn around two fingers on your left hand to make a circle, then pull the yarn through the circle with the knitting needle. Pull the ends so they are fairly tight.

1 & 2 Casting on

Start with the slipknot on the left needle. Push the empty right needle throught the loop on the left-hand needle, from front to back, so that it crosses behind the left needle. Wind the yarn from the ball around the point of the right needle, from below it to above it. Pull the right needle toward you and draw out the loop of the new stitch being formed. Pass the loop onto the left needle, in front of the previous stitch. Secure the stitch by pulling the yarn, but avoid pulling it too tightly. Repeat, using the first stitch on the left needle to form another new stitch, and so on until the required number of stitches has been cast on. You are ready to start knitting. The first row is a knit row.

3, 4 & 5 The knit stitch

Hold the needle with the cast-on stitches in your left hand. Push the empty (right) needle through the top of the first stitch, from front to back, so that it crosses behind the left needle. Wind the yarn from the ball around the point of the right needle, from below it to above it. Pull the right needle back and out of the cast-on stitch, still holding the yarn on its end. Drop the cast-on stitch off the end of the left needle. Repeat until you have reached the end of the row, then change the needles over.

The purl stitch

Make sure that the yarn is at the front of the needle. Holding the needle with the cast-on stitches in your left hand, push the empty (right) needle through the front of the first stitch, from front to back, so that it crosses in front of the left needle. Wind the yarn from the ball around the point of the right needle, from above it to below and back up again. Pull the right needle back and out of the cast-on stitch, still holding the yarn on its end. Drop the cast-on stitch off the end of the left needle. Repeat until you have reached the end of the row, then change the needles over to begin the next row.

Binding off/casting off

Knit (or purl) two stitches. Push the left needle into the first stitch that you worked on the right needle and lift it over the second stitch, and off the needle. Knit (or purl) the next stitch so that you again have two stitches on the right needle, and repeat until you have only one stitch left. Pull the yarn through this stitch to secure it.

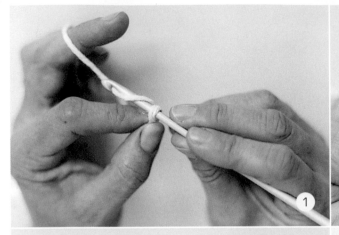

left-handers

If you are left-handed, simply hold the page up to a mirror to see all the instructions being performed with the left hand.

how to: Crochet

To start

Hold the hook in your right hand as you would a pencil. The left hand controls the flow of the yarn from the ball and the fingers maintain the tension. Holding the ball in your left hand, pass the yarn under your little finger and around the finger in a circle; then over the third, center and index fingers. The center finger supports the yarn in an easy position to be picked up with the hook. The yarn circled around the little finger maintains the tension to keep the stitches even. The index finger and thumb hold the work.

Slipknot

Make a loop, then hook another loop through it. Tighten gently and slide the knot up the hook.

1 & 2 Chain (ch)

Hold the slipknot between the thumb and center finger of your left hand. Insert the hook through the loop then under the yarn, which is supported by the center finger. Draw the yarn through the loop. This makes the first chain (1ch). Repeat this action to make as many chains as required.

3 Slip stitch (sl st)

Insert the hook into the next stitch. Catch the yarn with the hook and draw the yarn through the stitch and through the loop on the hook.

4 Single crochet (sc)

i) After making a chain, insert the hook into the 2nd ch from the hook. Wind the yarn over the hook.
ii) Draw the yarn through the stitch (you should now have 2 loops on the hook). Wind the yarn over the hook again. iii) Draw through the 2 loops on the hook. There is now 1 loop on the hook and 1sc made. Continue in this way, working into each remaining ch, to the end of the row. iv) To be able to start another row, work a single ch to bring you up to the correct height. This is called a turning chain. Turn the work around, keeping the hook in the right hand. v) For the next row, insert the hook under the 2 loops at the top of the last stitch of the previous row. Continue in this way to the end of the row. Work a single ch.

5 Double crochet (dc)

i) After making a chain, wind the yarn over the hook and insert the hook into the 4th ch from the hook. ii) Draw the yarn through the stitch (you should now have 3 loops on the hook). iii) Yarn over the hook, draw the yarn through 2 loops (2 loops left on the hook). iv) Yarn over the hook again, and draw through the remaining 2 loops. There is now 1 loop on the hook and 1dc made. Continue in this way, working into each remaining ch, to the end of the row. v) To be able to start another row, work 2ch to bring you up to the correct height. This is called a turning chain. Turn the work around, keeping the hook in the right hand. vi) For the next row, insert the hook under the 2 loops at the top of the last stitch of the previous row. Continue in this way to the end of the row. Work a single ch.

PRINTING SCREEN

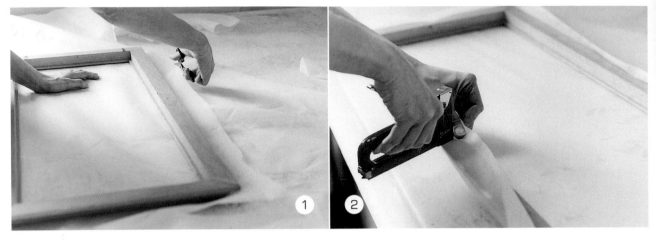

SQUEEGEE

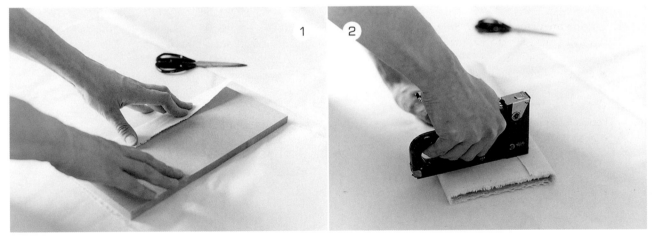

make your own: Printing screen and squeegee

to make the PRINTING SCREEN

You will need:
- A small wooden frame (such as an old picture frame or artists' stretchers, or four wooden battens)
- Polyester screen mesh about 4in/10cm larger all round than the screen, or polyester net drape fabric or organza
- Staple gun
- Scissors
- Strips of thick card
- Masking tape

1 If you are using four wooden battens, nail them together to make a sturdy frame. Stretch the mesh tightly and evenly across the frame. Staple, working from the center of each side to the corners.

2 Trim away excess fabric. Push the strips of card between the mesh and the frame to make the mesh very taut. Tape the back of the screen to seal.

to make the SQUEEGEE

You will need:
- Wooden battens
- Calico
- Staple gun

1 Cut a batten of thin, straight, inexpensive wood to about 2in/5cm wider than the width of your image and about 3in/8cm less than the width of the frame of your screen.

2 Wrap a piece of calico around it several times to soften the edge, then staple firmly. When you have finished printing, rip the calico off and attach a new piece for the next color.

Back stitch

Chain stitch

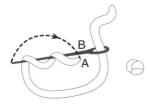

French knot

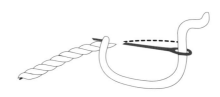

Stem stitch

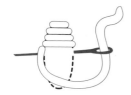

Satin stitch

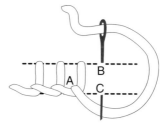

Blanket stitch

how to: Embroidery stitch guide

If you are new to embroidery, practice these simple stitches on scrap material until you feel confident about using them in your chosen project. You may find it easier to make even-size stitches if you place your work in an embroidery hoop before starting. This will keep the fabric taut while you stitch.

Fly stitch

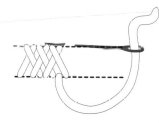

Basket stitch

Cross stitch

double cross stitch
To work double cross stitch first work a single diagonal cross stitch, then work a second straight cross over the top of the first.

Templates

Stenciling:
Devoré drape
pages 16–19

(photocopy and enlarge 1000%)

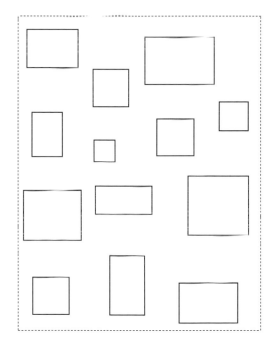

Stenciling:
Floor cushion
pages 20–3

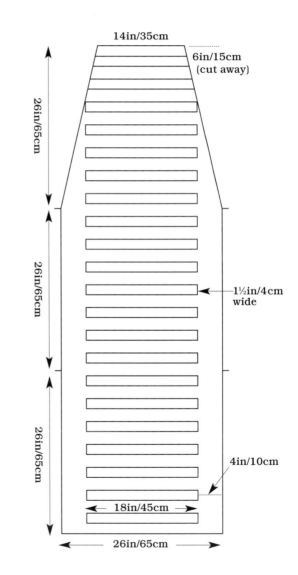

14in/35cm

6in/15cm
(cut away)

26in/65cm

26in/65cm

1½in/4cm
wide

26in/65cm

4in/10cm

18in/45cm

26in/65cm

Screen printing:
Wall hanging
pages 26–9

(photocopy and enlarge 1250%)

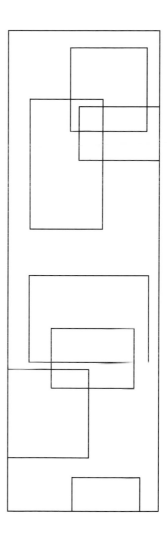

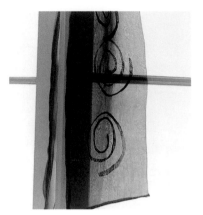

Screen printing:
Spiral scarf
pages 30–5

(photocopy and enlarge 200%)

Silk painting:
Wall hanging
pages 52–7

(photocopy and enlarge 1000%)

43in/110cm

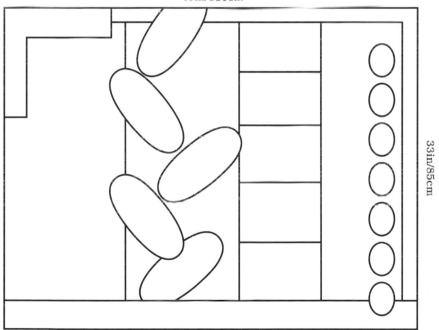

33in/85cm

Silk painting:
Abstract scarf
pages 58–63

(photocopy and enlarge 1000%)

18in/45cm

69in/175cm

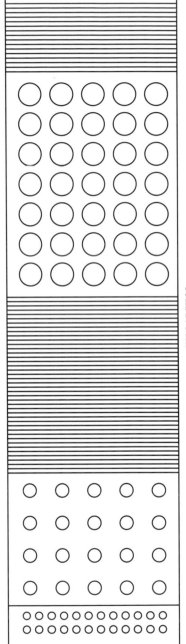

Hand embroidery:
Flower napkins
pages 106–11

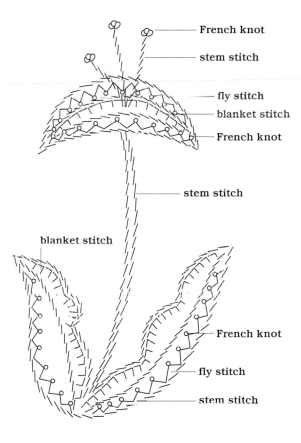

French knot

stem stitch

fly stitch

blanket stitch

French knot

stem stitch

blanket stitch

French knot

fly stitch

stem stitch

Hand embroidery:
Hot water bottle cover
pages 112–17

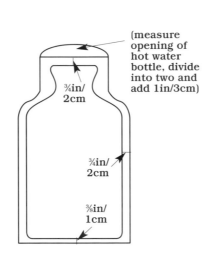

(measure opening of hot water bottle, divide into two and add 1in/3cm)

¾in/
2cm

¾in/
2cm

⅜in/
1cm

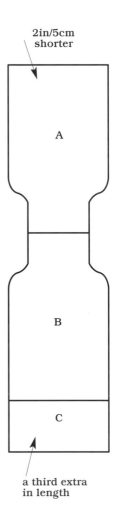

2in/5cm
shorter

A

B

C

a third extra
in length

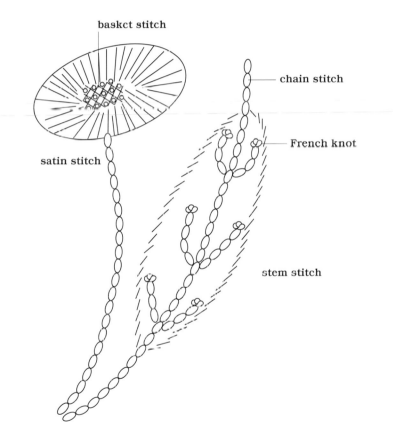

baskct stitch

chain stitch

French knot

satin stitch

(photocopy and enlarge 150%)

stem stitch

Appliqué:
Leaf placemats
and Kitchen tablecloth
pages 140–3; 144–7

(photocopy and enlarge 200%)

Appliqué:
Kitchen tablecloth
pages 144–7

(photocopy and enlarge 400%)

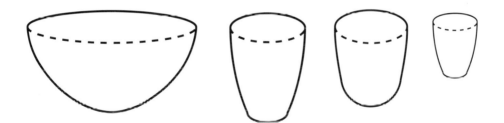

Complex textiles:
Flower cushion
pages 156–61

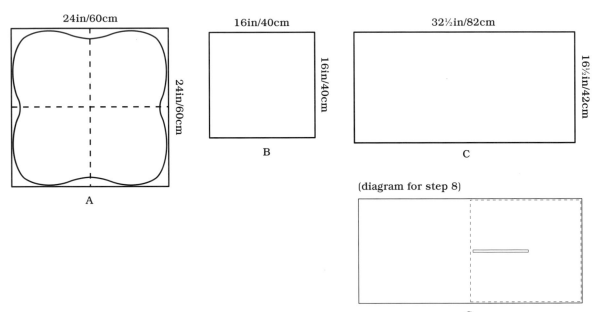

24in/60cm

24in/60cm

A

16in/40cm

16in/40cm

B

32½in/82cm

16½in/42cm

C

(diagram for step 8)

C

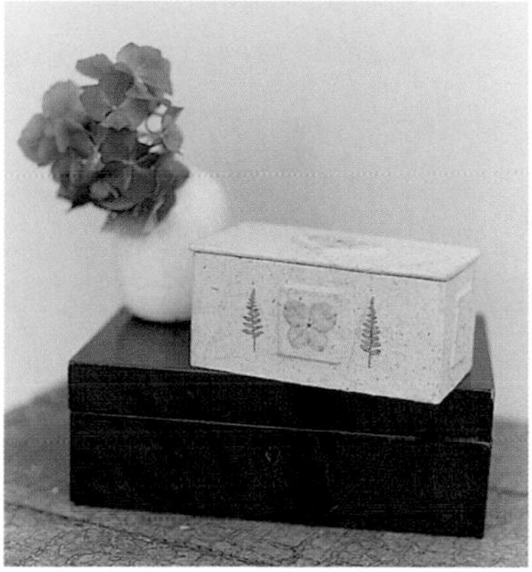

Papier mâché: Jewelry box
pages 268–73

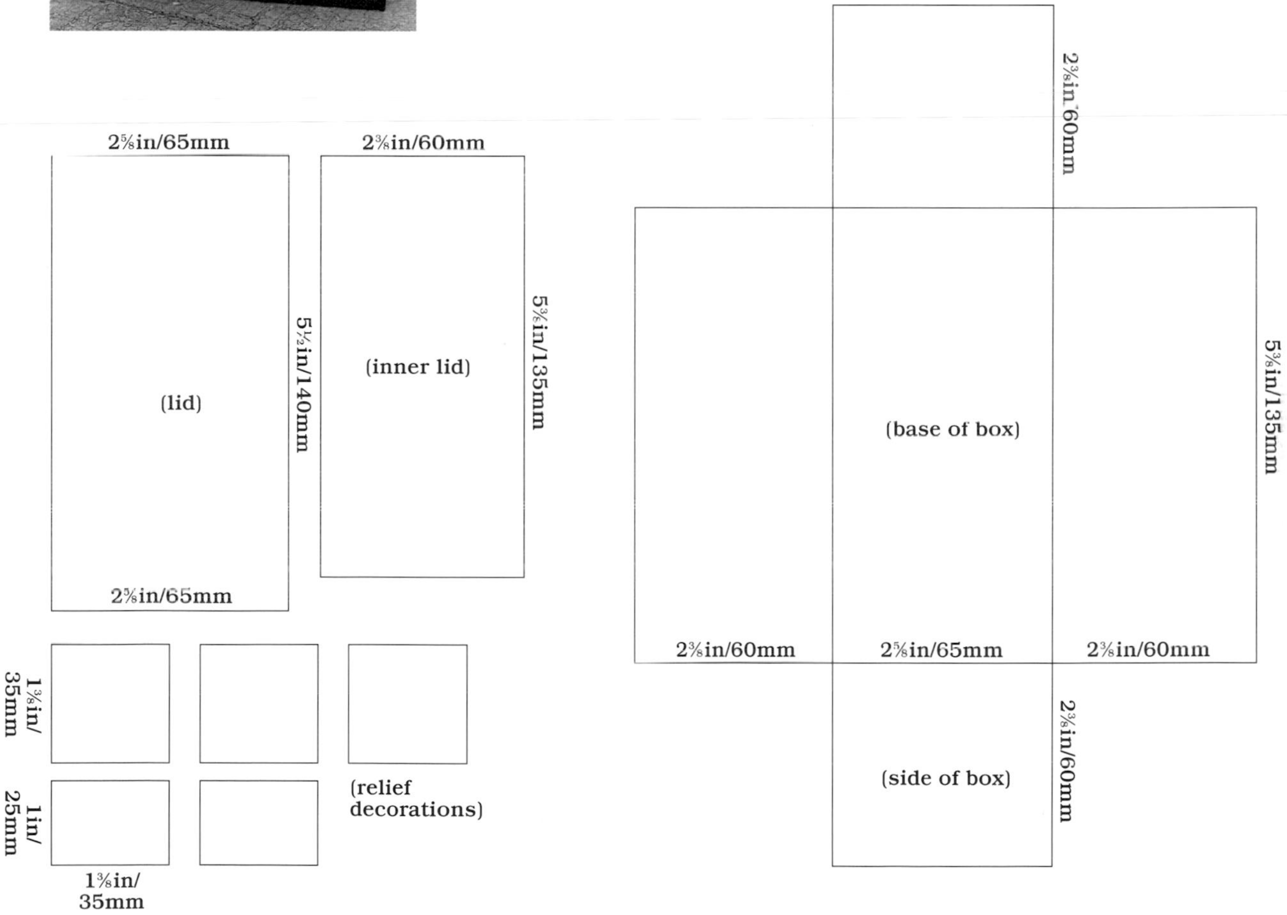

2⅝in/65mm
(lid)
5½in/140mm
2⅝in/65mm
2⅜in/60mm
(inner lid)
5⅜in/135mm
1⅜in/
35mm
1in/
25mm
1⅜in/
35mm
(relief
decorations)
2⅜in/60mm
(base of box)
5⅜in/135mm
2⅜in/60mm
2⅝in/65mm
2⅜in/60mm
(side of box)
2⅜in/60mm

Mosaic:
Decorative bowl
pages 320–5

(photocopy and enlarge 400%)

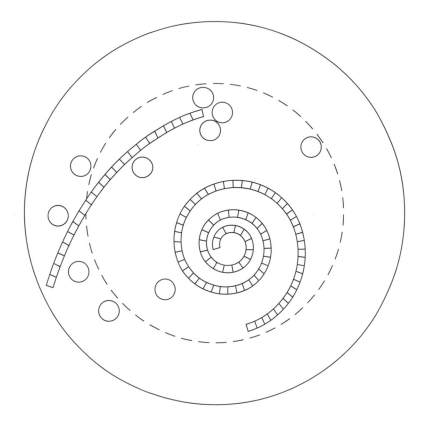

Soap making:
Zen soap
pages 372–5

(symbol for
water)

Contributors

STENCILING:
TRACY KENDALL WALLPAPER
116 Greyhound Lane,
London SW16 5RN
Tel: (020) 7640 9071
Fax: (020) 8769 0618
tracy@tkendall.fsbusiness.co.uk

SCREEN PRINTING:
TRACY KENDALL WALLPAPER
116 Greyhound Lane,
London SW16 5RN
Tel: (020) 7640 9071
Fax: (020) 8769 0618
tracy@tkendall.fsbusiness.co.uk

CYANOTYPE:
BARBARA JONES
barbara.a.jones@talk21.com
Mob: 07776 455913

SILK PAINTING:
SALLY WEATHERILL
11 Queen Street, Castle
Hedingham, Essex CO9 3EK

SHIBORI:
SARA KEITH
saraakeith@aol.com

KNITTING:
CATHERINE TOUGH TEXTILES
Suite 41, 63 Jeddo Road,
London W12 9ED
Tel/fax: (020) 8743 9186

CROCHET:
ERIKA KNIGHT
26 Great College Street,
Brighton, Sussex BN2 1HL
Tel: (01273) 702 220
Mob: 07970 539319
erika@eka.demon.co.uk

HAND EMBROIDERY:
HIROKO AONO-BILLSON
28 Han Street, Richmond,
Surrey TW10 7HT
Tel/fax: (020) 8940 2961
Mob: 07855 827111

MACHINE EMBROIDERY:
ANNETTE NAUDIN
Mob: 07957 471509
annettenaudin@hotmail.com

QUILTING:
JEANNE LAINÉ
1 Cleveland House, Hackford Road,
London SW9 0ET
Tel: (020) 7582 3420

APPLIQUÉ:
LISA VAUGHAN
Unit 258, The Clerkenwell
Workshops, 27–31 Clerkenwell
Close, London EC1R 0AT
Tel/fax: (020) 7250 0085
LVT@handbag.com

COMPLEX TEXTILES:
CORINNE PIERRE
Sycamore Cottage, Midway,
Chalford Hill, Gloucestershire
GL6 8EN, Tel: 01453 731 223
Mob: 07977 574 895
corinne@netgates.co.uk

FELT MAKING:
MARY KIRK
Studio 21, Great Western Studios,
Great Western Road, London
W9 3NY, Tel: (020) 7286 9530
Fax: (020) 8960 3924;
mary-kirk@bigfoot.com

USING FELT:
ANNE KYYRÖ QUINN
Tel: (020) 7486 2561
annekyyrodesign@aol.com

WEAVING:
Salt.®
OXO Tower, Bargehouse Street,
London SE1 9PH, Tel: (020) 7593 0007,
Fax: (020) 7401 6404
enquiries@salt-uk.com
www.salt-uk.com

RIBBONWORK:
HIKARU NOGUCHI TEXTILE DESIGN
Unit 2L, Cockpit Workshops,
Cockpit Yard, London WC1N 2NP
Tel: (020) 7813 1227
Fax: (020) 7813 0883

BEADWORK:
KAREN SPURGIN
39 Sundorne Road, London SE7 7PR
Tel: (020) 8355 4729
www.spurgin.co.uk

BASKETRY:
LIZZIE FAREY
8 Threave Road, Rhonehouse,
Castle Douglas DG7 1TD, Scotland
Tel/fax: (01556) 680473
lfarey@talk21.com

PAPER MAKING:
DAVID WATSON
Tel: (01273) 505201
d.a.watson@virgin.net

PAPIER MÂCHÉ:
CLAIRE ATTRIDGE
12 Ellicott Road, Horfield,
Bristol BS7 9PT
claire@attridge.co.uk

PAPERCRAFT:
ALEXANDRA GOUGH
Tel: (020) 7582 3420

CERAMIC PAINTING:
VICTORIA BRYAN
19, Northdown Avenue, Cliftonville, Margate,
Kent, CT9 2NL,
Tel: (01843) 227 494,
Fax: (01843) 297 919,
victoriabryan@hotmail.com

GLASS PAINTING:
KATE MAESTRI
Studio 2.11, Oxo Tower Wharf,
Bargehouse Street, London SE1 9PH
Tel: (020) 7620 0330
Fax: (020) 7928 9759

MOSAIC:
DONNA REEVES
33a Kay Road, London SW9 9DF
Tel: (020) 7733 7060
Fax: (020) 7737 0761
Mob: 07770 886 764

GILDING:
JANE CASSINI AND SANDRA LEE

SILVERWORK:
AMANDA DOUGHTY
Studio 2, Cockpit Workshops,
Cockpit Yard, Northington St,
London WC1N 2NP, Tel: (020) 7831 7390,
amanda@amandadoughty.com
www.amandadoughty.com

WIREWORK:
GEORGIE GLEN

SOAP MAKING:
SUE FLOCKHART
sue_flockhart@hotmail.com

PLASTIC DESIGN:
KATHIE MURPHY
1B Oldfield Road, London N16 0RR
Mob: 07973 249 852
Fax: (020) 7254 9528

ACRYLIC MOLDING:
MARLENE MCKIBBIN
118 Forest Road, London E8 3BH
Tel/fax: (020) 7683 0931

Index

First published in 2004 by Bay Books, an imprint of Murdoch Magazines Pty Ltd
Copyright© 2004 Murdoch Books®

ISBN 1 74045 500 2

Murdoch Books® is a trademark of Murdoch Magazines Pty Ltd

Commissioning Editor: Natasha Martyn-Johns
Project Editors: Dawn Henderson; Georgina Bitcon
Design and Art Direction: Cathy Layzell; Susanne Geppert
Photo Librarian: Bobbie Leah
Photographer: Howard Sooley
Stylist: Rebecca de Boehmler
with additional styling by Emeline Hudson
Illustrator: Christopher King
Production: Monika Paratore

Printed by Sing Cheong Printing Co. Ltd.
PRINTED IN CHINA